LANGUAGE AND LEARNING ACROSS THE CURRICULUM

Marion Crowhurst
University of British Columbia

Allyn & Bacon Canada
Scarborough, Ontario

To my husband, Otto Humele, in appreciation

Canadian Cataloguing in Publication Data
Crowhurst, Marion
Language and learning across the curriculum
ISBN 0-205-16134-0

1. English language – Study and teaching (Elementary).
2. English language – Study and teaching (Secondary).
I. Title

LB1576.C76 1994   428'.0071   C93-094701-0

© 1994 Allyn & Bacon Canada
A Division of the Paramount Publishing Education Group

1870 Birchmount Road
Scarborough, Ontario M1P 2J7

ISBN 0-205-16134-0

Acquisitions Editor: Clifford J. Newman
Developmental Editor: Lisa Penttilä
Copy Editor: Dick Hemingway
Production Editor: William Booth
Production Coordinator: Sharon Houston
Permissions: Erica Selby
Design: Alex Li
Page Layout: Jaytype Inc.

1 2 3 4 5   98 97 96 95 94

Printed and bound in U.S.A.

Every reasonable effort has been made to obtain permissions for all articles and data used in this edition. If errors or omissions have occurred, they will be corrected in future editions provided written notification has been received by the publisher.

CONTENTS

PART 1
LANGUAGE

PART 2
STRATEGIES FOR LEARNING THROUGH LANGUAGE

PREFACE

I decided to write this book after teaching a course at the University of British Columbia entitled "Language Across the Curriculum." This course is required for all students in the secondary education program. There were many excellent books available to us dealing with the various parts of the course — with language, with teaching the culturally different, with reading in content areas, with writing, and a few books that dealt with classroom talk and how it may be used to further learning. However, we could not find a book that dealt with all the topics our course addressed. Hence this book.

Though prompted by a course for secondary teachers, the subject matter of *Language and Learning Across the Curriculum* is important for all teachers from the primary grades through high school — and even (dare I say it?) for university teachers as well. In my teaching I find the material equally useful for both elementary and secondary teachers. I have written, then, for teachers from grade 1 through high school. My choice of illustrative material has been drawn from all levels in the school system and further examples will be easy for teachers to devise.

In writing this book, pre-service teachers were my primary target — both elementary teachers who teach many subjects, and specialist teachers in the high school who teach only one. However, I believe that the book will also be useful to in-service teachers at all levels and in all subject areas.

The book deals with language, and with ways of using language in all its forms to promote learning in all areas of the curriculum. Four of the chapters — those in Part 1 — are about language. We use language but, unless we are linguists, we don't often look at language and consider what it is and how it works. The four chapters about language encourage teachers to take that important look at language, at how it is acquired, and at the special characteristics of classroom language and of the language of various disciplines.

The seven chapters in Part 2 address pedagogy. They talk about ways of using talking, reading and writing to facilitate learning. One chapter deals specifically with applying these methods to teaching those who are culturally different — a subject of great and increasing importance in our country. (The chapters on language acquisition and evaluation also have special sections on second language learners.)

This book is based on unifying philosophy — a philosophy about learning and about the role of language in learning. That philosophy is presented in the first chapter and may be summed up in two propositions. The first is that students learn by making their own meanings; they do not learn in any meaningful way by memorizing meanings presented to them by their teachers. The second is that language plays a central role in such meaning-making. This philosophy is a unifying theme throughout the book and a determining factor in the discussion of evaluation and assessment in the last chapter.

In writing about "language in all its forms" I have confined myself, largely, to verbal language. In Chapter 8 I discuss visual representations of texts — representations that are not necessarily verbal or not mainly verbal — and mention dramatic representations of knowledge. The role of improvisation and of visual representations in facilitating learning deserve more detailed attention than this book could accommodate. I may address these topics in a later, expanded edition.

It is my hope that the teachers who use this text will use the methods described to teach the course for which the text is prescribed. The many strategies for teaching reading in content areas may be used in a methodology class using this book as the reading material. For example, I have my students work in groups of three to practise reciprocal teaching (see Chapter 8) as they read some important segment of text. I have them work in larger groups of four or five to graph a segment of text (see Chapter 8) and then present and explain their graph to the whole class. I have them engage in the various writing-to-learn activities described in Chapter 10. They work in groups discussing and applying the ideas presented in the text and in class. Sometimes the groups are subject area groups; often they are groups composed of people who have majored in different academic disciplines. If methods such as these are used, students experience demonstrations of the strategies recommended in the book. I hope that students will not be asked to memorize and regurgitate the material in the text.

I began teaching the language-across-the-curriculum course in 1988 with considerable trepidation. How, I wondered, could I tell music, physical education, science, and art teachers how to use writing as a means of learning in their courses? Many of these content areas were subjects I had never taught and knew comparatively little about. I discovered in that first year that I need not worry. Specialists are able to make their own applications — applications that would never have occurred to me. I have found teaching the course to be one of the most demanding, but one of the most rewarding experiences of my professional life. I hope that the text may help others find similar rewards.

ACKNOWLEDGEMENTS

Many of those to whom I am indebted are acknowledged in the numerous citations and references throughout the book. But there are others whose contributions I wish to acknowledge.

The idea for the book came originally from my colleague, Victor Froese, Head of the Department of Language Education at the University of British Columbia. Without his prompting, the book might never have been written. He has been generous with his advice whenever I have sought it.

My ideas about writing and about teaching writing have developed over many years in ways that are not easily documented. I pay special acknowledgement to my colleagues in the Department of Language Education at the University of British Columbia, with whom I cooperated over several years in conducting writing workshops for teachers and administrators in the Lower Mainland area of British Columbia. I note, in particular, Joe Belanger, Frank Bertram and Syd Butler, with whom I worked most frequently and with whom I have had innumerable conversations about writing.

The chapter on writing to learn owes much to illustrations drawn from the writing of students — students in elementary and high school classes, and my own students in the UBC Language Across the Curriculum course. I am indebted to all who have contributed, and to teachers who have shared the work of their students with me. I acknowledge in particular the assistance of Jennifer Belanger, for whom ideas about ways of using writing as a means of learning have been a regenerating influence in her teaching. She has been generous in sharing ideas, materials, and her specilized knowledge about science teaching.

Writing about subject areas that are not my specialty has required assistance from colleagues in other faculties and departments, assistance that has been readily given. Tom Schroeder in the Deparment of Math and Science Education at the University of British Columbia has been especially generous in sharing ideas and materials with me and in drawing to my attention important contributions by other mathematics educators. Early drafts of several chapters were used as readings in the UBC Language Across the Curriculum Course. I am grateful for useful comments passed on by course instructors. I note in particular the contributions of Jim Anderson, Syd Butler, Ellen Weber, Bernard Mohan, and my daughter, Megan Crowhurst, each of whom contributed their special expertise in commenting on drafts of one or more chapters. My teaching assistant, Marlene Asselin, shared her own rich understanding of reading processes and directed me to important source material.

Trevor J. Gambell of the University of Saskatchewan, Roderick Wm. McLeod of Lakehead University and Carolyn Pittenger of McGill University, the reviewers who read the completed draft of the book, made numerous valuable suggestions. I thank them for the painstaking care with which they read the manuscript and the thoughtfulness with which they responded.

Chapter 1

INTRODUCTION: AN OVERVIEW OF LANGUAGE AND LEARNING

CHAPTER OVERVIEW

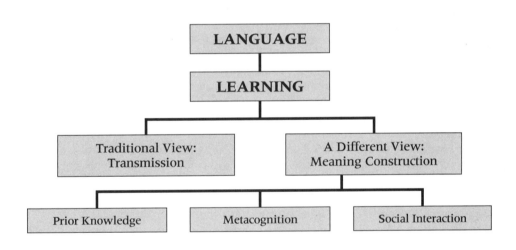

LANGUAGE

LEARNING

Traditional View: Transmission

A Different View: Meaning Construction

Prior Knowledge

Metacognition

Social Interaction

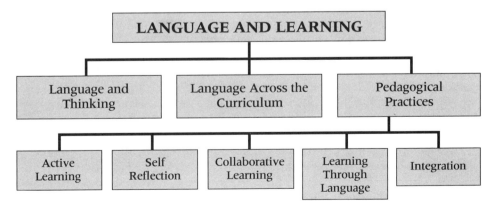

LANGUAGE AND LEARNING

Language and Thinking

Language Across the Curriculum

Pedagogical Practices

Active Learning

Self Reflection

Collaborative Learning

Learning Through Language

Integration

This book is about language, about learning, and about the interrelationships between the two. Teachers need to be aware of language and the way it works because it is through language, in its many forms, that most teaching and learning occur. Learning needs to be discussed because of the thin and inadequate understandings of learning that most of us have inherited. Language and learning are inextricably linked. To examine some of the ways in which they are linked is the task of this book.

LANGUAGE

Language, they say, is *transparent.* When we listen to talk or read print, we are aware of meaning. We rarely notice the language by which meanings are expressed. Two illustrations will make the point clear. Suppose that I am sitting in an airport coffee shop and hear mentioned the name of someone I know well who is being discussed by two people unknown to me who are sitting at the next table. Though I know that eavesdropping is not approved behaviour, the information being exchanged is very interesting, and I pay close attention. What I hear is not words and sentences, as such, but information. The information is expressed by words that are arranged in phrases and clauses. But I am not aware of the language, only of the meaning.

Suppose, however, that the two people leave, and I become aware of another conversation at a table behind me. This time, the language is one I do not understand — Cantonese, say. Now, the language is not transparent; I cannot look through the language to the meaning. As I listen, I am aware of the language. I may note sounds that are different from the sounds of English, and different rhythms of speech. It may seem to me that they speak very quickly. Even if I listen carefully, I cannot tell where one word leaves off and another begins. If we understand what we hear, we pay attention to meaning, not sounds and rhythm. We notice language only under special circumstances — if we do not understand it, or if we observe some oddity of expression, or difference of accent, or if we have some professional interest as a language teacher, perhaps, or a textual critic.

As teachers, we need to be aware of language and how it works because language is the currency of the classroom. Learning is mediated largely through language — through teacher talk and student talk, through the writing that students produce and the written language that they read. Throughout this book I encourage readers to look at language, at how it is acquired, and at the ways in which it is used for different purposes.

As competent language users, we have in our heads hundreds — indeed, thousands — of rules that determine how words may be used and how sentences must be structured. By and large, however, we are not aware of these rules. We obey them, and recognize infractions. We can usually correct errors, but often cannot explain the rule that is guiding our correction. One topic of interest, then, is the nature of the knowledge we have about the structure of the language.

We all speak many varieties of language, and change from one variety to another without even realizing that we do so. Lani, a graduate student from Lesotho, phoned home and spoke to her husband and her two elementary-aged children who had remained in Lesotho. Her roommate, reading in the same room, was aware that the language changed many times during the conversation, from English to Lesotho and back again. Interested, she asked Lani what the primary language of the home was. Lani, to her own surprise, could not answer the question. As the topic and purpose of talk changed, she and her family changed from one language to another without even being aware that they did so. Not all of us are bilingual. But all of us have many varieties of English that we use. As the topic, purpose, and situation of talk change, the kind of language we use changes. We use these varied forms of language automatically, without realizing that we do so.

Children master their mother tongue before they start school. By the time they enter kindergarten, they have learned all the basic sentence patterns, have a vocabulary of some thousands of words, and can use language for a wide variety of purposes. They perform this remarkable feat with virtually no formal instruction. The way children acquire language has important implications for many aspects of classroom learning.

There are major differences between spoken language and written language. Spoken language, when written down, often looks very strange. Most of us grew up with the idea that written language is correct language. We know that we do not always speak this way — in sentences, with correct grammar, without slang or vulgarisms, and so on. But we have a sneaking feeling that we ought to, that if we were doing the right thing, we would speak more carefully and correctly, more like the language that we see in print. Such beliefs, though widely held, are misguided. Written and spoken language are very different. Both written and spoken language are prominent in classroom use. A major task for children starting school is to learn to deal with written language. It is useful for teachers to be aware of the characteristics of these two uses of language and of the differences between them.

Language, then, is the topic of Part 1 of the book. Many topics are covered: the structure and use of language; varieties of language with special attention to the language of the classroom and the language of specific disciplines; language acquisition for both first and later languages; and the relationships between language and thought.

LEARNING

For most of the century, education has been dominated by an inadequate view of teaching and learning. According to this traditional view, learning is a matter of knowledge and skill acquisition; teaching is a matter of transmitting knowledge and skills, and of testing to see whether they have been acquired. This view of teaching and learning has dominated both school and university education. It is the view commonly accepted in the community at large. Developments in cognitive psychology have led to a different view of teaching and learning, one that emphasizes understanding and meaning construction rather than memorization.

THE TRADITIONAL VIEW: TRANSMISSION

Learning may be considered as a product or a process. If we consider the product of learning, the question is: *What is it* that has been learned. If we consider the process of learning, the question is: What is it that students *do* when they learn (Entwistle, 1984).

According to the dominant, traditional view of learning, the product of learning is factual knowledge. Learning is a matter of quantity. A historian is someone who knows a lot about history, who knows not only the year of an important event but also the exact date. A mathematician is one who can solve mathematical problems. According to this view, the process of learning is memorizing and applying information. *To know* means to be able to reproduce memorized information or practise memorized procedures.

Traditional views of knowledge, then, are quantitative (many facts are known) and reproductive (to know means to be able to call up memorized material). Such views are deep-rooted and widespread both in education and in the culture at large (Dahlgren, 1984). The quiz whiz is a person of great knowledge. She can answer "hard" questions that call for the knowledge of obscure details.

Quantitative, reproductive views of knowledge entail methods of teaching that emphasize memorization and testing. Teaching and tests emphasize discrete pieces of knowledge. Rewards (that is, marks and grades) are given for relatively simple performance, like the reproduction of memorized factual material, or the execution of memorized procedures in math. There is little emphasis on deeper understandings, which are harder and more time-consuming to measure. Even when teachers sincerely want their students to think broadly and deeply, their methods of teaching and assessment often convey a different message, and encourage the acquisition of detailed facts. Students are not slow to hear the message, and to engage in the behaviours that pay off in good grades.

Campione, Brown, and Connell (1988) have listed characteristic limitations of traditional teaching practice. They refer, particularly, to instruction in reading, writing, and mathematics — the staples of elementary education — though specialists in other disciplines will doubtless be able to draw comparisons to their own fields. The limitations are as follows:

1. *An emphasis on direct instruction with strong teacher control* The teacher determines the pace and order of instruction with little room for students to influence their own learning.

2. *Lack of on-line diagnosis* Studies in the teaching of both reading and math have shown teachers to be preoccupied with covering the curriculum content by moving students through a set of materials rather than diagnosing and addressing students' problems. However, diagnosis is central to the teacher's task. Teachers need to know not merely that students got the wrong answer, but also the cause of the error. Brown and Burtin (1978) describe a student whose teacher believed, throughout an entire school year, that he could not add since his answers seemed completely random. However, a diagnostic computer program revealed that the student had just one simple bug in the procedure he used. He followed his procedure for doing arithmetic virtually perfectly. Once the problem was diagnosed, his difficulty disappeared.

    Two anecdotes provide examples of conscientious teachers whose concern was to cover the curriculum rather than to diagnose the level of their students' achievement. The first was the remark of an experienced first-grade teacher who, some years ago, admitted in a class I was teaching how guilty she felt if she sent her first graders on to second grade without their having completed their reading workbooks. The second was related by a colleague who expressed surprise to his son's elementary school teacher that his son had received a *C* for reading. "I thought he was a good reader," my colleague said. "He's a very good reader," replied the teacher, "but he won't do his workbook activities." (Workbook activities, of course, were intended for the sole purpose of helping students to become good readers!) In both cases, the teachers saw their job as getting their students through a set of curriculum materials *whether the students needed the activities or not*. If they had already mastered the curriculum material, they must still do the work prescribed. If they completed the curriculum materials and had not learned, it was unfortunate but unavoidable.

3. *Basic skills before understanding* Traditional approaches to early reading instruction focus on decoding skills, that is, on translating written symbols into sounds. In early writing instruction, the focus of traditional approaches is on writing sentences with correct spelling and correct use of capitals and periods. In early math instruction, traditional approaches focus on the

acquisition of mathematical facts and the memorization of procedures for adding, multiplying, and so on. The emphasis on skills leads to inadequate views — that reading is decoding, that writing is mechanics, and that mathematics is executing algorithmic operations like multiplying or finding percentages. A sixth grade teacher told me with astonishment that several of his students, when asked to define reading, had written that reading was sounding out words. Certainly their teachers in earlier grades had not intended to convey that impression; but the focus on skills had prevented students from understanding what they were really supposed to be doing when they were reading, namely, constructing meaning, not merely sounding out words.

4. *An emphasis on instructing in subskills and a failure to instruct in more complex strategies* In order to assist students with the large task of reading comprehension, for example, the task is broken down into subskills such as finding topic sentences, picking out the main idea, and summarizing. The subskills are then practised in relative isolation. Students are not told how and when these skills should be used to make sense of large segments of text. Skills instruction takes place in reading lessons, occasions that are separate from the times when they are reading for real purposes such as getting information from a text for a social studies project. The result is that students learn to summarize and predict in reading classes when they are told to do so. But they cannot access the strategies when needed in real reading situations. It does not occur to them, for example, to say: "If I can get the main idea of every paragraph, I'll probably be able to understand the writer's argument." Competent readers learn for themselves how to use activities such as summarizing, paraphrasing, and predicting the author's argument in order to process difficult texts. But those most in need of such strategies — namely, weaker readers — do not make such discoveries themselves. They need specific instruction in how to use more complex strategies in the context of real, purposeful reading tasks.

In mathematics also the emphasis is on perfecting subskills like executing procedures for multiplying, or for solving equations. Many students who can calculate percentages flawlessly, do not recognize occasions when that skill should be used to help them solve problems. They need specific instruction in identifying appropriate contexts for using the skills that they have mastered.

5. *Differential treatment* Not only do poor readers not get instruction in complex strategies needed for comprehension or for solving mathematical problems, but also they receive prolonged instruction in basic skills. The weaker the students, the more likely they are to get extra instruction in basic skills and the less likely they are to develop the higher-level skills necessary for comprehending demanding text — and similarly in other subject areas.

Traditional approaches, then, emphasize memorization and knowledge acquisition. Teachers are the experts who direct and oversee the process. They are responsible for covering the curriculum and testing to determine the degree to which students have learned.

A DIFFERENT VIEW: MEANING CONSTRUCTION

Newer views of learning emphasize understanding and meaning rather than recognition and reproduction. Teaching is an activity that has students' learning as its goal (rather than covering a set of curriculum materials), and is carried out in a way that shows respect for the students' intellectual integrity and powers of reasoning.

Learning results not merely in *quantitative* change but in *qualitative* change. Learning results not merely in factual knowledge, but also in changes in the learner's understanding. Mastering factual or procedural details is often a prerequisite for deeper learning. But learning facts and procedures is not an end in itself but, rather, a means to more important ends.

The process of learning emphasizes active meaning construction by the learner rather than passive, unreflective memorization of material presented by others. As Bruner (1966, p. 72) has well said:

> We teach a subject not to produce little living libraries on that subject, but rather to get a student to think mathematically for himself, to consider matters as an historian does, to take part in the process of knowledge-getting. Knowing is a *process*, not a *product*. (italics added).

It may seem odd to describe active, meaning-centred approaches as "new" given that Bruner's comments were written thirty years ago, and that complaints about student passivity predate Bruner by many decades. Stevens (1912), for example, wrote more than 80 years ago:

> … the reason why our pupils gain so little in intellectual power is because our teachers do the intellectual work (p. 22) … (T)here is very little effort put forth to teach our boys and girls to be self-reliant, independent mental workers (p. 26).

Despite periodic calls for change, traditional approaches to teaching and learning have persisted. Goodlad (1984), for example, conducted a comprehensive, eight-year investigation of schools in the United States. His researchers visited more than 1000 classrooms. He comments on the extraordinary degree of student passivity. Not even 1% of instructional time was spent on activities that required responses involving reasoning or even opinions from students. There is no good reason to believe that things have been much different in the average Canadian classroom.

If learning is to go beyond the memorization of facts and procedures, learners need to be active meaning makers rather than passive recipients of information. Teaching must foster independent, self-directed learners who are capable of reflecting upon their understanding and upon their learning processes. Key concepts in active, constructivist views of learning are: (a) the importance of prior knowledge for learning; (b) the importance of metacognitive awareness; and (c) the interactive, social nature of learning.

Prior Knowledge

Prior knowledge refers to all the knowledge and experience the learner brings to the learning situation. All learning takes place in terms of what we already know. Learning involves making connections between our existing knowledge and new information. We remember more of what we hear or read about topics that we know a good deal about, than about topics about which we know very little. Students often have relevant prior knowledge that they do not connect with the topic under consideration. It is important, then, for relevant prior knowledge to be activated so that the known can serve as a bridge to what is to be learned.

Another reason for paying attention to prior knowledge is that misconceptions act as a filter for new information. If students hold beliefs contrary to new material being studied, their old beliefs are likely to interfere with their acquisition of new understandings. Marshall (1989) cites an example of fourth and fifth graders who read a social studies passage about responsibilities at home and at school. The authors had avoided sexual stereotyping by using examples of boys helping in the kitchen and of girls doing yard work. Yet the students reported that the text said that boys should mow the lawn and that girls should help with the dishes. Their understanding of the text was shaped by their prior experience. The literature of science teaching is rife with examples of how students' everyday beliefs interfere with their ability to develop a more scientific perspective (e.g., see Osborne and Freyberg, 1985). Indeed, students show a remarkable ability to keep their school learning and their everyday knowledge separate, using school-learned "knowledge" to answer school exams, but retaining their everyday knowledge for practical purposes outside the classroom. Prior beliefs are remarkably resistant to change. It is important for teachers to understand the ideas that students bring to class because those ideas will influence the way they think about new material.

Metacognition

Metacognition has to do with understanding what you are doing. There are two important aspects of metacognition: (a) *knowledge* about one's own cognition or thinking processes; and (b) *control* of one's cognitive processes (Flavell 1976, p. 232).

The first perspective on metacognition deals with questions like: What do I know? How do I know what I know? How did I come to know what I know? You are engaging in metacognitive thinking, for example, when you note that you are having trouble learning a given body of information or solving a given mathematical problem, or when you realize that you are likely to forget an address or a phone number if you do not write it down.

The second perspective on metacognition focuses on monitoring and regulating our cognitive processes. It goes beyond knowing about one's learning to the management of learning.

Considerable work on the second aspect of metacognition — the self-monitoring and self-regulation of learning — has been done by Ann Brown and her colleagues (e.g., Brown, Campione, and Day, 1981; Campione, Brown, and Connell, 1988). They were moved to this kind of emphasis because of repeated findings that, although students' learning and memory skills could be improved by instruction, they were unable to make use of their newly learned skills once they were removed from the experimental situation. They have therefore concentrated on teaching students how to monitor and oversee their learning by applying the strategies that have been learned. Most work on self-regulation of learning has been done in the areas of reading comprehension — with implications for a variety of subject areas — and mathematics (Campione et al., 1988).

Social Interaction

Sociocognitive views of learning emphasize the role of social interaction in cognitive development. Learning takes place within a social context in which the interaction supports and extends learning. The Russian psychologist, Vygotsky (1978), stressed the importance of collaborative interaction with experts — adults and more capable peers — by means of which the learner is helped to higher levels of understanding and performance. The Swiss psychologist Piaget (1980) believed cognitive conflict to be indispensable for intellectual development. Cognitive conflict occurs when one engages in interaction with peers and is confronted with their conflicting points of view. It is through the resolution of such conflict that cognitive growth takes place. The American psychologist Jerome Bruner (1966; 1975a; 1975b) also stresses the role of verbal interaction in both language acquisition and cognitive development.

LANGUAGE AND LEARNING

Language, thinking, and learning are intimately related. Relationships between the three have been discussed by psychologists such as Bruner, Piaget, and Vygotsky, by philosophers such as Popper (1979), and by curriculum theorists such as James Moffett (1968a; 1968b) and James Britton (1970). In making sense of the world, language is the major means by which we represent experience to ourselves and to others. Language plays a central role in thinking, knowing and learning.

LANGUAGE AND THINKING

Britton (1970) points out that speech quickly becomes the young child's principal instrument for exploring the world. Children question endlessly as they engage actively in their search for information.

Young children use language also to help them direct their activities as they execute tasks. They talk to themselves as they draw, build with blocks, or play with toys. ("Now I'm going to draw a house." "I'm going to build a swimming pool." "I'm putting the dolly to bed.") Action is accompanied by talk of this kind even when there is no one to listen or respond. As Vygotsky (1962, p.228) has said, such talk "does not merely accompany the child's activity; it serves mental orientation, conscious understanding; it helps in overcoming difficulties…" Their running commentary about what they are doing seems to focus their attention and keep them on course.

Language serves to clarify meanings and make them more precise. The things we know that we can express in words are the things we know most surely. Moreover, putting what we know into words helps us to clarify our thoughts and to come to know more clearly.

Language plays a major role in information storage and retrieval. Experience is encoded largely by means of language. Moreover, ideas that are encoded in words are more easily retrieved later.

Language enables us to go beyond present experience (Bruner, 1966). It enables us to consider what is not immediately present thus allowing us to free ourselves from the immediate context. Language enables us to talk about what happened in the past and what might happen in the future. It enables us to predict, to hypothesize, to imagine, to generalize.

What we know may be represented in ways that do not involve language — in images or patterns, for example. Some things that we know are not easily or not well represented in words. To illustrate the difficulty of representing some kinds of knowledge verbally, Flower and Hayes (1984) invite their readers to consider how they might put into words: a cognitive map of a city; how to dance your way across a crowded floor; or the song of a bird. They point out that when the call of the whiskered owl is described as "4 to 9 high pitched *boos* slowing at the end," the description may serve as an aid to memory for someone who knows the call already, but it does a poor job of representing the call to someone not already familiar with it.

There are, then, other ways of representing knowledge. It remains true, nonetheless, that language plays a role of central importance in thinking, knowing, and learning. As Lindfors (1987, p. 285) has well said:

> language aids thought; language reflects thought; language refines thought; language extends thought; language creates thought. And language even enables us to become aware of our own thinking and thus, to some extent..., to direct it.

LANGUAGE ACROSS THE CURRICULUM

Given the importance of language for thinking and learning, it is hardly surprising that there has been, in several countries, a widespread movement to stress the role of language in learning across all areas of the curriculum. Important precursors of the movement were curriculum theorists, James Moffett in the United States and James Britton in England. Moffett's (1968a; 1968b) influential books on curriculum reflected the important work of psychologists and psycholinguists on language acquisition, and the relationship between language and learning. He emphasized the importance of students' expressing their experience in words, both written and spoken. The work on language across the curriculum, begun in the 1960s by James Britton and his colleagues at the University of London Institute of Education (Barnes, Britton, and Torbe, 1990; Martin, D'Arcy, Newton, and Parker, 1976), influenced national policy in the United Kingdom. Publications of the Department of Education and Science in 1975 and 1985 (The Bullock Report and The Swann Report), contain clear statements about the importance of language in the learning process, and about the need for school policies on language and learning across the curriculum. In Canada, one of the clearest statements of language across the curriculum policy was made by the Ontario Ministry of Education in 1984. This policy is cited in Figure 1.1.

The major beliefs that characterize language-across-the-curriculum approaches are that:

1. Language plays a central role in learning.

2. Students must be actively engaged in meaning-making processes. (A corollary is that teachers will less frequently occupy centre stage as transmitter of information.)

3. Active learning commonly involves listening, talking, reading and writing.

4. Students should be encouraged to use their own language to express and explore their understanding of curriculum content. Corson (1990, p. 73) interprets *language* more broadly than listening, talking, reading, and writing, and suggests that four additional meaning-making processes be added:

Figure 1.1   Language Across the Curriculum Policy
Ontario Ministry of Education

Language plays a central role in learning. No matter what the subject area, students assimilate new concepts largely through language, that is, when they listen to and talk, read, and write about what they are learning and relate this to what they already know. Through speaking and writing, language is linked to the thinking process and is a manifestation of the thinking that is taking place. Thus, by explaining and expressing personal interpretations of new learning in the various subject fields, students clarify and increase both their knowledge of the concepts in those fields and their understanding of the ways in which language is used in each.

It follows, then, that schools should provide an environment in which students are encouraged to use language to explore concepts, solve problems, organize information, share discoveries, formulate hypotheses, and explain personal ideas. Students need frequent opportunities to interact in small group discussions that focus on the exploration of new concepts. In addition, they should be encouraged to keep journals in which they write thoughts, questions and speculations that reflect on their learning.

Principals should provide leadership by encouraging all teachers to participate in developing and practising a school language policy, which is, in effect, a school learning policy. By allowing students to discuss and write in the language they already control, teachers can gain new insights into the difficulties that students are encountering in particular subject areas. In this way teachers can help students to avoid rote learning and to gain clear understandings.

Source: Ontario Ministry of Education (1984). *Ontario Schools: Intermediate and Senior Divisions* (Toronto: Ministry of Education), p. 7.

moving: using facial expression, gesturing and whole-body movements to express meaning;

watching: attending to and interpreting the movements of others;

shaping: using visual effects to express meaning;

viewing: attending to and interpreting the visual effects created by others.

PEDAGOGICAL PRACTICES

The kinds of teaching strategies advocated in this book are those that encourage active, constructivist, meaning-centred learning. Characteristic features of classrooms where such teaching and learning go on are described in this section.

Active Learning

Students spend much time actively engaged in making meaning, and spend little time as passive recipients of predigested knowledge from the teacher-as-expert. Some of the ways in which they are active are as follows: predicting, observing, discussing, solving problems, writing, reading, and transforming and applying what they read and hear into written and visual forms.

Self Reflection

Students are encouraged to reflect upon their knowledge and their learning. They are invited to comment on what they know and how they know it; on what they do not know or do not understand. A major means for encouraging self reflection is writing — spontaneous, unpolished, unedited writing of the kind done in a course log or journal. They should also be asked to reflect upon their knowledge and understanding in conferences with the teacher and in talking with peers.

Collaborative Learning

Cooperative and collaborative learning (Johnson and Johnson, 1987; Slavin, 1983; 1989) come in a variety of forms; all involve small, mixed-ability groups working collaboratively on tasks, problems, or projects. In the kind of class envisaged, students spend a considerable amount of class time working in pairs and small groups. Sometimes they work on tasks devised by the teacher and sometimes on tasks that they set themselves. Some tasks take only a portion of a period; some take many days to complete and require a division of work among group members. Sometimes the class as a whole engages in discussion or problem solving. The teacher facilitates and supports discussion without dominating.

Sometimes collaborative learning involves an older, more able tutor who engages in what Bruner (1975b) calls **scaffolding**. The teacher or tutor assists a child in learning a complex task in the following ways: (1) by segmenting a task; (2) by modelling the component parts; (3) by giving as much help as is needed for success but no more; and (4) by gradually withdrawing assistance as the learner acquires skill. **Reciprocal teaching** (Brown and Palincsar, 1987; Campione, Brown, and Connell, 1988) involves both cooperative learning within a small group and expert scaffolding (See Chapter 8 for a full description.) The basic notion behind all these procedures is that learning is a cooperative, collaborative, interactive procedure.

Learning Through Language

Many of the means by which students engage in meaning-making are language activities. Language is a primary way of sorting out one's thoughts. When students put things into words — spoken or written — they discover what they think and mean, and come to understand in new ways. Purposeful talking, reading, and writing are central activities in classrooms where students are active learners. Language, more broadly interpreted, includes also making meaning by moving and by creating visual representations, and by interpreting the movements and visual representations of others (Corson, 1990).

Integration

Integration refers to many aspects of school and learning. One kind of integration is the integration of knowledge. School learning has commonly been marked by compartmentalization. What students learn in one subject is rarely applied — or even remembered — in another. Their everyday knowledge often remains intact even though they learn incompatible information in school. School knowledge has been described as "inert" knowledge (Whitehead, 1916), of little use except to pass a test in the subject in which it is learned, and not available for other purposes. Learning occurs when students actively assimilate new information and integrate it with what they have learned in other ways and in other contexts.

Integration refers also to language activities. Students talk, listen, read and write in most classes. Talking and writing prepare them to read. Reading prepares them to talk or to write.

A third kind of integration is the mixing of different kinds of students in groups large and small. Students who have not yet learned can benefit from interaction with their more able peers. Those who are more able can profit by explaining to their less proficient peers. Students whose mother tongue is other than English will improve their English language skills as they talk and interact in groups with their peers.

Integration refers to wholeness. Knowledge is whole and should not be rigidly compartmentalized into subjects, or into what is known from experience outside the classroom versus what is learned in school. Education needs to deal with students as whole persons and encourage inquiring attitudes both in the classroom and in the world.

CONCLUSION

Language and learning are intimately related. As teachers, we need to understand both language and learning, and how language in all its forms can be used to promote learning.

Traditional learning with its emphasis on memorization and the accumulation of factual knowledge will not serve students in this world of rapid change and exponential increases in knowledge. Students must be helped to become active, engaged learners who construct their own meanings. Classrooms where active learning is fostered are cooperative, interactive environments where learners struggle constantly to solve problems and put their thoughts into words both written and spoken, and into other forms of representation like improvisations, skits, and visuals of varying kinds. The teacher is actively engaged in assessing and promoting learning, but is less often the central performer than is the case in more traditional classrooms.

Many beginning teachers have themselves been educated in classrooms where traditional approaches to teaching and learning dominate. Moreover, since traditional approaches remain all too common, some beginning teachers may not have seen newer approaches to teaching and learning in the classrooms where they completed their student teaching practicum. Learning new ways of teaching is not easy when few models have been available for observation. The chapters of this book present many suggestions for teaching in ways that encourage active learning. Beginning teachers are encouraged to hasten slowly, gradually introducing and mastering ways of teaching and learning that produce classrooms filled with active, involved learners.

REFERENCES

Barnes, D., J. Britton and M. Torbe (1990). *Language, the Learner and the School* (4th ed.). Portsmouth, NH: Boynton/Cook.

Britton, J. (1970). *Language and Learning*. London: Penguin.

Brown, A.L., J.C. Campione and J.D. Day (1981). Learning to learn: On training students to learn from texts. *Educational Research*, 10, 14-21.

Brown, A.L., and A.S. Palincsar (1987). Reciprocal teaching of comprehension strategies: A natural history of one program for enhancing learning. In J.D. Day and J. Borkowski (eds.), *Intelligence and Exceptionality: New Directions for Theory, Assessment and Instructional Practice* (pp. 81-132). Norwood, NJ: Ablex.

Brown, J.B., and R.R. Burton (1978). Diagnostic models for procedural bugs in basic mathematical skills. *Cognitive Science*, 2, 155-192.

Bruner, J. (1966). *Toward a Theory of Instruction*. Cambridge: Mass: Harvard University Press.

Bruner, J.S. (1975a). The ontogenesis of speech acts. *Journal of Child Language*, 2, 1-20

Bruner, J. (1975b). Early social interaction and language acquisition. In H.R. Schaffer (ed.), *Studies in Mother-Infant Interactions* (pp.271-291). London: Academic Press.

Campione, J.C., A.L. Brown and M.L. Connell (1988). Metacognition: On the importance of understanding what you are doing. In L.R. Charles and E. Siwer (eds.), *The Teaching and Assessing of Mathematical Problem Solving* (pp. 93-114). Resto, VA: National Council of Teachers of Mathematics.

Corson, D. (1990). *Language Policy Across the Curriculum*. Clevedon, Avon: Multilingual Matters.

Dahlgren, L. Outcomes of learning. In F. Marton, D. Hounsel and N. Entwistle (eds.), *The Experience of Learning* (pp. 19-35). Edinburgh: Scottish Academic Press.

DES (Department of Education and Science) (1985). *Education for all: Report of the committee of inquiry into the education of children from ethnic minority groups* (The Swann Report). London: HMSO.

DES (Department of Education and Science) (1975). *A language for life* (The Bullock Report). London: HMSO.

Entwistle, N. (1984). Contrasting perspectives on learning. In F. Marton, D. Hounsel and N. Entwistle (eds.), *The Experience of Learning* (pp. 1-18). Edinburgh: Scottish Academic Press.

Flavell, J.H. (1976). Metacognitive aspects of problem solving. In L.G. Resnick (ed.), *The Nature of Intelligence* (pp. 231-235). Hillsdale, NJ: Erlbaum.

Flower, L., and J.R. Hayes (1984). Images, plans, and prose: The representation of meaning in writing. *Written Communication*, 1, 120-160.

Goodlad, J.I. (1984). *A Place Called School*. New York: McGraw-Hill.

Johnson, D., and R. Johnson (1987). *Learning Together and Alone: Cooperative, Competitive, and Individualistic Learning*, 2nd ed. Englewood Cliffs, NJ: Prentice Hall.

Lindfors, J.W. (1987). *Children's Language and Learning*, 2nd ed. Englewood Cliffs, NJ: Prentice Hall.

Marshall, N. (1989). The students: Who are they and how do I reach them? In D. Lapp, J. Flood, and N. Farnan (eds.), *Content Area Reading and Learning: Instructional Strategies* (pp. 59-69). Englewood Cliffs, NJ: Prentice Hall.

Martin, N., P. D'Arcy, B. Newton and R. Parker (1976). *Writing and Learning Across the Curriculum 11-16*. London: Ward Lock Educational.

Moffett, J. (1968a). *Teaching the Universe of Discourse*. Boston: Houghton Mifflin.

Moffett, J. (1968b). *A Student-Centered Language Arts Curriculum K-13: A Handbook for Teachers. Boston*: Houghton Mifflin.

Ontario Ministry of Education. (1984). *Ontario Schools: Intermediate and Senior Divisions*. Toronto: Ministry of Education.

Osborne, R., and P. Freyberg (1985). *Learning in Science: The Implications of Children's Science.* Auckland, NZ: Heinemann.

Piaget, J. (1980) Foreword. In C. Kamii and R. Devries, *Group Games in Early Education.* Washington, DC: National Association for the Education of Young Children.

Popper, K. (1979). *Objective Knowledge: An Evolutionary Approach.* Oxford, England: Clarendon Press.

Slavin, R. (1983). *Cooperative Learning.* New York: Longman.

Slavin, R. (1989). *School and Classroom Organization.* Hillsdale, NJ: Erlbaum.

Stevens, R. (1912). *The question as a measure of efficiency in instruction: a critical study of classroom practice.* Teachers College, Columbia University. Contributions to Education N. 48. New York: Bureau of Publication, Teachers College, Columbia University. Cited in J.R. Baird and I.J Mitchell (eds.) (1987). *Improving the quality of teaching and learning: An Australian case study—The PEEL project.* Melbourne, Australia: Monash University Printer.

Vygotsky, L.S. (1978). *Mind in Society: The Development of Higher Psychological Processes.* (edited by M. Cole, J. Scribner, V. John-Steiner, and E. Souberman). Cambridge, MA: Harvard University Press.

Vygotsky, L.S. (1986). *Thought and Language.* Cambridge, MA: M.I.T. Press.

Whitehead, A.N. (1916). *Address to the British Mathematical Society.* Manchester, England.

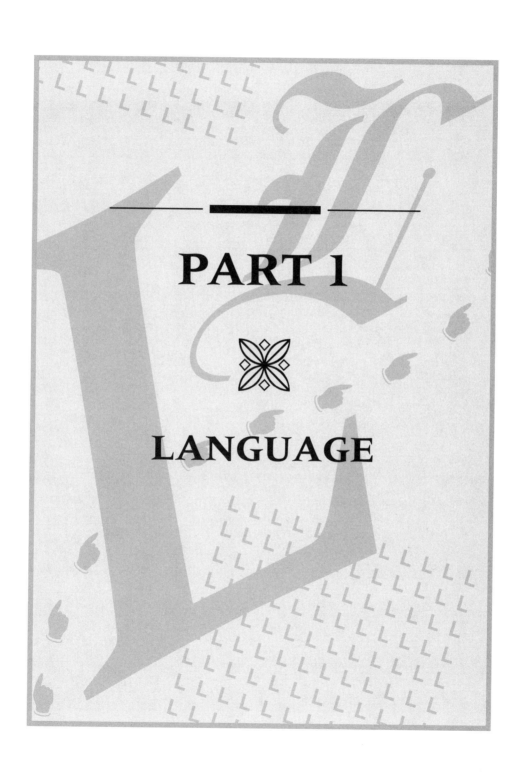

PART 1

LANGUAGE

Chapter 2
LANGUAGE: ITS STRUCTURE AND USE

THE STRUCTURE OF LANGUAGE

- The Sound System
- Words and Their Meaning
- Sentence Structure

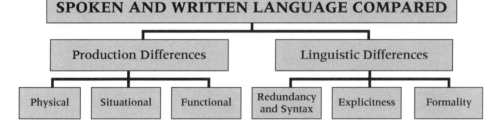

SPOKEN AND WRITTEN LANGUAGE COMPARED

- Production Differences
  - Physical
  - Situational
  - Functional
- Linguistic Differences
  - Redundancy and Syntax
  - Explicitness
  - Formality

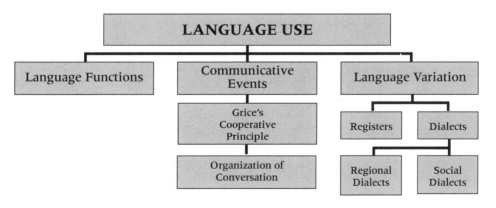

LANGUAGE USE

- Language Functions
- Communicative Events
  - Grice's Cooperative Principle
  - Organization of Conversation
- Language Variation
  - Registers
  - Dialects
    - Regional Dialects
    - Social Dialects

Learning a language involves two different kinds of learning. We must learn how the language is structured — what makes a well-formed sentence, for example. Secondly, we must learn appropriate uses for various forms of the language — for example, how to make a request to a friend versus a stranger, and under what circumstances it is acceptable to use the first names of those we interact with.

Both structure and use are governed by rules — quite strict rules. Learning a language involves learning thousands of rules that govern its structure and use. However, most of these rules are not consciously known by native speakers of a language. Native speakers often cannot articulate the knowledge that governs their language production and use.

A colleague related an interesting anecdote about a task she had given a class composed of francophones who were learning English and anglophones who were learning French. She first asked them to write down all the verbs in English that have the same form for the past tense as they do for the present tense. The anglophones looked puzzled and could not immediately think of any examples, whereas the francophones busily wrote down the list: *beat, bid* (as in bridge), *burst, cast, cost, cut, hit, hurt, let, put, quit, set, shed, shut, slit, split, spread, thrust.*

She then asked the class to write down the French verbs that are conjugated in the *passé composé* with the auxiliary *être* rather than the more usual *avoir.* The francophones looked puzzled while the anglophones busily wrote down *aller, arriver, devenir,* and so on — the list painstakingly learned when they had learned the *passé composé.*

The knowledge we have of our native language governs our language performance and prevents us from saying *The batter hitted the ball to the boundary.* However, we are often not aware of the knowledge that guides our language production, and have trouble articulating that knowledge. When I was writing this chapter, I called on several colleagues in my department — professors in the Department of Language Education, all with Ph.D.s — to help me try to figure out the list of verbs like *hit.* Our best efforts enabled us to list only six or seven of them. It was a colleague who had learned English as a second language who finally provided me with the complete list. The knowledge that we have of our native language is, for the most part, implicit rather than explicit. When we learn a foreign language, however, we lack the intuitive knowledge that guides the native speaker and must learn explicitly lists, rules, and exceptions to those rules.

We also internalize rules for using language in appropriate ways. Think of all the ways you might ask a person to go away:

Go away

Get lost

Would you please leave

I wonder if you would be so kind as to excuse me while I take this phone call

and many other variants, both more polite and less. A class of mine once came up with more than thirty different versions of the request in both verbal and nonverbal forms. If you were to ask elementary school children to categorize such a list of expressions on a chart to indicate which they might address to various people — the teacher, their mothers, their younger brother, a stranger — they would almost certainly show good awareness of the situations in which each might be appropriately used.

Each of us has many varieties of language available for use in different situations. A major distinction may usefully be made between written language and spoken language. Spoken language and written language are based on the same system but there are major differences between the two modes. Each mode is used for a range of functions and there is some overlap. Nonetheless there are overall differences between speech and writing that are important for educators to consider.

To learn a language as a native speaker, then, involves the largely unconscious acquisition of knowledge that governs both the structure of the language and its use, in both written and spoken forms, for various purposes and in various settings. In this chapter three main topics are addressed: (1) the structure of language — the structure that underlies all forms of the language; (2) a comparison between written language and spoken language; and (3) language use.

THE STRUCTURE OF LANGUAGE

As noted above, languages are highly structured, governed by thousands of rules. The rules I am talking about are not the prescriptive rules found in grammar books but rules in the heads of native speakers. For the most part, these rules have never been taught or explained to native speakers. Native speakers do not need to be taught rules of this kind. They are known intuitively; these rules constitute the native speaker's knowledge of his or her language. Usually native speakers cannot articulate the rules. They are well aware, however, when a rule is violated. Let me give some examples of the kind of rule I am talking about.

I have a colleague who speaks several languages. His native language is Greek; he is fluent in English and French and understands some German and some Arabic. Despite his great facility with languages, as a non-native speaker of English he sometimes speaks in ways that deviate slightly from the expected. One day, seeing him for the first time in a month, I said, "I haven't seen you for ages, George!" He replied, "I haven't seen you too, Marion." Any native speaker recognizes the sentence as deviant. An eight-year-old knows that if you say, "Lisa likes bananas" you may say "Laurel likes them too." But if you say "Lisa doesn't like bananas" you say "Laurel doesn't like them either" rather than "Laurel doesn't like them too." Most native speakers, however, are likely to have difficulty explaining why.

Colleagues of mine collected the following examples of signs seen in foreign countries:

peanuts vendor

shoes repair

letters box

Note that the signs make perfect sense. A peanut vendor does, indeed, sell peanuts; a shoe repair person repairs shoes; and a letter box is for holding letters. However, the use of the plural forms, *peanuts*, *shoes*, and *letters*, strikes us as odd. Though we may not be able to explain why, we know that it violates the way English works.

Three major kinds of knowledge about our native language are addressed in this section of the chapter: knowledge of the sound system or **phonology**; knowledge about meanings or **semantics**; and knowledge about the way words are combined into longer structures like phrases and sentences — known as **syntax**.

THE SOUND SYSTEM

Part of the knowledge native speakers have about their language is a knowledge of the sounds of the language. We can, of course, *make* all the sounds of the language, and we are aware of the difference when a non-native speaker substitutes a slightly different sound. If a native speaker of French or German pronounces *three* as if it were *tree*, we note the difference and realize that the speaker is probably not a native speaker of English.

The native speaker also knows how sounds may be combined in English. If you are asked how many "possible" English words could be created from the letters *g*, *l*, *p*, and *a*, you would probably come up with

g l a p

g a l p

p l a g

If you had to make up the name of a new product, for example, you might consider any of the above, but you would certainly reject the following as impossible combinations: *glpa, alpg, apgl, pgal*.

Let us take another example of your knowledge of the sound system of English. The sound spelled in English as *ng* — and written in phonetic script as /ŋ/—may occur at the end of a word as in *sing*, or within a word as in *singer*, but it may not occur at the beginning of an English word. The native speaker's knowledge about the sound /ŋ/ is much more complex than this.

If, for example, the sound / η / occurs *within* a word it is sometimes followed by the sound /g/ and sometimes not. Compare, for example, the pronunciation of *hanger* and *anger*. In the case of *anger*, the sound / η / is followed by the sound /g/, whereas in the case of *hanger* there is no /g/ sound. This you know well if you are a native speaker of English. Now consider the following imaginary scenario. You meet someone at a party and, in the course of conversation, you ask, "What do you do for a living?" She answers, "I pling wobs." "You what?" you ask, and she says, "I am a plinger of wobs." Though you have, presumably, never seen the non-word *plinger* before, you have no doubt, as your read this anecdote, about how to pronounce it. You know that it rhymes with *singer* and not with *finger*. You are guided in your pronunciation by knowledge that you probably cannot articulate. Our knowledge of the sound system of our native language includes a large number of rules that we do not know that we know.

WORDS AND THEIR MEANINGS

Our knowledge about the meanings of the words of our native language is complex. Our knowledge of the meaning of *apple*, for example, enables us to tell an apple from orange or a chair. We know that apples and oranges are related but that apples and chairs are not. We know that apples and poppies are also related in some kind of way, but not as closely as apples and oranges. We know that skin, core, seeds and pulp are parts of an apple, and that spartans and golden delicious are kinds of apples. We know that you can eat an apple but that you cannot drink one. You *peel* an apple when you remove its skin; but if you remove the skin from a chicken or a bear, you *skin* it. In other words, our knowledge of the meanings of words enables us to do much more than pick out and name objects; our knowledge tells us how a word fits into complex networks of other related words.

Our knowledge of words enables us to make subtle distinctions among words of similar meaning. Consider the following list of verbs that are all somewhat related to *say*:

remark	hint	yell	mumble	murmur
roar	relate	cry	announce	whisper
declare	state	assert	maintain	confide
contend	mutter	grumble	complain	bellow

Each word has the same basic meaning of *say*, but each has additional features of meaning that indicate a specific manner of saying or suggest a certain kind of situation. If you think about it, you can describe the special feature or features of meaning for each word

Our knowledge of the words of the language includes knowledge about the word classes they belong to. Teachers sometimes complain that their students do not know what a noun is, or an adjective, or a verb. Perhaps students cannot name a given word as a noun or a verb, but they certainly know what nouns, verbs, adverbs and adjectives are. If they did not, they could neither speak nor understand the language.

Visiting in a third-grade classroom one day, I showed individual students the following nonsense sentence:

The mitty wirts fommed tiply.

I explained that it was a silly sentence because it was made up of words that are not real words at all. "But suppose," I said, "that I wanted to make this silly sentence into a real sentence. Can you tell me a real word that could go in place of *fommed*?" Not one of those eight-year-olds gave me anything but a verb. When I asked them to replace *wirts*, not one of them gave me anything but a noun. All of them replaced *mitty* with an adjective and *tiply* with an adverb. Perhaps they could not have named *fommed* as a verb, but they knew that a verb had to go in the slot in the sentence that *fommed* occupies, and they were able to pick out a verb from their mental lexicons and tell it to me when I asked. If we did not have words categorized as nouns, verbs, and so on, we could not perform a task like this and we could not form acceptable sentences.

We not only have verbs categorized as verbs. We make fine distinctions among kinds of verbs. Consider the following sentences:

The boys were playing.

The boys were making.

The first sentence is acceptable; the second is not because it is not complete. It is not complete because *make* is a verb that requires an object. Third graders can recognize that the first of the following sentences is acceptable but that the second is not:

Tom tripped his grandmother.

Tom stumbled his grandmother.

They may not be able to explain that *tripped*, a transitive verb, may be followed by an object whereas *stumbled*, an intransitive verb, may not. But they can use the words correctly and can recognize improper usage because they have the verbs correctly categorized in their mental lexicons.

The discussion thus far has treated words as if they were the basic unit of meaning in the language. But actually, words are often made up of smaller meaning units called **morphemes**. Sometimes two root words are combined as in *afternoon* or *sunflower*. It is easy to see the two meaning units in each of these words. It is not quite so easy to see the two morphemes in *flowers* or *walked*.

Flowers is made up of *flower* and the plural morpheme *-s; walked* is made up of walk and the past tense morpheme *-ed.* Morphemes that carry grammatical meaning of this kind are called **inflectional** morphemes.

Another kind of morpheme is the **derivational** morpheme. Look at each group of words in the accompanying table and see if you can find a meaning element that is common to the words in each group.

1	2	3	4	5
trivialize	childishness	driver	flaky	contractible
familiarize	modesty	writer	rosy	reducible
actualize	boldness	keeper	wily	visible
polarize	naturalness	founder	gory	manageable
realize	density	dancer		noticeable
	rarity			comprehensible
	honesty			

The suffixes that appear on the words in the table are called derivational morphemes. Such suffixes usually change the word class to which the word belongs. *Trivial* is an adjective; the *-ize* suffix changes it into a verb that means "to make trivial" — and so with all words in group 1. The *-y, -ity* and *-ness* morphemes in group 2 change adjectives into nouns, and so on. Note that you may not simply pick any noun-making morpheme and add it to an adjective; *boldity* and *modestness* are not acceptable (though my intuitions tell me that *modestness* has more chance of being accepted than *boldity*).

Only a few aspects of meaning have been considered in this brief discussion. Enough has been said, however, to indicate the complexity of the meanings we have for the words of our native language. Clearly, learning the meaning of a word is not a one-time event. We learn these complex meanings as we meet the words many times in different situations.

SENTENCE STRUCTURE

Our knowledge of our native language includes not only knowledge of the sound system and knowledge of the words of the language but also knowledge of how words may be combined into phrases and sentences. Consider the following "sentences":

1. Has sheep little her lost Bo Peep.

2. Has lost her sheep.

3.   James put the newspaper.

4.   Eliza has to her grandmother a letter written.

All four sentences are deviant in some way. Sentences 1 and 4 are not ordered correctly. Sentences 2 and 3 are incomplete. In other words, certain elements are required for a complete sentence, and elements in a sentence (or, indeed, in a phrase) must be ordered in certain ways in order to be acceptable.

As to completeness, the elements required in a sentence are determined by the kind of the verb, as suggested above. An intransitive verb requires nothing more than a subject and verb for a complete sentence (e.g., *Jack ran; Marie cycled*). A transitive requires an object after the verb (e.g., *Janice saw a plane*). Transitive verbs that are like *put* require not only an object, but an adverbial (e.g., *Mark put the baby **in the crib***).

Word order is critically important in English. Apart from adverbials, which have some ability to move in the sentence, the order of words is highly constrained. Consider the four words *eyes*, *Helen*, *her*, and *closed*. There are twenty-four possible orders. Yet if native speakers are asked to order the words so as to form an acceptable sentence, all will agree on the same order: *Helen closed her eyes*. In English, the order of the elements of a sentence is strictly governed. Not only sentences, but the order of smaller structural elements is strictly ordered. Suppose you are given the following set of five words, *sweaters*, *those*, *woollen*, *torn*, *five*, *red*, and are asked to order them in such a way as to form an acceptable phrase that ends with *sweaters*. There are 120 possible word sets, but it is unlikely that you will come up with any other phrase than: *those five torn red woollen sweaters*. Even though word order is critical in English syntax, it is not talked about in formal grammar lessons delivered to native speaking children. No instruction is needed. Native speakers internalize the strict rules that govern the ordering of words in phrases and sentences, and never give word order a thought until they hear a deviant sentence by a non-native speaker.

SUMMARY

The brief description of the structure of language set out above illustrates the kinds of knowledge that native speakers have of their language. Our production of language and our understanding of the language we hear and see are determined by our knowledge of the structure of our language. Native speakers' knowledge of their language is referred to as their **linguistic competence**. A native speaker's knowledge is vast and complex. It enables us to produce sentences that have never before been uttered and to understand novel sentences that we have never before heard or read. Our knowledge is acquired, for the most part, unconsciously.

Spoken and Written Language Compared

Several years ago, a student in an applied linguistics course I was teaching tape recorded — with my permission — two samples of my oral language. One was a portion of a formal lecture to the class; the other was an informal interview I had with him in my office. The purpose was to provide data that he could analyze in order to write a short paper describing differences between formal and informal oral language. I remember with amusement his discomfiture when he talked to me, later, about the transcript he had made of my informal oral language in the interview situation — a transcript that was rife with fragments, false starts, repetitions and even errors. He was a courteous man who struggled to be polite. But he finally blurted out that he was astonished that an educated woman, a university professor, no less, should have talked in such a way.

During his early years in office, former United States president, George Bush, was criticized in a number of newspaper articles because of his inadequate control of the English language. In one critical article that I read, many of the examples cited were off-the-cuff remarks in response to reporters' questions — utterances that would have sounded perfectly acceptable in the flow of spoken language where they occurred, but which looked odd indeed when written down.

Few of us — university graduates, English teachers, presidents of the United States, included — are pleased to have our informal oral language presented in written form. Language that is entirely appropriate in spoken exchanges looks very strange when transcribed and presented in written form. Oral language and written language are different forms.

It is an oversimplification to divide language merely into oral and written categories. Some oral language forms are much closer to written language than others. A lecture that has been carefully prepared will be closer in form to written language than will conversational exchanges in the cafeteria during coffee break; the messages I send to friends by electronic mail exhibit some of the informality of spoken language. Nonetheless there are important characteristic differences between written and spoken language. It is important for teachers to be aware of the characteristics of spoken and written language and the reasons for those characteristic forms. The influential Bullock Report produced by the Department of Education and Science in the United Kingdom noted that "not enough account is taken of the fundamental differences that exist between speech and writing" (DES, 1975, p. 143). Teachers who understand those differences will be in a better position to help students in a variety of ways.

Two major kinds of differences between written language and spoken language are discussed: production differences and linguistic differences. By and large, the linguistic differences are due to the production differences.

PRODUCTION DIFFERENCES

Production differences arise from physical differences, situational differences, and functional differences (Perera, 1984).

Physical Differences

An obvious difference between the two is that writing is visual language, whereas speech is audible language. Writing consists of marks arranged in space; speech consists of sounds produced in time. This most obvious of differences between the two modes has consequences both for the producer of language and for the receiver.

Speakers have little time in which to produce their utterances. They cannot polish spontaneous speech as they can their written sentences. This makes for less varied vocabulary and simpler sentence structures in spoken language than in written. Speakers have little time to search for the best word and make do with whatever words come quickly to mind.

The syntax of spoken language tends to consist of clauses strung together in chains by means of *and*, *but* and *so*.

Chafe (Chafe and Danielewicz, 1987) examined four kinds of language from each of twenty academics: conversations, lectures, letters, and academic papers. He found that vocabulary was least varied in conversations, followed, in order, by lectures, letters, and academic papers. He found that syntax was simplest in conversations, followed by lectures, letters, and academic papers. In other words, both kinds of spoken language had less varied vocabulary and simpler syntax than either kind of written language.

The mode of production has consequences for the receiver as well as for the producer. Listeners must process speech as it is produced. They cannot speed up to get the gist of a speech or conversation, as they can with written language. They cannot slow down to allow extra time to process difficult material; and they cannot run speech through a second time to get what they missed the first time, as they can with a written text. The less demanding vocabulary and sentence structure that is a normal consequence of the mode of production of oral language has benefits, then, for the listener for whom more complex language would be more difficult to process.

A further major difference between speech and writing arises from the fact that speech has certain ways of conveying meaning that are not available in writing. Oral language is partially composed of sounds like /t/ and /f/; these sounds are represented in writing by letters. In addition, however, oral language also makes use of what are known as paralinguistic features like stress and intonation which have no clear parallels in writing. Consider the simple sentence

Jeremy drove to Calgary on Friday.

If the sentence is uttered with falling intonation on the last syllable, the sentence functions as a statement giving information. If, however, the sentence is uttered with rising intonation on the last syllable, the sentence becomes a question. Moreover, the meaning of the question changes each time we stress a different word:

> *Jeremy* drove to Calgary on Friday? (Was it Jeremy who drove to Calgary or was it someone else?)

> Jeremy *drove* to Calgary on Friday? (Are you sure he didn't fly?)

> Jeremy drove *to* Calgary on Friday? (Are you sure he didn't drive *from* Calgary?)

> Jeremy drove to *Calgary* on Friday? (Are you sure it wasn't to Edmonton?)

> Jeremy drove to Calgary on *Friday*? (Are you sure it wasn't on Thursday?)

Paralinguistic features, in other words, often reveal something about the speaker's attitude. In the sentences above, the speaker has some doubt about the information that has been given. To take another example, if a wife says to her husband

> *You paid one hundred dollars for that sweat shirt?*

with a marked fall in pitch on the first syllable of *dollars* and a marked rise in pitch on the second syllable, she is not primarily asking a question for verification. She is expressing her attitude towards the expenditure — astonishment, perhaps, or disapproval. The kinds of meaning so easily conveyed in spoken language by stress and by the rise and fall of intonation patterns cannot easily be conveyed in writing. Stress may be indicated by underlining or italicizing a word, but such devices must be used sparingly, and are usually discouraged altogether in more formal writing. Other means must be found to convey such meanings in writing.

Situational Differences

Oral language is usually produced in face-to-face situations and is received immediately, whereas writing is produced in isolation from the receiver who is separated from the writer by time and distance. Listeners are usually active participants in the speech situation. They can interrupt with their own examples or contributions to the subject under discussion. They can ask questions if they do not understand. Listeners' facial expressions and body language advise us about their reception of what we say. Even if we are addressing a large audience where interruptions and questions are not appropriate, facial expressions and body language may indicate puzzlement or restlessness.

Facial expressions and body language are used by speakers also to help get their message across. The shrug of a shoulder or raised eyebrows can convey meaning that does not need to be put into words. Writers have to express all their meaning through the words they choose and the way they organize those words on the page. They must take pains to be clear so that receivers who cannot ask questions will be able to understand the message.

Functional Differences

By and large, speech and writing are used for different functions. Some functions can be performed in either mode. A story, for example, may be told orally or in writing. But many functions are restricted to one mode or the other. Lists and legal documents are written; conversations and marriage ceremonies are conducted in spoken language. An invitation may be issued either orally or in writing; but note that the kind of occasion for which you issue a formal written invitation is very different from the kind of occasion for which an oral invitation is appropriate. Compare, for example, an invitation to drop in for a drink on Friday night and an invitation to a large, formal, catered wedding reception.

Differences between speech and writing are caused, then, by various factors associated with the production of each of the two modes. Speech and writing are physically different. The situations in which they are produced and received are different. They are used for different functions. We now turn to the specific linguistic differences between speech and writing that are largely caused by these production differences.

LINGUISTIC DIFFERENCES

There are four major kinds of linguistic differences between spoken language and written language: (1) the degree of redundancy; written language is less redundant than speech; (2) syntax, which must be discussed in conjunction with redundancy; (3) the degree of explicitness required; and (4) the degree of formality.

Redundancy and Syntax

Oral language is usually produced spontaneously with little time for planning. One result of this production factor is that speech is highly redundant. In spoken language, a lot of words are used to convey a given amount of information with many instances of hesitations, false starts, incomplete utterances, repetitions, hedges (e.g., *sort of*), fillers (e.g., *well, you know*), and frequent pauses, sometimes filled with *er* or *umm*. Goldman-Eisler (1961) has pointed out that, in spoken language, up to 50 per cent of the time is occupied by pauses.

Casual spoken language does not segment easily into sentences. Spoken language is produced in brief spurts that have been called **idea units** or **intonation units** (Chafe and Danielewicz, 1987; Perera, 1984). They are marked as units by their intonation contour and are usually followed by a pause. They usually consist of a single clause or a syntactic fragment of some kind and are strung together in chains, usually by means of coordination. (It is worth noting, in passing, that one of the major tasks for children beginning school is to learn what a sentence is because spoken language does not consist of sentences. Children who have been read to a great deal will find the task easier than those who have had little or no exposure to written language before they start school.)

Spoken language is less varied than written language both in vocabulary and in the structure of intonation units, as already mentioned. The simple structure of intonation units and simple, repetitive vocabulary do not become tedious in speech because speakers achieve variety by paralinguistic devices (stress and intonation patterns) and by body language (gestures, facial expressions, etc.).

Written language is much less redundant than spoken language. False starts are not tolerated. Repetition is irritating. The writer makes use of more varied sentence structure and vocabulary for several reasons. One is that writers have time to find the right word and to construct more complex sentences. They can take time as they produce their written text, and can revise, at a later time, as many times as necessary. A second reason is that overuse of coordinated clauses and reliance on a limited vocabulary makes for boring prose.

A major factor affecting written language is the value placed upon economy of expression. It is expensive to print two pages if the same information can be conveyed in one. Moreover, readers are reluctant to plough through unnecessary verbiage in order to get information. It is a waste of time. If we have difficulty understanding a paragraph or a page, we can always adjust our reading rate or reread the passage.

In order to achieve economy of expression, constructions are used that contribute to compression. The result is that written language tends to have long sentences loaded with information. This is especially true of writing that serves the function of transmitting information, like the writing in textbooks. Some of the constructions favouring compression that are common in writing but not in spoken language are: **nominalizations**, **attributive adjectives**, **prepositional phrases**, **non-finite subordinate clauses**, and **ellipsis**.

1. *Nominalizations* A nominalization is the formation of a noun from a verb or adjective as with the words *maintenance*, *verification*, and *availability*. Nominalizations allow a whole sentence to be compressed into a phrase.

   > *Critics of the Green Revolution claim that the **increase** in grain **production** has been achieved at the **expense** of social **justice**.*

In conversation this would probably have sounded something like:

> *More grain has been produced. It's called the Green Revolution. But it's cost a lot of money and some people don't think it's right to spend all that money on producing more grain. They think the money should have been spent on better social programs.*

2.   *Attributive Adjectives*   appear before the noun as in:

> *Both movements viewed creativity as a **conscious, goal-directed** activity in which **problem** definition plays a **crucial** role in the **creative** act.*

Attributive adjectives have the effect of making longer, more informative noun phrases.

3.   *Prepositional Phrases* are often piled on top of each other in written sentences:

> *By 1937, this debate on the future of humanity between the defenders of an old order and the advocates of a new was swallowed up in a new struggle for survival.*

4.   *Non-Finite Subordinate Clauses* have several words omitted, the introductory conjunction, the subject, and auxiliary verbs as in:

> ***Satisfied with the deal**, the union's negotiator confidently presented the package to the membership.*

In speech, the non-finite clause would be more fully expressed as *because he was satisfied with the deal*, or, more likely still, *he was satisfied with the deal so he …*

5.   *Ellipsis* occurs when repeated elements are omitted from a clause. The words in parentheses were omitted in the following sentence:

> *World timber production would rise by seven times; fertilizer use (would rise by) thirteen times; and all energy use (would rise by) fourteen times.*

It is not important that you be able to remember or name these various constructions. It is important, however, to understand that written language makes use of a variety of constructions that allow writing to convey a lot of meaning in fewer words than would be normal in speech. The compressed nature of written language contributes to the processing load and can make for comprehension difficulties as discussed further in Chapters 5 and 7.

A further factor that affects syntax is the absence of paralinguistic features in written language. As noted above, speakers can make use of stress and intonation and body language to express many kinds of attitudinal meanings. Writers must express all their meaning through words and the way they organize them. Writers use several constructions to achieve the kinds of meaning conveyed by stress and intonation in speech. For example, whereas a speaker stresses the city to which Jeremy went by stressing *Calgary* in the sentence *Jeremy went to Calgary on Friday*, the writer achieves the same kind of stress by using the following construction:

It was to Calgary that Jeremy went on Friday.[1]

Explicitness

Written language is more explicit than speech because it is addressed to a reader who is separated in time and space from the writer. The reader cannot ask questions to clarify misunderstanding. The writer must therefore take care to give all the information the reader is likely to need. Moreover, speech is supported by a context that is shared between speaker and listener. This results in a considerably greater use of pronouns and inexplicit adverbials like *here, there,* and *like this*. A speaker may say *It's over there* and be understood; but a writer must be explicit about what is where, as in, for example, *The slipper was half hidden beneath the chair.*

Formality

There are varying degrees of formality in both speech and writing. In general, however, writing serves more formal purposes than speech. There are a number of constructions widely accepted in speech that are less acceptable in writing. For example, a speaker would not be harshly judged if he said, *The Hungarians won more medals than us in the 1992 Olympics even though their population is smaller.* In writing, however, a majority of educated people would expect to read *than we* or *than we did.*

SUMMARY

While speech and writing are based on the same system, there are notable differences between the two. Whereas the sentence is the basic unit of written language, the idea unit is the basic unit of spoken language. Speech is marked by simpler syntax and vocabulary, and is highly redundant, marked by fragments, false starts, hedges, fillers, and repetitions. These characteristics are especially marked in informal, interactive speech, but are noticeable, as well, in formal speech situations like lectures. Written language is much less redundant than speech and, in many of its forms, is characterized by constructions that favour compression. Written language — especially the language of textbooks — is

---

[1] Those interested in further examples of constructions used for this purpose might see Perera's (1984) excellent chapter on differences between speech and writing.

heavily loaded conceptually. The compressed, conceptually-loaded nature of written language can make for comprehension problems for poor or inexperienced readers.

The differences between speech and writing are not always obvious. One reason for this is that, when we are involved in conversation, we note content and not form. We pay scant attention to fragments, false starts, repetitions and so on. Another reason is that a good deal of the spoken language that we hear — on the radio and on television newscasts, for example — is actually written language delivered orally. The differences between spoken and written language are significant in schools. It takes children some years to become competent in handling both the production and the comprehension of written language. If teachers are aware of the differences, they are in a better position to offer support and help.

LANGUAGE USE

The discussion of the structure of English in the first major section of this chapter addresses the question of how language is organized in the human mind. Our knowledge of the structure of our language is called **linguistic competence**. It is our linguistic competence that enables us to produce well-formed or grammatical sentences.

In order to communicate, however, more is required of our utterances than that they be well-formed. They must also be appropriate. Our ability to produce utterances that are both well formed and appropriate has been described as **communicative competence** (Hymes, 1974). Our linguistic competence enables us to produce well-formed sentences like *Excellent wheat is grown in Saskatchewan.* Our communicative competence tells us that such a sentence is an inappropriate response to the question *Where's the bread?*

Our linguistic competence is part of our communicative competence. In order to communicate, we must be able to produce sentences that conform to the linguistic rules of the language. The other part of our communicative competence is a complex set of rules that guide us in our attempts to communicate. These rules give guidance about such things as when and how we speak, and about initiating, sequencing, and terminating various kinds of discourse. We know we have such rules because we recognize violations. Let's look at an example:

> Anita meets Susan in the library. Anita has been trying to find a book in the stacks and cannot locate it. She says to Susan: "I can never find anything here." Susan responds:

1. Why don't you ask the librarian to help you.

2. It's raining.

3. I'm going skiing tomorrow.

4. That's a bit of an exaggeration, I think.

5. I often have the same problem.

We easily recognize that 2 and 3 are inappropriate because they introduce a topic unrelated to the topic of Anita's complaint. We know, furthermore, that 4, while related to the topic, is somewhat inappropriate because it treats Anita's complaint more literally than Anita may have intended. We could not make such judgements if we did not have rules that guide us in making appropriate conversational moves.

Our communicative competence enables us to use language to do things. We do not speak or write merely to compose sentences. We speak or write to request, to inform, to entertain, to invite, to greet, to complain, and for dozens of other functions. Our communicative competence allows us to use language appropriately in performing a large variety of *speech acts*.

We use language differently in different situations. The rules that guide us in ways of speaking and writing that are appropriate to the situation are acquired largely unconsciously through experience. An interesting illustration of a child's natural acquisition of communicative rules was passed on to me by a former student, a francophone living in Brandon, Manitoba. I met her after a period of years. She told me that she had married a francophone and that they had two daughters aged twelve months and three years. Since there were few francophones in Brandon, they had made French the language of the home, but their older daughter, Therese, spoke English as well as French, having learned it from anglophone children in the neighbourhood. She showed excellent ability in deciding which of her two languages she should use in a given situation. She had many dolls, her mother told me, most of them with French names (Marie, Jeanne, Monique, Yvette, and so on), and one doll with an English name, Daisy. All of her dolls she spoke to in French with the exception of Daisy to whom she spoke English!

Not all of us are bilingual. But all of us have access to a variety of ways of speaking (and writing) that are appropriate to different situations. Forms of language that vary according to situation are called *registers*. Our language varies according to what we are talking or writing about, who our addressee is, and what our purpose is.

Another kind of language variation derives from differences among language users. For this kind of language variation the term *dialect* is used. Dialect differences are caused by such factors as region, ethnicity, social status, age, and gender.

In this section, then, we consider language use — the rules that enable us to use language appropriately, and the ways in which language varies in different situations and with different speakers. Each of the following is considered in turn: (1) language functions — the uses we make of language; (2) the rules that govern the organization of communicative events such as conversations; (3) registers — or varieties of language that are appropriate for various situations; and (4) dialects — the variation in language due to differences among speakers.

LANGUAGE FUNCTIONS

We speak or write not merely to *say* things but to *do* things (Austin, 1962). We use language to question, to report, to swear, to rebuke, to insult, to flatter, and for many other purposes. Those who are authorized to do so use language to marry, to sentence, and to make laws. The sentences we use in our speech and writing are forms that perform various functions. It is useful to make the distinction between form and function as separate components in a communicative act.

FORM	**FUNCTION**
(what X says)	(what X is doing in saying it)
1. (Mother calls sons Rob and Dan and confronts them with a broken vase.) Dan says, "Rob broke it."	Dan is *accusing*.
2. Rob says, "It was an accident."	Rob is *explaining* (excusing)

There is no one-to-one relationship between a language form and a language function. The same sentence may function in one way in one context and in a different way in another as the following examples illustrate.

1. Sarah answers the phone. The caller asks to speak to her mother. Sarah calls her mother who is digging in the back garden. She then returns to the phone and says: "Mummy's coming."

2. Sarah plays with her 15-month-old sister while her mother slips next door to borrow an egg from her neighbour. Her infant sister, missing her mother, goes to the front door and begins to sob. "Mummy's coming," says Sarah.

3. Sarah, reading in her bedroom, is disturbed by the noisy play of her brother and cousin who are yelling and banging about in the room next to hers. Sarah goes to the door of their room and says, "Mummy's coming!"

Sarah used the same sentence, *Mummy's coming*, to perform three different functions. In the first case she used it to *inform* the telephone caller. In the second case, she used it to *comfort* or *reassure* her sister. In the third, she used it to *threaten* or *warn* her misbehaving brother and cousin. The meaning of the sentence is the same in all three examples. But it is used to serve different purposes in three different contexts.

You probably learned in school that there are three kinds of sentences: declarative, interrogative, and imperative. You probably learned, also, that declarative sentences are used to make statements, that interrogative sentences are used to ask questions, and that imperative sentences are used to give orders or directions. This explanation of the uses of the forms of sentences is inadequate. It is based on the inaccurate assumption that there is a one-to-one relationship between form and function. If I ask: "Can you tell me the time?" I do not expect you to treat my utterance as a yes/no question about your ability to tell the time. It has the form of a question but is functioning as a request. Statements may also function as requests. When my elderly aunt says, "I can't hear you," she is not speaking to inform me, but to request me to repeat my comment. Sometimes interrogative sentences are used to make statements. Suppose a friend asks "Are you working this weekend?" and you reply "Is the Pope Catholic?" Your reply has the form of a question but is clearly a vigorous affirmative to your friend's question.

Note that certain conditions must be fulfilled in order for an utterance to function in a given way. These are called **appropriateness conditions**. Any person may say, "I now pronounce you husband and wife." But the words will have the effect of uniting the couple in matrimony only if an authorized person utters the words in a certain context after various conditions have been met. If I promise to lend you my car on Friday night, I must have a car to lend, I must be willing to lend it, and I must believe that you would like the use of my car. If, for example, I know that you have your own car and that it will be available on Friday night, one of the appropriateness conditions for a promise has been violated. (If I know, further, that you are taking out a special friend on Friday night, and that your car is a late model BMW whereas mine is an ancient VW bug, you will probably conclude that I am joking rather than promising.) A question requires that the questioner does not know the answer, wants to know the answer, and believes the person questioned does know the answer. As we will discuss later, teachers' questions commonly violate these appropriateness conditions.

We speak and write, then, to *do* things with language, to achieve purposes such as informing, questioning, greeting and complaining. Language forms are used to perform various functions. There is not a one to one relationship between form and function; the same utterance may perform different functions in different contexts.

COMMUNICATIVE EVENTS

Communicative events are cooperative undertakings. Participants cooperate in engaging in conversations, interviews, lectures, and other forms of oral discourse. In conversations and interviews, participants take turns speaking; but in lectures and sermons, members of the audience do not expect to have a turn and usually remain cooperatively silent — except for a chuckle in response to a joke, or perhaps a question if one is invited. Communication through written language is also a cooperative venture. Both the writer and the reader have certain obligations and each expects the other to fulfil those obligations. Readers expect writers to write clearly, relevantly, and coherently, and writers expect readers to read in ways that enable them to construct meaning from the written text.

Discourse analysis is a vast and fascinating field of study still in its infancy. We do not usually think of conversations, telephone calls, interviews, and classroom lessons as being rule-governed forms of behaviour. However, researchers have begun to describe the implicit rules that we follow in such communicative events. In this brief introduction, only two aspects are treated. The first is the underlying principles that guide our behaviour as we engage in communicative events. Secondly, we discuss briefly the rules that govern our participation in conversations.

Grice's Cooperative Principle

Philosopher Paul Grice (1975) has suggested that speakers adhere to a set of cooperative principles when they converse. His four **maxims** or principles have contributed greatly to our understanding of the way people behave when they engage in conversations and other communicative events.

The Maxim of Quantity states that speakers are expected to give as much information as necessary for their listeners to understand them, but to give no more than is necessary. If you ask a friend, "Have you seen Harvey lately" and he replies, "I saw him two weeks ago," you are entitled to assume that he has not seen Harvey in the past two weeks. If he has seen Harvey more recently, his answer conceals relevant information and thus violates the maxim of quantity.

If, on the other hand, you ask a passerby how to get to Victoria Avenue and she replies:

> Ah, Victoria Avenue. That's a lovely old street. I used to live there myself. Well, there are two or three ways you can get there from here. You could drive north to Broadway then turn right and go about three kilometres. You'll pass x, y and z, then you'll come to Victoria which is a main cross street with traffic signals. If you kept going you'd come to a, b, and c which are other main streets that cross Broadway. The other way you could go is to drive south to Prince Edward — that's about six blocks from here — and

then turn left. You go about three kilometres past p, q and r and you'll come to Victoria.

In providing too much information, the woman is violating the maximum of quantity. People who give too much information are bores.

The Maxim of Relevance Speakers are expected to make comments that are relevant. If your friend is about to leave the building in a heavy rain storm without a raincoat or umbrella, and you say, "Would you like the loan of an umbrella?" she has a right to expect that you have an umbrella that you are willing to lend. Otherwise your question would be irrelevant.

Sometimes an apparently irrelevant comment is interpreted — and perhaps intended — to convey a different message. If a teacher writes a letter of reference for a former student who is applying for a job as a computer programmer and comments that he is a tall man who writes very neatly, the recipient of the letter may conclude that the applicant has few good qualities to recommend him, since the writer is expected to make comments that are relevant to the position applied for and has failed to do so.

The Maxim of Quality requires that speakers and writers be truthful. Sometimes we violate the principle in order to make a joke, or when we are being ironic. But usually in such cases the context indicates that the "truth" principle has been suspended. Generally we speak and write what we believe to be true.

The Maxim of Manner the fourth principle, requires that speakers and writers be clear.

Conversation

We do not usually think of conversations as being organized. Researchers have found, however, that conversations are governed by clearly recognizable rules. When we converse, for example, we observe Grice's maxims: we make relevant comments; we are usually truthful; we keep the length of our "turn" within acceptable limits; and we are more or less clear in what we say. We take turns. We give and read signals that indicate when a turn is over and another speaker may begin. We have socially accepted ways of beginning and ending conversations. We have ways of repairing glitches when they occur.

Turn taking, a major feature of conversations, is governed by two simple rules. The first is that speakers signal when they wish to end their turn. The second is that the next speaker takes the floor by beginning to speak.

Speakers may signal the end of a turn in a variety of verbal and nonverbal ways. A tag question (*wasn't she? don't they?*) may explicitly invite another to take the floor. Sometimes a speaker nominates a specific speaker by turning to another or by addressing the next speaker directly. If this is not done, anyone may take the floor. A complete sentence followed by a pause is another kind of signal for a change of turn since pauses quickly become awkward. Sometimes speakers sharply raise or lower the pitch of their voice to mark the end of a turn, or end with the phrase *or something:*

Speaker 1: She acted as if she thought she was in charge or something.

Speaker 2: Just imagine!

Gestures and eye gaze are examples of nonverbal signals. Gestures are used to support verbal utterances. As long as we continue gesturing, we indicate that we have more to say. When we stop gesturing, we indicate that our turn is over. In mainstream culture in Canada and the United States, speakers do not normally fix their gaze on the person they are speaking to. Rather, they alternate between meeting the listener's gaze and staring off, briefly, into space. When a speaker ceases doing this and gazes fixedly at her conversational partner, she is signalling the end of her turn.

Researchers have examined many aspects of conversational exchanges: beginnings and endings, ways of changing topic, ways of resolving glitches like too lengthy a pause, or simultaneous attempts by more than one speaker to take the floor. These and other aspects of conversation are clearly guided by internalized rules. Usually, we are unaware of the unspoken rules that guide our behaviour. But we recognize that we have such rules when we note violations. For example, if I meet a friend or acquaintance that I have not seen for some period of time and he says, "Hi, Marion, how are you?" his greeting is an appropriate conversational opener. But if I pick up the phone and, in response to my "Hello," hear someone say "Hello, Mrs. Crowhurst. How are you today?" I recognize a violation of the rules for telephone conversation. Telephone callers are expected to identify themselves when they take their first turn. When I hear this particular violation, I immediately suspect that someone is about to make a solicitation since telephone solicitors frequently begin in this not-quite-acceptable way.

Not only conversations, but all kinds of discourse, both written and spoken, are structured according to fairly well-established principles. We learn the rules for kinds of discourse largely through our experiences with many examples of the discourse type. When they begin school, for example, children must learn the rules for classroom discourse—a topic to be taken up in a later chapter.

LANGUAGE VARIATION:
REGISTERS

All of us have access to many varieties of language that we match to the situations in which we use them. Language varies with different aspects of speech situations such as the participants, the setting, and the purpose.

Language varies according to who is speaking to whom and what their relationship is. Finocchiaro (1974, p.12) illustrates the different forms a message may take by imagining a doctor describing a very sick patient to a variety of people:

> To her husband: *His condition's not good. I'm worried.*

> To the patient: *You're doing pretty well. It'll take a while but you should be up and about in no time.*

> To the patient's family: *I can't be too optimistic. He may have to be hospitalized for at least a month.*

> To a colleague: *These are the x-rays. What do you think? I'm pessimistic. Should I try some … ?*

> In a written report: *X-rays showed lesions … He is not reacting to the prescribed medication. The prognosis is guarded.*

A second factor affecting language use is the setting. A man speaks to his boss in one way if they are in a meeting at the office, and in another if they to go to a pub for a drink after work. Even in the same location, language changes as the topic changes. If a matter related to the office comes up in the pub, the change in topic will produce a change in the kind of language used. It may even put them back, temporarily, into the employer/employee relationship, with consequent effects upon the language used.

A third factor is the kind of language event. Some examples of language events are: sermons, interviews, trials, conversations, and ceremonies. The written mode is also used to deal with a variety of language events: legal opinions, business letters, poems, recipes, and shopping lists, to name a few.

The degree of formality is a major determinant of the kind of language used. Registers vary along a continuum from very casual to very formal. How formally we write or speak is a function of the factors already mentioned.

Registers differ at all grammatical levels — semantic, phonological, and syntactic. Note the different word choices made by the doctor mentioned above to describe her opinion about the patient's condition: *worried* to her husband; *not too optimistic* to the patient's family; *pessimistic* to her colleague; *prognosis … guarded* in the written report. Note the contractions used in oral language (*I'm, you're*, and so on). Research shows that speakers articulate more carefully in formal situations; they are more likely to use contractions and to "drop their *g*'s" (i.e., pronounce words like *singing* as *singin'*) in casual speech than in formal. Syntax is more varied and more complex in more formal situations. Consider the following sentence:

> Given the demonstrated critical role of capacity demands and automaticity in children's performance in other areas of cognition, Brown's model appears to be a fruitful framework for future metattentional research.

It is marked as formal academic language both by its syntax (e.g., long noun phrases), by its specialized vocabulary (e.g., *automaticity, cognition,* and *metattentional*), and by more formal choices such as *children's performance* rather than more casual choices such as *the way kids act* which might have been made in casual conversation, or in an informal note from one colleague to another.

It is usual for all aspects of language to fit the situation. If they do not, the result sounds odd or, sometimes, humorous. In the musical *My Fair Lady*, a beautifully-garbed Eliza, drinking tea at the home of Professor Higgins' mother, announces, in an impeccable upper class accent, *He done her in*. The humour of the situation is caused by the mismatch between her elegant appearance and accent, on the one hand, and her colloquial language and nonstandard syntax, on the other.

Those who are fluently bilingual, when speaking to others who are fluent in the same two languages, vary not only the register in which they speak but also the language. They move from one language to the other according to the topic and purpose of their talk. My Greek colleague referred to earlier always spoke Greek to his son, George. One day at a picnic, he rebuked George in English for some minor misbehaviour. It was the first time in ten years that I had heard him speak to George in English, and I commented on the fact. My colleague had to think about it. He then explained that, because he was angry with George, he had used English as a distancing technique rejecting the use of Greek which was the language of closeness and intimacy between them. Variation between languages for bilingual speakers is the same kind of phenomenon that appears in monolinguals as register variation.

DIALECTS

Dialect is the term used for language variation caused by regional and social differences. The two major regional varieties of English are British and American, each with many subdivisions. The major sources of social variation in language are social class, ethnicity, age, and gender.

Regional Dialects

Regional dialects come about because languages change, and because changes that occur in one area do not always occur in another. Dialect differences include pronunciation differences (often called *accents*), vocabulary differences, and syntactic differences. British and American English also have a number of differences in spelling. Vocabulary differences between British and American English are numerous, for example: *braces* versus *suspenders*; *lift* versus *elevator*; *torch* versus *flashlight*. Syntactic differences are fewer in number. One example is illustrated in the following pair of sentences:

British English: *We used not to take the bus.*

American English: *We didn't use to take the bus.*

Well-known spelling differences are the British *centre, metre, colour* and *analyse* versus the American *center, meter, color* and *analyze*. Somewhat less well known are differences involving doubled letters, for example, *counselled* and *marvellous* in British English versus *counseled* and *marvelous* in American. There is considerable variability among Canadians in the degree to which they follow either British spelling or American. A majority probably follow American spelling in *analyze* and British in *centre*; it is less easy to speak with any certainty about prevailing habits for words like *counselled* and *marvellous*.

Both British and American English have many subdialects. Canadian and Southern dialects are regional subdialects within American English; Australian, Indian English and Scottish are regional subdialects within British English.

Canadian English differs from American English in a number of ways. The largest number of differences is in vocabulary. Vocabulary differs both in items derived from British English, like *solicitor*, and in items that are uniquely Canadian either in origin or in use like *Mountie, cache, mukluk, tuque,* and *patriation* (of the constitution). The best known pronunciation difference between Canadian and American English is found in the pronunciation of words like *life* and *house*. Syntactic differences are few. The one most often quoted is the use of *eh* as in *He lives in Regina, eh* where *eh* has no particular meaning. *Our Own Voice* by Ruth McConnell (1978) provides a rich source of information on Canadian English.

One of the most interesting dialects in Canada is Newfoundland English, which differs markedly from general Canadian English in syntax, pronunciation, and vocabulary. A syntactic difference is illustrated by the following examples: *I runs, I knows*. There are numerous words that are common in Newfoundland but generally unknown in the rest of the country. Examples are: *dwye*, a brief shower of rain or snow; and *flanker*, a live spark from a wood fire. The *Dictionary of Newfoundland English* (1990) is a rich source of information on the many words and phrases unique to Newfoundland English. A well known pronunciation difference is the use of /t/ and /d/ for the sounds that are spelled *th* in *think* and *this*; another difference is the pronunciation of *does* to rhyme with *choose* rather than with *buzz*.

One reason for the uniqueness of Newfoundland English is that the island was settled primarily by immigrants from Ireland and from the West Country of England. A second reason is that it was relatively isolated from other North American language communities for much of its history. Indeed, there is considerable dialectal variation on the island itself caused by the fact that many communities have lived in relative isolation from other communities.

Social Dialects

Just as physical separation of groups of speakers leads to regional dialects, social barriers and social distance cause social dialects. Age, social class and gender are three major social sources of language variation.

Age   There are obvious age differences in vocabulary, syntax and pronunciation between young children and adults. These differences are due to the obvious fact that language is still developing in children. There are also language differences between younger and older adults. Older adults are generally more conservative than younger adults and less likely to change their way of speaking. They are less likely, for example, to introduce trendy new words and expressions into their language. The difference is most clearly seen in vocabulary. Slang is one of the clearest marks of age differences. Each age generates its own favoured expressions. Since slang quickly become outmoded, the use of particular slang terms tends to date a person.

Social Class   Social class differences in language use are usually discussed in terms of *standard English*. Both social class and standard English are slippery concepts, not easily defined. Social class is often determined using such indicators as education and income, but anomalies are not difficult to think of—for example, the clergyman with a Ph.D. who is the modestly-paid pastor of a church; or the multi-millionaire hockey player who did not finish high school.

Standard English is variously described. It is the language used by educated people in more formal situations. It is the language used in the media and taught in schools. Trudgill (1974, p. 17) points out that

> The difference between standard and non-standard ... has nothing in principle to do with differences between formal and colloquial language, or with concepts such as "bad language." Standard English has colloquial and well as formal variants, and standard English speakers swear as much as others.

Webster's Dictionary (1976, p. 2223) describes standard English as follows:

> ... the English that with respect to spelling, grammar, pronunciation and vocabulary is substantially uniform though not devoid of regional differences, that is well-established by usage in the formal and informal speech and writing of the educated, and that is widely recognized as acceptable wherever English is spoken and understood.

Standard English is the prestige variety of English because it is the variety used by the educated and powerful. It is not clearer, more logical, or more expressive. *I never seen him* is quite as communicative as *I didn't see him*. However, the speaker who uses non-standard forms is likely to be negatively judged as being less well educated, less intelligent, and of lower social status than those who speak standard English. Teachers are not exempt from the prejudices and stereotypes elicited by non-standard speech. There is considerable evidence that teachers' evaluations and expectations of students are negatively influenced by non-standard language associated with social class or ethnicity (Corson, 1990; Edwards, 1982). Since inaccurate expectations and evaluations may hinder children's progress in school, teachers need to be aware of the danger of stereotyping poor and minority-group children on the basis of the way they speak.

There are other major questions for teachers to grapple with. To what extent, for example, should teachers commit their energies towards seeing that their students acquire standard English? And how and when should they work towards the goal of standard English for all? These are questions that are not easily answered. There is no single answer that will fit all cases.

Gender   Myths about linguistic differences between men and women have a long history. It is only in the past two decades that gender differences in language have been the subject of sustained serious research. Since the area of research is fairly recent, many questions remain to be answered. There are, however, a number of differences that are fairly well documented (Berryman and Eman, 1980):

1.   Women's speech is more likely than men's to be characterized by correctness. They are less likely, for example, to "drop their *g*'s" or to use non-standard syntax.

2.   Men and women tend to use language for different purposes. Language serves a socio-emotional or expressive function more often for women than for men; men more often use language for task-related purposes.

3.   In mixed-sex interactions men interrupt more and talk more than women.

4.   Women's voices are higher pitched than men's, and women use more variable, more expressive intonation patterns than men.

In her influential and entertaining book, *You Just Don't Understand*, Tannen (1990) discusses contradictory opinions and evidence about which group speaks more. The contradictions are to be explained, she claims, by the fact that men and women talk at different times, in different places, for different purposes.

> More men feel comfortable doing "public speaking," while more women feel comfortable doing "private" speaking … For most women, the language of conversation is primarily a language of rapport: a way of establishing connections and negotiating relationships. Emphasis is placed on displaying similarities and matching experiences … For most men, talk is primarily a means to preserve independence and negotiate and maintain status in a hierarchical social order. This is done by exhibiting knowledge and skill, and by holding center stage through verbal performance such as story-telling, joking, or imparting information. (pp. 76-77).

CONCLUSION

Our language use is governed by complex, systematic knowledge that we are usually unaware of. Our linguistic competence enables us to formulate utterances that conform to the grammar of the language. Our communicative competence enables us to use utterances appropriately in a variety of situations.

Language use varies with the situation and with speakers. Situational varieties are referred to as *registers*. For language variation caused by differences among users the term *dialect* is used. Two major kinds of dialects are regional dialects and social dialects.

Both spoken language and written language have a variety of forms from very formal to very informal. While there is some overlap, written language and spoken language have characteristic differences. A major objective of schooling is to teach students to read and write at increasingly demanding levels. It is important for teachers to be aware of the differences between written and spoken language in order to understand the nature of the task students face in learning both to produce and to comprehend written language.

EXERCISES

1. Consider the following sentence from a history text:

    Daunted neither by the reports in the capitalist press of brutalities and murders committed in Russia to manure the soil for the future harmony of mankind, nor by the atrocities committed by both sides in the Spanish Civil War, the advocates of a new order clung tenaciously to their belief that bad conditions rather than innate depravity were the cause of human evil.

    a. Can you find examples of constructions listed and described on pp. 32-33 that the writer has used to lengthen the above sentence? Discuss your answer in your group.

    b. Try your hand at rewriting the sentence as it might have appeared in spoken language. You might want to think not only of syntactic constructions but also of choice of vocabulary. Share you attempt with a classmate.

2. For each of the examples below, complete the function column as indicated. Express the function in any way that seems appropriate. There is not necessarily a single correct word for each function.

FORM	**FUNCTION**
1. (Two adults meet in a restaurant.) One says, "Sorry I'm late:"	He is _____ing.
2. Teacher, addressing her students, says, "I will not accept any assignments after Friday."	Teacher is _____ing.
3. Father, to misbehaving child, "I'll send you to your room if you don't behave."	Father is _____ing.
4. Employer says to employee, "This work is full of mistakes."	Employer is _____ing.
5. (Parents attend son John's baseball game. Jack hits the ball.) Parents say, "Run, John!"	Parents are _____ing.
6. (Two women at a party.) One says, "Look at that dress she's wearing! That's her new boyfriend with her. I hear he's married."	The woman is _____ing.

3. A register has been described as "a language *variety* associated with a particular situation of use. Examples: baby talk, legalese" (Finegan and Besnier, 1989, p. 531). Describe as fully as you can each of the following registers. You may be able to observe instances of the register and record your observations:
   a. A religious ceremony; think, for example, of a marriage ceremony.
   b. Sportscasting.
   c. A news broadcast.

4. Describe as fully as you can the register of teacher talk in school. You might consider whether or not it is a single register. If not, list various teacher registers and describe one of them in detail. Consider such aspects as the purposes for which they speak; special vocabulary; special expressions.

5. Observe a conversation. See if you can see examples of each of the following:
   a. Long pauses and how they are ended.
   b. Changes of topic. Who changes? How? Are attempts at shifting topics always successful? If not, why not?
   c. Resolution of a situation where two people speak at once.
   d. Terminating the conversation. Do you observe any routines?

REFERENCES

Austin, J.L. (1962). *How to Do Things With Words*. Oxford: Oxford University Press.

Berryman, C., and C. Eman (1980). *Communication, Language and Sex*. Rowley, MA: Newbury House.

Chafe, W., and J. Danielewicz (1987). Properties of spoken and written language. In R. Horowitz and S.J. Samuels (eds.), *Comprehending Oral and Written Language* (pp. 83-113). New York: Academic Press.

Corson, D. (1990). *Language Policy Across the Curriculum*. Clevedon, Avon: Multilingual Matters.

DES (Department of Education and Science) (1975). *A Language for Life* (The Bullock Report). London: HMSO.

Edwards, J.R. (1982). Language attitudes and their implications among English speakers. In E. B. Ryan and H. Giles (Eds.), *Attitudes Towards Language Variation: Social and Applied Contexts* (pp. 20-33). London: Edward Arnold.

Finegan, E., and N. Besnier (1989). *Language: Its Structure and Use*. New York: Harcourt Brace Jovanovich.

Finocchiaro, M. (1974). *English as a Second Language: From Theory to Practice*. New York: Regents.

Grice, H.P. (1975). Logic and conversation. In P. Cole and J. Morgan (eds.), *Syntax and Semantics: Volume 3: Speech Acts* (pp.41-59). New York: Academic Press.

Goldman-Eisler, F. (1961). The significance of changes in the rate of articulation. *Language and Speech*, 4, 171-4.

Hymes, D. (1974). *Foundations of Sociolinguistics: An Ethnographic Approach*. Philadelphia: University of Pennsylvania Press.

McConnell, R.E. (1978). *Our Own Voice: Canadian English and How It Came to Be*. Toronto: Gage.

Perera, K. (1984). *Children's Writing and Reading: Analysing Classroom Language*. Oxford: Basil Blackwell.

Story, G.M., W.J. Kirwin and J.D.A. Widdowson (eds.) (1990). *Dictionary of Newfoundland English* (2nd edition with supplement). St. John's, Newfoundland: Breakwater.

Tannen, D. (1990). *You Just Don't Understand: Women and Men in Conversation*. New York: Ballantine Books.

Trudgill, P. (1974). *Sociolinguistics*. Harmondsworth: Penquin.

Webster's Third New International Dictionary of the English Language (1976). Springfield, MA: G. and C. Merriam.

Chapter 3
LANGUAGE ACQUISITION

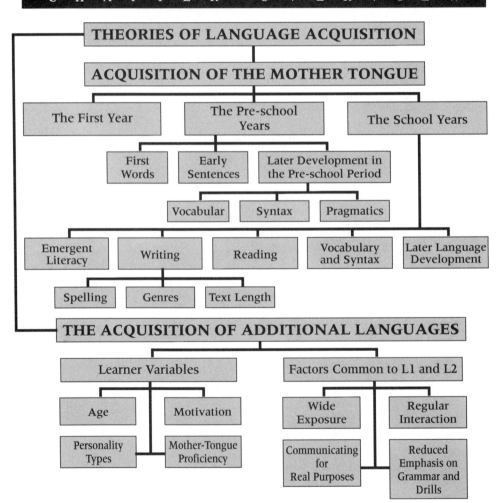

THEORIES OF LANGUAGE ACQUISITION

ACQUISITION OF THE MOTHER TONGUE

- The First Year
- The Pre-school Years
  - First Words
  - Early Sentences
  - Later Development in the Pre-school Period
    - Vocabular
    - Syntax
    - Pragmatics
- The School Years
  - Emergent Literacy
  - Writing
    - Spelling
    - Genres
    - Text Length
  - Reading
  - Vocabulary and Syntax
  - Later Language Development

THE ACQUISITION OF ADDITIONAL LANGUAGES

- Learner Variables
  - Age
  - Motivation
  - Personality Types
  - Mother-Tongue Proficiency
- Factors Common to L1 and L2
  - Wide Exposure
  - Regular Interaction
  - Communicating for Real Purposes
  - Reduced Emphasis on Grammar and Drills

By the age of five or six, when they start school, children have already performed one of the most remarkable feats of learning of their lives. They have learned their native language. This they do without formal instruction. Indeed, if they are raised in a bilingual environment, they will probably learn both languages with native-like competence.

The understanding of first language acquisition that has been achieved in recent decades has powerful implications for several areas of learning. The learning of a second language has much in common with learning the first. There are important parallels between language acquisition and learning to read and write. Our knowledge of language acquisition has led to changes in approaches to remedial work for those who have difficulty acquiring literacy skills. As they grow, children master a variety of *registers* or ways of using language that are appropriate for different situations. In school, they must learn the languages of various disciplines, the language of math, for example, and the language of the various sciences. Our understanding of the ways in which they acquire language as young children can help us to use procedures that will facilitate the acquisition of the language of the disciplines we teach.

The purpose of this chapter is to trace the development of the first language from birth through the school years, and to look briefly at the learning of other languages.

THE ACQUISITION OF THE MOTHER TONGUE

During their first year of life, babies make remarkable progress acquiring language. Most will speak only a word or two by the age of twelve months, but all have acquired important knowledge about the language and how it is used. By the age five, when they start school, children's ability to use the language approaches adult-like competence in many ways. They have mastered all the usual sentence patterns and can form questions, negatives, and complex sentences with subordinate clauses. They have learned many words and may have a vocabulary of as many as 8000 words (Gleason, 1989). Moreover, they know how to use the language for many purposes and in many social situations.

The school years bring new tasks for language learners. One of the most important is learning to deal with written language. Vocabulary continues to increase as they are faced with new domains of knowledge. During the school years, they learn to use language, in both spoken and written forms, for many new purposes.

Even the end of schooling does not see the end of language development. Adults continue to learn new words, probably as long as they live. They learn the specialized vocabularies of their professions or vocations, and of their hobbies. They learn ways of using language that are appropriate to new situations they encounter. We are language learners as long as we live. The focus of this section, however, is language learning through the school years.

THE FIRST YEAR

During the first year, few children master more than a few words. Nonetheless, it is a period of much learning about language. Humans appear to be born with a special capacity for language learning that manifests itself, at a very early age, in the way they respond to language. Within the first few weeks of life, infants show special interest in the human voice. As early as the third day, babies can distinguish their own mothers' voices from those of other mothers. At one month, they can distinguish between similar sounds such as /b/ and /p/. This ability has been revealed by an ingenious test (Eimas, Siqueland, Jusczyk, and Vigorito, 1971). Babies are given a pacifier which is attached to a sound-generating system. When the baby sucks, she hears "ba." Initially, she sucks busily to produce the sound but gradually loses interest as she hears the same sound again and again. If, however, the "ba" is now replaced by "pa," the baby takes renewed interest and begins sucking with vigour again. The clear inference of the baby's behaviour is that she can detect the difference between /b/ and /p/. The ability to make such distinctions is critical to language learning.

At about six months, infants begin to babble. Late in the babbling period, the sounds produced are marked by intonation and stress patterns that sometimes make babbling sound very much like speech. A child may make eye contact with her mother as she babbles, and act as if she thinks she is actually speaking. Episodes of conversational babble are often marked by turn-taking. If the child's mother responds to the child's turn with a neutral comment such as "Fancy that" or "Yes, I agree," the child is likely to produce another round of babbling. Though she cannot yet speak, her babbling shows two important kinds of learning: she has started to learn the intonation patterns of English[1]; and she has started to learn about turn taking, the basic rule governing conversation.

THE PRE-SCHOOL YEARS

From the age of one year to the age of five when they begin school, children's language develops rapidly. During this period, they acquire large vocabularies, learn all the regular sentence patterns, and learn to use language for a variety of purposes.

---

[1] It is to be noted that intonation patterns are one of the earliest language features learned by the young child but are learned late and with difficulty by those who try to learn a language as adults.

First Words

Late in the first year or early in the second, children produce their first words. They understand words before they produce them. Benedict (1979) reported that the children in his study *comprehended* their first 50 words at about 13 months, but did not *produce* 50 words until about 19 months.

Several factors affect the words they learn first. Words that are easy to pronounce become part of their vocabulary before more difficult words. Many of their early words are nouns. They are more likely to learn the names of objects they interact with like toys, clothing, and items of food, and are less likely to learn the names of immovable objects like *window*, *wall*, and *table*. Though nouns are most numerous, early vocabularies also include a variety of other word classes such as action words like *up* and *sit*, and modifiers like *pretty* and *mine*. The words they learn are also related to their cognitive development. For example, at about the time that children learn about **object permanence** — that is, that objects that disappear from sight continue to exist somewhere else — they begin to use words such as *gone* to comment on the disappearance of an object (Pease, Gleason, and Pan, 1989).

Many examples of **overextensions** occur in children's early speech. For example, a child may use the word *moon* to refer to many round objects like round shapes in books, postmarks, and the letter O, or the word *doggie* to refer to any four-legged, furry animal. One explanation for children's overextensions is that they understand a word to refer to one (or two) particular features of meaning. According to this explanation, the child assumes that *moon*, for example, means roundness. A different explanation is that when children do not know the appropriate word to express a concept, they make do with whatever word they know that shares some features of meaning with the unknown word. One child, for example, used the word *dog* for pictures of many animals in his book. But if he was asked to find the picture of the dog, he always selected the dog and never pointed to any of the other animals that he sometimes called "dog." Note that the second explanation attributes greater semantic knowledge to children than the first one does.

Early Sentences

Towards the end of the second year or early in the third year, children begin putting words together. At first, most of the child's sentences are two words long. Examples of early sentences from different children are:

Get truck.	See boy.
No bed.	Eve lunch.
No down.	Throw Daddy.

More car.	Sat wall.
More sing.	Car garage.

Several points are to be noted. First, content words — nouns, verbs, and adjectives — predominate. Secondly, the sentences are not imitations of adult speech; many of the sentences children use at this stage would never have been spoken by an adult and are unlikely to have been heard by the child. Thirdly, children's early sentences have few function words (e.g., prepositions, conjunctions, articles, pronouns, and auxiliary verbs) and do not have inflections that mark plural nouns (as in *boys*) or different forms of the verb (e.g., *walks, walked, walking*). The predominance of content words, especially nouns and verbs, and the omission of most function words makes children's early sentences sound somewhat like the sentences adults used to write in telegrams. Hence, children's language at this early stage has been called *telegraphic* speech.

The final important point to be noted about children's early sentences is that they reflect the same word order as English sentences. Agents come before verbs (e.g., *Daddy sit*). Objects come after verbs (e.g., *Drive car*). The possessor comes before the thing possessed (e.g., *Mommy dress*).

Children gradually add **grammatical morphemes** *to* their language. Grammatical morphemes are endings to nouns and verbs (like the plural *-s* and the possessive *'s* on nouns, and tense endings like *-ing* and *-ed* on verbs) and function words (like the prepositions *in* and *on* and the articles *a* and *the*). Roger Brown (1973) of Harvard University conducted a longitudinal study in which he examined the acquisition of fourteen morphemes by three children to whom he gave the pseudonyms *Adam, Eve,* and *Sara*. One of Brown's most important findings was that the children acquired the fourteen morphemes in almost identical order. The first morphemes to be acquired by all three were the plural *-s* on nouns, the *-ing* on verbs, and the prepositions *in* and *on*. Subsequent studies involving larger numbers of children confirmed the order of acquisition that Brown reported.

A second interesting point to note about the acquisition of grammatical morphemes is that children acquire rules. This is well illustrated by the acquisition of the past tense morpheme which is *-ed* for regular verbs (e.g., *talked*) but which has a variety of different forms for irregular verbs (e.g., *ran, came, saw*). Children first use irregular past tense forms like *came* and *went*. These forms are probably learned as single vocabulary items rather than as *come*-plus-past-tense-marker. Later, children begin to form the past tense of regular verbs by adding the past tense morpheme *-ed*. We know that it is a rule they have learned, because once the past tense morpheme appears, it is added to irregular verbs as well, and forms like *comed, singed, goed,* and even *wented* appear in their speech. Moreover, the rule, once learned, inhibits them from imitating correct forms even when they are encouraged to do so. The following conversation is cited by Cazden (1972, p. 92):

Child: My teacher holded the baby rabbits and we patted them.

Adult: Did you say your teacher held the baby rabbits?

Child: Yes.

Adult: What did you say she did?

Child: She holded the baby rabbits and we patted them.

Adult: Did you say she held them tightly?

Child: No, she holded them loosely.

During their third year, children learn to use negative and interrogative forms of sentences. As with grammatical morphemes, negatives and questions follow similar patterns of acquisition for all children, and children are often unable to imitate well-formed questions or negatives before these structures appear in their own spontaneous speech. Consider, for example, the following delightful exchange between a child and his mother recorded by McNeill (1966, p.69):

Child: Nobody don't like me.

Mother: No, say "Nobody likes me."

Child: Nobody don't like me.

(Exchange is repeated eight times.)

Mother: No, no listen carefully; say "Nobody likes me."

Child: Oh! Nobody don't LIKES me.

LATER DEVELOPMENT IN THE PRESCHOOL PERIOD

Children's language development continues at a rapid pace during the later preschool years, so rapidly that it is not easy to characterize the major changes. Their vocabulary expands at a great rate. Their sentences become longer as their knowledge of syntax increases. They continue to learn to use language for a variety of purposes.

Vocabulary

Children's vocabularies develop rapidly. During the peak preschool ages of 2½ to 4½, they add, on average, between two and four new words each day. In addition to adding new words in general, children master special categories of words in years three to six. One category of interest is relational words for which the meaning is not fixed but varies according to the object described — words such as *big/little, my/your, this/that.*

One set of relational words that has been studied a good deal is the set of spatial relational adjectives: *big/little, tall/short, high/low, long/short, wide/narrow, thick/thin,* and *deep/shallow.* The earliest of these pairs to appear in children's speech is *big* and *little.* These words are commonly used before the age of three. However, the full relational meanings of the words take some time to develop. If two- or three-year-olds are shown a small shot glass, they are likely to identify it as a "little" glass rather than a big glass. If that shot glass is subsequently placed in front of a doll on a small toy table such as might be used in furnishing a doll's house, young children will still call it a little glass. Four-year-olds, on the other hand, are likely to comment that the glass is big — big for the doll, or too big for the table. They are able to adjust the meaning according to the context (deVilliers and deVilliers, 1978).

The relational pairs listed above are acquired in the following order: *big/little, tall/short* and *long/short, high/low, thick/thin, wide/narrow,* and, finally, *deep/shallow.* Many five-and six-year-olds have difficulty providing the opposite for a word from the *wide/narrow* and *deep/shallow* pairs.

Two factors are thought to contribute to the order of acquisition. One is the *frequency of occurrence* of the adjectives in adult and child language. *Big* and *little* are very commonly used. The second factor is the *conceptual complexity* of the words. *Big* and *little* are the most general of the terms. An object may be big by virtue of its height, its width, or its thickness. The other relational words require more specific knowledge to be used correctly. *Tall,* for example, must be associated specifically with the vertical dimension.

Children between ages three and six also acquire *deictic* expressions such as *this* and *that, here* and *there,* and *my* and *your.* Most children have mastered the *I, me, my/ you, your* distinction before the age of three.

Mastering relational words is no easy task. It is easy to take for granted the remarkable achievements of children in acquiring these and other features of language. When things go awry, it sometimes helps us realize the magnitude of the task they face in learning language. For example, Jamie, aged two years and nine months, was told that his friend Yorgo was coming to visit later in the day. An hour or so later, Jamie enquired when "my go" would arrive. "Not *my go*," replied his mother. "It's *Yorgo.*" Jamie offered no comment. But in subsequent mentions of Yorgo, he played it safe and referred to him as "the go". No doubt he was confused when a hypothesis he had thought confirmed was thrown into question by the accident of acquiring a friend with an unusual name. One realizes with awe the amount of hypothesizing and hypothesis testing that goes on as children acquire language.

Here/there and *this/that* also appear early. However, full understanding of these terms is not acquired until age seven or older. For example, seven-year-olds have difficulty understanding the distinction between *this* and *that* if they do not share the perspective of the speaker. If the speaker is on the opposite side of the room from the child and refers to objects that are near him but not near the child as *this one* and *that one*, the child will have difficulty understanding.

Vocabulary development involves more than adding new words. It involves also the reorganization of the meanings of words so that they are more like conventional meanings. Children also develop in their ability to recognize interrelationships among words. They first learn the names of specific items like *dog, cat,* and *elephant*; later they learn that these all belong to the category of *animals,* and that *poodle* and *collie* are kinds of dogs. Such interrelationships among words are referred to as **semantic networks**. Vocabulary development, then, involves adding new words, adding new meanings and new shades of meaning for old words, and establishing links between words.

Syntax

In the later pre-school period, children begin to acquire more complex syntactic constructions than the simple sentences they use first. They begin to learn such syntactic constructions as passives (e.g., *The child **was bitten** by a snake*), relative clauses (e.g., *Bring me the pencil **that's on the table***), and coordinate constructions (e.g., *You can read this book and I can read that one*). These constructions are not completely mastered, however, by the time they begin school. Easier cases are understood before more difficult cases. For example, a passive sentence like *The car was driven by the boy* is understood before a passive like *Marie was hit by James*. Note that the first sentence does not make sense if *car* and *boy* are reversed in the sentence but the second sentence still makes perfect sense if Marie and James are reversed. It is thus easier to misunderstand the second sentence with its *reversible passive* than it is to misunderstand the first sentence which is irreversible.

Children's difficulty with reversible passives like the second sentence is shown in a delightful sequence in the film *Out of the Mouths of Babes* (Archibald and Cook, 1975). Becky, aged three and a half, is asked to act out sentences with toys. "The car is bumped by the truck," says the researcher. Becky takes the car and bumps the truck. "Now," says the researcher, "show me *The car bumps the truck.*" "Again?" she asks with a puzzled look. When the researcher repeats his request, she takes the car a second time and bumps the truck. She interpreted the sentences as being exactly the same.

Pragmatics

In addition to learning how to compose acceptable sentences, children must learn how to use the language to communicate effectively in various situations. They must learn how to inform, request, describe, deny, and so on, and how their language needs to vary for different kinds of people. The study of the use of language in context is called *pragmatics*.

Some studies have used controlled laboratory settings to examine children's use of language. One aspect of language use studied in controlled experiments is children's ability to compose messages appropriate for their listener. Simple games like the following have been used. Two participants are seated at a table separated by an opaque screen. In front of each is a set of six blocks each decorated with a novel design such as the following (Glucksburg and Krauss, 1967):

The task of the speaker is to select the blocks, one at a time, and to describe each block so that the listener on the other side of the screen can pick out the appropriate block from the set in front of her. Kindergartners and preschool children do not perform well on such tasks. Their descriptions are short, and, often, highly idiosyncratic: for example, *mother's hat*. Moreover, young children do not usually rephrase their messages if their listener does not understand. If a listener expresses a failure to understand, an older child or an adult gives a more detailed description. Young children, however, simply repeat their descriptions or remain silent. The failure of young children in tasks such as these has been attributed to their egocentrism — their inability to consider the needs of their listeners.

However, researchers who observe children in more natural situations see a good deal of evidence that children are able to adapt their communication to their listeners when they are in familiar situations. For example, Mueller (1972) introduced pairs of three- and four-year-olds to each other and observed their communication as they played together. They were able to communicate successfully with their listener as evidenced by the fact that, eighty-five percent of the time, they received a reply or at least attracted their listener's attention. Other researchers have observed that pre-school children are able to maintain topics as they converse, and to take turns appropriately in conversations.

Even young children adapt their speech to their listeners in natural situations. Four-year-olds use shorter, simpler sentences when speaking to two-year-olds than they do to adults (Shatz and Gelman, 1973), and even two-year-olds talk differently to their infant siblings than to adults (Dunn and Kendrick, 1982). Anderson (1984) asked children aged 4 to 7 to adopt various roles, and found that they adapted their language according to their role as speaker and the role of their partner. They used more imperatives and shorter sentences when pretending to speak to younger children, and they used more directives when pretending to be the teacher than when playing the role of student. Of course, young children have much to learn about adapting their speech to their listeners. Preschoolers on the phone, for example, are apt to answer questions or comments with nods of the head, or by pointing. Nonetheless, it seems clear that by school age they have made considerable progress in their ability to communicate with others. Certainly, they are better able to adapt their speech to their listeners than early laboratory experiments suggested. Many factors affect their performance — for example, fatigue, hunger, and the degree of their involvement in the task. Children are most likely to show sophisticated language adjustment if they are passing on well-known information in a familiar context such as their own home, to a familiar listener such as a friend or a family member.

A further aspect of children's knowledge of the way language varies with situation involves politeness and register variation along the formal-informal dimension (Warren-Leubecker and Bohannon, 1989). Some studies have examined children's understanding and use of various forms of requests. The language allows many ways of making a request from the abrupt imperative (e.g., *Give me your pencil*) through the more polite request (*May I borrow your pencil*) to the even more polite indirect request (*I don't have anything to write with*). By the age of three or four, children are able to understand indirect requests made by peers or parents. Shatz (1978), for example, reports that when a mother said *The window is open*, her young child correctly understood it as an indirect request and closed the window. In the late pre-school years, children who listened to pairs of requests such as the following, *I want a candy* and *I would like a candy*, were able to judge which of two requests was "nicer" (Bates, 1976). In an interesting experiment Bates (1976) had children request a candy from a hand puppet dressed as an elderly, grey-haired woman. When a child had made the request, the experimenter whispered with the elderly woman and then told the child that "Mrs. Rossi" liked children to be very, very nice, and that she would certainly give a candy if the child asked her again even more nicely. Even 2-year-olds were able to increase the politeness of their requests.

In summary, then, even young children are able to adjust their communication in a variety of ways. Their ability to do so is greatly influenced by the context. Their ability to adjust their speech improves over time. Indeed, it is likely that development continues through the whole of life as we continue to develop skill communicating in an ever wider range of registers.

THEORIES OF LANGUAGE ACQUISITION

Children make remarkable progress towards the acquisition of their native language during the preschool years. They acquire their language without formal instruction and with very little informal instruction or correction. A question of considerable interest is how they manage to achieve such a remarkable feat of learning.

A commonsense explanation, widely accepted some decades ago, was that children modelled their words and sentences on the language they heard around them. It was assumed that, when they made errors, their parents or other adults would correct them. The explanation was one of imitation and reinforcement.

A couple of interesting facts throw this explanation into question. One is that children produce sentences that they could never have heard, sentences that are not the result of imitation, like *Daddy goed* and *allgone sticky*. Secondly, when they are asked to imitate sentences that are beyond the present level of their grammatical ability, they often cannot do it, as in the example above of the child who could not say *Nobody likes me*. Thirdly, parents of young children do remarkably little by way of correction. They are quite likely to correct their child on a matter of fact but not likely to correct a young child's syntax. Roger Brown and his colleagues (Brown, Cazden, and Bellugi, 1969) reported that Eve's mother responded with *That's right* when Eve said *He a girl* and *Her curl my hair*. The mother responded positively because the sentences were factually accurate; the fact that they were ungrammatical was irrelevant.

An extended discussion of theories of language acquisition is beyond the scope of this book.[2] Several points are, however, of interest and relevance to educators:

1. Most theorists agree that language acquisition is the result of both innate capacities and linguistic experience. The young human is predisposed to learn language. Evidence for this is seen in very early responses to the human voice and in the fact that the course of early development is very similar for children learning the same language, and for language learning across many different languages. Despite this biological predisposition,

---

[2] For a brief, readable discussion, see Bohannon and Warren-Leubecker, 1989.

however, children who are isolated from language — like the normal children of deaf parents — do not learn to speak.

2. Children learn to *use* language. Children know what language is because they know what language does (Halliday, 1973). They learn language because it does things for them. They do not learn to speak because their parents teach them to speak for speaking's sake. They learn to speak because speaking enables them to request, to greet, to inform, to question, and so on.

3. They acquire words and structures gradually. They understand words before they produce them. The meaning they have for a word, initially, will be more limited than the meaning they eventually acquire as they meet the word many times in varied contexts. Mistakes are made, initially, as they learn grammatical structures like negatives or questions or various forms of the verb; but these mistakes disappear over time as they have more experience with the structure.

4. The language they hear — especially the language that is addressed to them by their mothers, for example — is a simplified form of language.

5. Interaction plays a critical role in language acquisition, especially interaction between mother and child (Bruner, 1981; Wells, 1986). Communicative interaction begins early in the first year. Mothers treat babies' early cries and, later, their babbling as if the child intends to communicate. They follow their baby's gaze and comment on what the child fixes his eye on. They use interactive games and formats such as "What's that?" to help the child learn to name objects in books and in the room. Bruner (1981) cites evidence that, if mothers are highly responsive to their very young children's baby talk, the children make fast progress with language development.

Conclusions about the ways in which children learn language in the preschool years have implications for the ways in which they continue to learn language during the school years. There are implications also for remedial work in language for those who make less than desirable progress in language and literacy in school, and for the learning of additional languages.

THE SCHOOL YEARS

The acquisition of the mother tongue by pre-school children seems almost miraculous. With very little instruction, they learn, by the time they start school, all the basic sentence patterns of the language and a considerable vocabulary. They can use language for a variety of purposes, and are able to adjust their language appropriately to suit a variety of social situations. Nonetheless, major tasks in language learning need to be achieved during the school years.

A major task of the school years is learning to deal with written language. Students must learn to read and write. Literacy is rooted in oral language and its beginnings occur before the start of formal schooling. Reading and writing development continue throughout the school years and well beyond for many.

Interesting interrelationships exist between oral language, reading, and writing. Oral language is the foundation upon which literacy develops. The better their oral language development, the more easily children are likely to learn to read and write. However, once children learn to read and write, their reading and writing, in turn, affect their oral language. Moreover, their reading affects their writing; those who read a lot tend to be better writers. And their writing influences their reading. The interrelationships among reading, writing, and oral language are complex and fascinating. The story of those inter-relationships can be touched upon only briefly here. In this section we look at the following topics: emergent literacy; writing development; reading development; vocabulary and syntax.

EMERGENT LITERACY

The topic of emergent literacy might well have been placed in the section on the pre-school years. By the time they begin school, children from literate homes have made huge strides in their development of oral language and have acquired a great store of knowledge about written language. Their knowledge of oral language and of reading and writing gives them a huge advantage over children who come to school with less knowledge. Let me illustrate this by telling you about Emily.

Emily has just turned four. Her brother, Joshua, is two and a half. Her mother, who is university educated, does not, at the moment, work outside the home. Her father is a doctoral student at a Canadian university.

Emily has been read to daily since she was twelve months old. She owns many dozens of books and makes regular visits to the library to borrow others. Both parents read to her frequently — several books each day — and talk about the stories and pictures in the books they read. Over a period of three years, the number of books read to her already numbers several hundred, most of which have been read over and over again. When she goes to the library, the librarian sometimes reads the children stories. Emily plays librarian at home, and "reads" books to Joshua. She owns many tapes of children's songs — which she is able to play for herself on her own sturdy children's tape recorder — and a few favourite children's videos. At least once a week, she speaks on the phone to her grandparents who live in another city; she has done so since before she was two. At first she merely listened and smiled when her grandmother said "Hi, Emily." Then she could say "Hi." Now when she picks up the phone she says "Hello" and then "Who would you like to speak to?" She volunteers information, answers questions, makes requests, and responds appropriately to her grandmother's comments (Grandmother: "We had a bad storm last night and our lights went off." Emily: "That's too bad."). She always ends the conversation by saying, "Bye, Nana."

She owns a vast array of writing implements — crayons, felt pens, chalk — and spends a lot of time drawing. She received her first letter from her grandmother at the age of two and a half and shortly after that began sending occasional letters back to her grandmother and grandfather whom she calls "Obu." Three-year-old Emily was wildly excited when her grandmother explained in a letter the reciprocity of letter exchanges. "You write me a letter," said her grandmother, "and then I'll write one back to you." Emily sat down at once and wrote fifteen letters to various relatives.

Her first letter, written when she was two years and nine months, was written on both sides of a sheet of paper. On one side, long, extended bursts of squiggles stretched across the page. These squiggles said — so Emily told her mother — "Dear Obu, Thank you for the bunny soaps" (referring to a recent gift). The other side had a completely different appearance; large scribbles filled the page. When asked what it said, Emily replied, "I just wrote a picture just for Obu and Nana." It seems that she knew already that writing that says something looks different from drawings. Shortly after she turned three, Es (for Emily) and Os (for Obu) started to appear in her letters. A few months later, strings of Ns and Os at the top of the page said —so she reported — "Dear Nana and Obu." A string of letter-like symbols said "hugs and kisses." At three years and four months she attempted to sign her name, and learned to write it —perfectly spelled though usually written backwards — a few months later. By her fourth birthday, she was able to write several words, for example, *OBU, JOSHUA, BELL* (for Belle in "Beauty and the Beast"), *NNAA* (for Nana).

Before she was three, she pointed to a *b* and asked her father, "What noise does that one make?" She was able to recognize letters addressed to her, when she collected them from the mail box, because she could recognize the *E* at the beginning of her name. At three, when her grandmother visited, she was able to sort a bag of gifts according to whether the wrapping was marked *J* for *Joshua* or *E* for *Emily*. At four, she enjoyed playing the game of naming the sounds that words start with.

A year before she is due to begin kindergarten, Emily already has great competence with oral language and considerable knowledge about written language. The words and expressions of the books that are read to her appear constantly in her speech. She can use language for many purposes, not only in face-to-face situations, but also on the phone. She has begun to learn the forms and etiquette of telephone discourse: she knows how to greet, how to terminate, and how to enquire who the caller wants to speak to, and how to exchange information. In recognizing *E* and *J* (and other letters as well) she has started to read. She can write several words accurately, and makes a good effort at writing several others. Indeed, writing started when all she could do was write lines of indecipherable scribble that she translated into messages. She knows a great deal about the discourse of letter-writing: that letters start with a salutation ("Dear Nana and Obu"), that they carry a signature, that "hugs and kisses" is one way you can end a letter to a relative, and that a letter is supposed to bring a letter in response. The hundreds of stories she has heard have taught her what a story is like. When her mother, in the middle of a story, asks, "What do you think is going to happen?" she is able to make good predictions. She can tell little stories that have a setting, characters and events or episodes. When her writing skill develops, she will be able to write them. She knows that writing is used for many purposes: to tell stories, to communicate with distant relatives, to make signs (like the *happy birthday* on the wall for Joshua's birthday), to make lists for shopping, to send invitations to parties and to reply to them; she knows that her father does writing for school on his computer and that he prints out what he writes. She knows that reading is used for various purposes: for entertainment; to enable communication with distant grandparents; her father reads to study; her mother reads the paper and the phone book for information, and recipe books to find out how to make a cake. Long before entering school, Emily has already made significant progress towards reading and writing, two of the most important goals of schooling.

Emily is learning to read and write almost as naturally as she learned to speak. She is learning to read and write because they are daily activities in her home where both her parents read and write for many purposes. Her reading and writing development are closely interrelated, and are rooted in her oral language.

THE DEVELOPMENT OF WRITING

Children learn to write naturally when they write regularly for meaningful purposes and when they get responses to the *meaning* of what they are trying to say rather than the *form*. When children learn to speak, they gradually acquire the pronunciation, vocabulary, syntax and discourse forms of the oral language around them. Similarly, as children learn to write, they gradually acquire the conventional forms of written discourse.

Spelling

Children who start to write before they go to school use what is known as **invented spelling**. The invented spelling used by children aged, roughly, four through seven, shows remarkable similarities for children in widely separated areas in Canada, the United States, the United Kingdom, Australia, and New Zealand. One much-quoted example of invented spelling is the message that five-year-old Paul wrote to his mother when she failed to answer his questions. The message read "RUDF" which his mother easily understood as "Are you deaf?" (Bissex, 1980). Children progress in recognizably similar ways from their earliest invented spellings until their words approximate conventional spelling. Note the progression of the two first grade students whose writing appears in Figure 3.1 and Figure 3.2.

Figure 3.1
Writing of First-Grade Student #1

e K S h I A K R A N e O (Nov. 8)

(I can see a rainbow.)

I M V a S M (Dec. 7)

(I made a snowman.)

I   S a S e m e N i l k e m N i s e   (Jan.5)

(I saw a superman and I like him and I say help.)

I see the cuboy Fut I saw the cuboy is did (Feb.)

(I see the cowboy fight I saw the cowboy is dead.

Figure 3.2
Writing of First-Grade Student #2

I W T N A R P N (first day of school)

I want an airplane.

For an extended period of time, the child wrote only rows of looped squiggles. When he "emerged" from this period, his writing was much more mature:

This is Sata kas hE sz Ho Ho Ho hE GV AS Las av Pazs (Nov. 10)

(This is Santa Claus. He says Ho Ho Ho. He gives us lots of presents.)

The docs uv hasrt or rNEN iWAY froM The coPS (Jan. 7)

(The dukes of hazzard are running away from the cops.)

This SNAK IS jIST LaEnD hr eggs in the souol aNd tr hgoe in spren (Jan. 19)

(This snake is just laying her eggs in the soil and they're hatching in spring.)

At first, the letters children use in their writing show little or no correspondence with the sounds of the words they say the writing represents, as in the November 8 sentence of Student 1. When sentences begin to show correspondences between sounds and letters, the sentence is likely to be a string of consonants, each consonant representing a word or a syllable as in the December 7 and January 5 sentences of Student 1. Conventionally spelled words in common use are incorporated into students' letter strings as they become familiar with those words in the classroom. Thus Student 2 above spells *this, is, the, from, in,* and *and* conventionally. Gradually, vowels are added. An early strategy for vowels is to use the letter name that has the same sound as the required vowel sound. Using this principle, a child will spell *lady* as LADE and *feet* as FET.

Primary teachers who understand the way that children progress from invented spelling to conventional spelling usually encourage children to spell familiar words accurately and to spell other words as they sound. If children are encouraged to use, in their writing, words they know but cannot spell, it tends to increase the number of different words they use in their writing (Gunderson and Shapiro, 1988). Note, for example, the words that six-year-old Harold attempted to use in his writing presented in Figure 3.3, words like *tornado, weather forecaster, Pompeii, Vesuvius,* and *spectacular.*

Figure 3.3
The Writing of 6-year-old Harold

The RAcon FOL UP inTo The TonATO The wiTHr FocaTR woz RoiT
(The racoon flew up into the tornado. The weather forecaster was right.)
PoMPaY woz hom FoR The PePL FO VsoveIs. nAW The RmAnings Fo The PePL TIL os aLoT abot The PePe.
(Pompeii was the home for the people of Vesuvius. Now the remains of the people tell us a lot about the people.)
won Day To Frinz wr Plaine win a BLD Egl kam aLoog Anb The Egl DiD A SPiTkyLr shoT AnD TheoT wz a HoPE Day.
(One day two friends were playing when a bald eagle came along and the eagle did a spectacular shot and that was a happy day.)

Genres

It was long assumed that narrative and personal writing were the easiest and most natural forms of writing for young students to attempt. The chronological order of narratives and personal experiences is certainly easier than the logical structure that exposition requires. The ability to write well-structured exposition does not develop early. However, recent research into the writing of children in primary and elementary grades challenges the assumption that narrative and personal writing is the most natural form of writing for young students. Students in early grades compose in many forms and for diverse purposes. They write, for example, plays, stories, poems, essays, letters, journals and reports. They are especially likely to use a variety of genres if they are encouraged to find their own topics and purposes for writing rather than writing to complete school assignments (Hudson, 1986). Newkirk (1987) suggests, moreover, that the non-narrative writing that young students produce is the seed from which later successful expository writing develops.

Text Length

Children's compositions are, of course, very short when they first begin to write. However, children who are encouraged to write about things they know about and on topics that interest them rapidly increase in writing fluency. It is not uncommon for students to write compositions of a page or more by the end of grade one.

Composition length is affected not only by the topic but also by the type of writing. Students at all levels in the school system write longer stories than arguments or reports (Crowhurst, 1990; Langer, 1986). They write more when they are writing for authentic purposes than when they are writing to meet the requirements of school assignments. Greenlee (Greenlee, Hiebert, Bridge, and Winograd, 1986) found that second graders who exchanged letters with pen pals wrote longer, more complex letters than those who wrote to imaginary readers and received comments from their teachers. Crowhurst (1992) describes dramatic increases in length in letters that sixth graders wrote to pen pals who were education students. Initial letters averaged only 67 words whereas the average length of the next seven was 160. Many children wrote letters of 300 words and more. The teacher reported that students who had previously been unwilling to write even a paragraph for a school-assigned task willingly wrote one and two pages to their pen pals.

THE DEVELOPMENT OF READING

Reading is a complex process. Research theorists have constructed various competing models that describe the reading process. There are also competing theories about how to teach beginning reading. Some place great emphasis on comprehension from the beginning while others stress the importance of phonic skills, that is, the ability to recognize various letters and the sounds those letters represent. Instructional programs that involve children in writing and reading from the very beginning tend to emphasize both phonics and meaning.

In general, it may be said that children pass through various stages as they learn to read. In the later pre-school period and during kindergarten, most children are in the pre-reading stage. During this period, they learn to recognize (and write) numbers and letters; they can recognize their own names and a few other words. During the first year or eighteen months of the primary grades, children learn to decode simple texts. From grades 2 to 4, they develop fluency in reading and greater skill in extracting information from print. From grades 4 to 8, students learn to deal with increasingly demanding text. Content area reading materials place heavier demands in terms of content, vocabulary, and text organization. The demands of content area texts increase significantly throughout the remainder of secondary school. Students are called upon, increasingly, to draw inferences and to make applications of what they read. Strategies for helping students to deal with the demands of content area texts are described in Chapter 8.

VOCABULARY AND SYNTAX

Vocabulary development continues throughout high school and beyond. New words are added; old words take on new meanings; and students develop organized networks of semantically related words.

Throughout the elementary years, students' spoken vocabularies increase by about 3000 words a year (Nagy and Anderson, 1984). At about the fourth grade, reading becomes an important means of vocabulary development. Students who read a lot develop more extensive vocabularies than those who do not.

The burden of vocabulary learning is heavy in some content areas, particularly the sciences. In many content areas, known words are used with new meanings. Teachers need to take particular care that students understand the specialized meanings given to words in a particular discipline. When students use a given term, it is easy to assume — sometimes wrongly — that they understand the specialized meaning appropriate to the subject area. (See Chapter 5 for a fuller discussion.)

Learning a given word is a gradual process rather than a single event. All of us have words in our vocabularies for which we have partial meanings. Students recognize words in print before they can use those words in their own speech or writing. They may be able to recognize and use words and yet not be able to perform the still more demanding task of defining them. In helping students to learn vocabulary, teachers need to supply many opportunities for students to use the words in their own speech and writing. Having students talk, in pairs and small groups, about the concepts they are learning is a particularly useful way of encouraging them to make specialized vocabulary their own.

By the time they begin school, children have basically mastered syntax. They can produce all the basic sentence patterns and can transform them into questions and negatives. However, written language is characterized by many syntactic forms that do not usually occur in spoken language. This has consequences for both writing and reading. The development of children's written syntax occurs over many years. In reading, comprehension difficulties may result from sentence patterns that occur commonly in written language but not in spoken language. This section deals briefly with syntactic development in children's writing. Syntactic structures that make for difficulty in reading comprehension are discussed in Chapters 4 and 7.

When children start to write, they commonly string clauses together with *and* and *but.*

> *Then they saw the reindeers, and so the children made presents and they road on the reindeers, and they delivered it.* (grade 3)

> *In the front room I triped on my sock and I fell and hit my head on the sharp edge of a table and my father called a ambulance.* (grade 5)

This kind of construction is common and appropriate in speech, even for adults. However, the overuse of *and* and *but* to coordinate sentences makes for tedious prose. As children grow older, they gradually learn to use syntactic constructions that increase variety and economy in their writing. Two indicators of syntactic development in writing are longer noun phrases and the use of various kinds of subordinate clauses.

Young students tend to use short simple noun phrases, especially in subject position. Pronouns (e.g., *I, they, he*) and determiner/noun constructions (e.g., *a boy, the goalie*) are common. Note the short noun phrases in the following composition by a third grader:

> *Farmers once had troubles with bagers (badgers). So one of them got a pit bull, then all got pit bulls. One day two farmers wanted to see wicth of there pit bulls was best. So they agreed on a fight and colected bets. That night they all gathered around and watched to see who would win. In those days it was not aginst the law and it is today.*

As they grow older they lengthen noun phrases by the use of attributive adjectives, prepositional phrases, and relative clauses, and, occasionally, appositives. Some examples of expanded noun phrases from the writing of students are:

> *There was **the biggest animal he'd ever seen, the legendary Giant Unicorn!*** (grade 3)

> *He smelled **the fragrance of home-made Valentine shaped cookies**.* (grade 3)

> *We rented **a small cabin in a small fishing village called Dosan**.* (grade 5)

> *He grinned **a kind of I won grin**. (grade 6)*

> *...holding **the elastic he had been aiming at May Lou's head**.* (grade 6)

As they grow older, students use an increasing variety of subordinate clauses. Relative clauses have already been mentioned as one means of lengthening noun phrases. Hunt (1965) found that the use of relative clauses increased steadily from grade four through grade twelve. Certain kinds of adverbial clauses appear early in children's writing. The earliest to appear are adverbial clauses of time (often beginning with *when*) followed by adverbial clauses of reason beginning with *because*.

LATER LANGUAGE DEVELOPMENT

The remarkable progress in language acquisition made in the first decade of life must not blind us to the fact that language development continues through the high school years and beyond. Students continue to add words to their vocabularies and to refine the meanings of words previously learned. By the end of high school, the average graduate has learned the meanings of at least 80,000 words (Miller and Gildea, 1987), and learning continues especially for those who pursue higher education.

Some common words are not well understood until adolescence. Connectives are one category of words that are acquired late. Some connectives may be used by young children, but many are not fully understood until well into adolescence. Among those words acquired late are: *but, although, unless, thus,* and *however* (Nippold, 1988). Connectives like these are commonly used in intermediate and high school texts. Teachers need to be aware that some students will not understand them.

Writing development occurs both at the sentence level and the discourse level. Older, more competent students are more likely to use, in their sentences, constructions that make for economy and variety of expression. They use longer noun phrases, a greater variety of verb phrases, and non-finite clauses. They are more likely than younger students to use a wide variety of adverbial clauses and may also use rare kinds of adverbial clauses introduced by *although, even if, unless, provided that*. They use more relative clauses and different kinds of relative clauses — for example, non-finite relative clauses (Perera, 1984).

Development occurs also at the discourse level. Students' knowledge of the structure of various kinds of writing (for example, argument and report writing (Crowhurst, 1990; Langer, 1986)) improves with age as does their performance in these genres. Even at the end of high school, however, there is room for considerable development in all aspects of writing for most students.

Reading at the high school level and beyond imposes heavy demands. Readers must learn to deal with the difficult sentence structures commonly used in texts (see Chapters 2 and 5). They must also learn to recognize various ways of organizing expository prose (see Chapter 5). Reading literature requires an ability to understand figurative language and to respond in a variety of ways. In a major study of adolescents' responses to literature, Squire (1964) found that scores on a standardized reading test he administered were not a reliable indicator of his students' ability to interpret literary selections. Different kinds of reading tasks impose different kinds of demands.

In order to understand the demanding texts that must be read in high school and post-secondary institutions, students need to be able to use, simultaneously, a variety of strategies including:

> activating and refining predictions, maintaining and varying focus, interrelating ideas, self-questioning, attending to important information, dismissing irrelevant information, following topical development, recognizing relationships, evaluating understandings, considering the worth of ideas …, sensing mood and tone, sometimes visualizing, sometimes adding information, redefining, analogizing, editing, and reshuffling ideas. (Tierney, 1982, p. 98.)

Reading difficult texts is a demanding task.

Throughout the high school years, students continue to develop reading skills especially when specific instruction is given. It is common, however, for little or no instruction to be given beyond the elementary years of school. Many students both in high school and beyond have not mastered the skills needed to make them fluent, competent readers of the kinds of demanding texts that they are required to read in high school and post-secondary institutions.

SUMMARY

Children learn their mother tongue virtually without instruction. Learning a language means learning the sounds of the language, the vocabulary, and the sentence patterns of the language, and learning ways of using the language to achieve a variety of purposes in a variety of different situations. Humans are innately predisposed to learn language. However, the course of language development is dependent upon the experience the child has with language and upon cognitive development. Interaction between the child and others, especially the primary care-giver, plays an important role in language acquisition.

Children have made great strides in language learning by the time they start school. During the school years, language development continues. A major task for the school-age student is the development of literacy. Recently-acquired understanding of literacy development indicates many similarities between learning to speak and learning to read and write. Children from literate homes often learn to read and write with little formal instruction. However, reading and writing are complex skills that continue to develop through the school years and beyond.

THE ACQUISITION OF ADDITIONAL LANGUAGES

In English Canada it is commonly expected that most children in school will be native speakers of English. Those who are not are often regarded as deviations from the norm. However, it is becoming increasingly common, in our multicultural society, for classrooms to have many students whose mother tongue is other than English. Approximately 50 percent of school students in Vancouver are ESL (English-as-a-second-language) students. Toronto, Calgary, Winnipeg, and other large urban centres in the country also have large numbers of ESL students. The presence of large and increasing numbers of ESL students in classrooms has made it mandatory for school systems and teachers to pay attention to their needs. It is relevant, then, to consider the acquisition of second and later languages and ways in which such language acquisition is similar to and different from the acquisition of the first language or mother tongue.

Two facts of interest are to be noted in passing. The first is that a large percentage of the world's children are educated in a language other than their mother tongue. It may seem normal in Canada for children to be educated in their mother tongue, but on a world basis, it is not the norm. The second fact of interest is that major population movements have occurred in recent years as political and economic refugees have sought safer or better living conditions. Many countries are like Canada in having substantial populations of immigrant school-age children who need to be educated in English (or French, or German) as a second language. This situation has prompted a good deal of research into the acquisition of additional languages and into teaching those who have a different mother tongue from the dominant language of the school and society.

A distinction needs to be made between those who acquire two (or more) languages simultaneously and those who learn another language after they have acquired their first. Children who are raised in a bilingual environment usually acquire both languages naturally as described above for the learning of the mother tongue (Piper, 1993). This chapter deals with learning languages sequentially rather than simultaneously.

Learning a second language shares many similarities with learning a first language. It also has some differences. A major difference is that people come to their first language as new-born infants and go through somewhat similar patterns of acquisition in their first four or five years. Additional languages, on the other hand, may be taken up at any point in life. Children may become second language learners when they start school at age five or six, or when they immigrate to a new country during childhood, adolescence, or later in life. Second language learners come to the task, then, not only with a wide range of individual differences but also with great differences in their background knowledge and experience. These differences are referred to as **learner variables**.

LEARNER VARIABLES

Learner variables that affect the learning of an additional language are: age, motivation, personality types, and proficiency in the mother tongue.

Age

It is generally assumed that young children have a considerable advantage over adolescents and adults when it comes to learning a second language. In actual fact, older learners have an initial advantage. This is largely due to their better-developed cognitive skills. If young children and adults were instructed in the same class in an unknown language, the adults would initially make greater progress. Over time, however, if both have continuous experience using the language in natural situations in a community where the target language is used, young children will eventually acquire native-like proficiency whereas the adults probably will not. Older learners can reach high levels of proficiency in additional languages. It is difficult, however, for them to acquire nativelike pronunciation and grammar in the new language.

Motivation

Motivation and attitude are of central importance in acquiring an additional language. Students are likely to make good progress if they have positive attitudes towards the language and its native speakers, and if they want to learn the language so that they can participate in the life of the new community. Their learning of the language is likely to be slower, however, if they perceive a lack of congruence between their traditions, attitudes, and lifestyle and those of the mainstream community whose language they are learning. It is important, then, that children's mother tongue and native culture be respected in the new school and classroom, and that they be made to feel part of the mainstream school from the beginning.

Personality Types

People learn in different ways. There is no single best way for students to learn an additional language. Wong-Fillmore (1976; 1983) observed nearly 50 five-year-olds — native speakers of Spanish and native speakers of Cantonese — as they learned English in their first few years of school. She found that the group she identified as *good learners* included children of various personality types. Some were sociable, outgoing children who spoke English from the beginning. However, other successful learners were quiet, scholarly children who talked little. Teachers should not be unduly concerned if new arrivals to the class spend considerable time observing and listening without trying to speak the language. Research shows that, for some learners, a "silent period" — a time when they listen a great deal and speak little or not at all — seems to be beneficial.

Mother-Tongue Proficiency

Second language development is influenced by students' proficiency in their mother tongue (Cummins, 1979). Students who have good skills in their first language make better progress in school than students whose first language is not well developed. Students who are able to read in one language learn more quickly to read in a second language; moreover, first and second language reading skills are highly correlated. Concepts developed in the first language are easily transferred to the second. For these reasons, it is important for teachers to encourage students to maintain their first language. Cummins argues that the loss of their first language may hinder them in developing proficiency in their second. For this reason, the parents of young children should be encouraged to use the mother tongue in the home both before and after the children start school. This is especially important if the parents' English is less than proficient.

Learning an additional language, then, is different from learning the first partly because learners come to the task at an older age and bring with them a considerable amount of knowledge and experience that influences their learning. There are, however, a number of notable similarities between learning the first language (L1) and learning a second language (L2).

FACTORS AFFECTING BOTH L1 AND L2

Many factors that are influential in learning a first language also affect the learning of additional languages. The following factors, in particular, are to be noted (Scarcella, 1990):

1. Wide exposure to both written and spoken English.

2. Regular interaction in English, especially with peers.

3. Frequent opportunities to communicate for real purposes in both written and spoken English.

4. Reduced emphasis on grammar instruction and drill.

Wide Exposure

Children do not learn their first language as a result of instruction. They learn sentence patterns as a result of hearing, reading, and using the language. They learn words not primarily because parents or teachers instruct them in vocabulary, but because they meet the words, repeatedly, in meaningful contexts. Similarly, second language learners need wide exposure to written and spoken English used for meaningful purposes. Specific instruction may support but cannot substitute for wide exposure.

The language to which infants are exposed tends to be simplified language — often referred to as *baby-talk* or *motherese*. It is marked by simple syntax and vocabulary, careful articulation, a slower rate of speaking, higher than normal pitch, and frequent repetition and restatement. Topics of conversation centre on the here and now. Adults speaking to second language learners adjust their speech in similar ways. Second language learners need exposure to written and spoken language that is comprehensible to them. Krashen (1985) suggests that the language they hear and read should contain structures just a little beyond their current competence.[3]

Regular Interaction

Students need not only exposure to the language but opportunities to produce language in interactive situations. "Being a witness at the feast of language is not enough of an exposure to assure acquisition. There must be ... interaction" (Bruner, 1978, p. 64). Both first and second languages are acquired through interacting with others. Second language learners need experience speaking for many purposes in a wide range of contexts.

ESL students need, in particular, frequent opportunities to interact with their peers. The value of peer-group interaction for both language development and content-area learning is an oft repeated theme in this book. It is important for all students to engage often in cooperative, collaborative learning in small groups. It is especially important for ESL students. In small groups they have opportunities to practise speaking in a less threatening environment than the whole class situation. They can ask questions and clarify misunderstandings. As they interact in small groups on tasks associated with content area topics, they hear and use new vocabulary repeatedly and so make it their own. Finally, there is evidence that peers are especially important as language models. Children choose peers as models rather than teachers; their language development may even be hampered if the only available models are adults (Piper, 1993, p. 153).

---

[3] When students are plunged into a second language environment in upper elementary or secondary school, they often have to cope with language well beyond their level of comprehension. Teachers need to take special measures to help them both with their language development and with the demanding language they meet in content area texts and lectures. Specific suggestions are made in Chapter 11.

Communicating for Real Purposes

Children learn their first language because they find out that language does things for them. Language can get them a drink when they are thirsty or a story when they are bored. Language gets them information and enables them to make contact with others. Studies of early literacy have taught us astonishing things about children's ability to learn to read and write when they are encouraged, from earliest years, to read and write for authentic purposes. Communicating for authentic purposes is of critical importance in acquiring spoken and written forms of the first language. In similar fashion, second language learners need to be actively engaged in real communication if their language development is to be facilitated. Teachers facilitate students' second language development when they provide interesting, challenging, relevant tasks that call on students to speak and write for real communicative purposes.

Reduced Emphasis on Grammar and Drills

Along with increased understanding of the role of interactive communication in second language acquisition has come decreased emphasis on formal grammar instruction and the grammatical drills and exercises that formerly played a prominent role in second language instruction. A commonsense approach might suggest that, if students make many grammatical errors in their speech and writing, they need instruction and drill in grammar to eliminate the errors. Three points need to be made. The first is that grammatical errors are an inevitable part of second language development — even as they are of first language development. The second is that many grammatical errors disappear as the student acquires greater familiarity with the language, even as the small child's *runned* and *brang* give way to *ran* and *brought* when her experience increases. The third point is that grammatical instruction is especially unlikely to help if students are not psychologically ready to acquire the grammatical structure.

That said, it should be noted that recent years have seen a reevaluation of the role of grammar instruction in second language acquisition. Several researchers have suggested that appropriate grammatical instruction may assist students in acquiring their second language (Long, 1988). In general, teachers' major focus should be on meaning. They should avoid over-emphasis on forms of language and on formal errors, while yet realizing that appropriate instruction in grammar will help some students. In general, adolescents and adults will benefit more than younger students.

Conclusion

Children acquire their first language naturally as they interact with others, especially their primary care givers. While great progress is made in the pre-school years, language development continues throughout the school years and beyond. Reading and writing are major aspects of language learning that develop during the school years. Early literacy develops naturally in children who grow up in highly literate environments.

The development of additional languages shares many similarities with the acquisition of the first language. For both, wide exposure to both written and spoken language are important as are opportunities to use language for authentic purposes, especially in interactive situations. Since learners generally come to a second language older than to a first, learner variables like age and motivation are much more significant in learning a second language than in learning a first. A further factor influencing second language learning is previous experience, and, especially, proficiency in the mother tongue.

EXERCISES

1. Observe the speech of parents or caregivers with infants of several ages — for example, 6 months, 12 months, 2 years, and 4 years. If possible compare the speech of a mother with two young children of different ages. What differences do you notice?

2. Ask children aged 4, 5, 6 and 8 to define *word*.

3. Ask children of different ages to tell you the meaning of particular words, for example: *mother, building, animal, husband, cold, old*. What differences do you notice?

4. Tape record a 30-minute naturalistic interaction between a child aged 20-30 months and his/her care-giver. Make sure to provide a good supply of toys that are likely to produce comments by both child and care-giver. Make detailed notes of the session as it proceeds. Listen to your tape recording in conjunction with reading your notes. What observations can you make about the child's language development?

5. If possible, obtain some samples of the writing of children in grade 1 and grade 2 classrooms where the teachers encourage the children to spell the best way they can without asking for adult assistance. What do you observe about the children's invented spellings?

6. The following entries were written in a journal in a grade 11 biology course by an ESL student who had come to Canada from Hong Kong eight months previously. He had learned some English in Hong Kong before coming to Canada.

Monday

Today we have play the team tournament again. Today's questions some are quite tricky, but anyway after I did this competition I had a basic membrance for all questions and help me to have a little review.

Tuesday

Today I had took the exam, I think it's quite hard for me so I can't pass the exam. Sometimes I think Biology is difficult because the questions are not go straight from the text book.

a. In responding to his journal, would you correct or refer to errors he has made? Why or why not?

b. Would you note errors he made so that you could give him some remedial help with English at some point? Why or why not? Which particular errors would you select for instruction, if any?

c. Are there errors in these entries that would cause you concern for a student with his experience of English? If so, which errors? If not, why would his errors not concern you?

REFERENCES

Andersen, E.S. (1984). The acquisition of sociolinguistic knowledge: Some evidence from children's verbal play. *Western Journal of Speech Communication*, 48, 125-144.

Archibald, N. (Producer) and H. Cook (Director) (1975). *Out of the mouths of babes* (Film). Toronto: Canadian Broadcasting Corporation.

Bates, E. (1976). *Language and Context: The Acquisition of Pragmatics*. New York: Academic Press.

Benedict, H. (1979). Early lexical development: Comprehension and production. *Journal of Child Language*, 6, 183-200.

Bissex, G. (1980). *Gyns at Work*. Cambridge, MA: Harvard University Press.

Bohannon, J. N., and A. Warren-Leubecker (1989). Theoretical approaches to language acquisition. In J.B. Gleason (ed.), *The Development of Language*, 2nd ed. (pp. 167-223). Columbus, Ohio: Merrill.

Brown, R. (1973). *A First Language*. Cambridge, MA: Harvard University Press.

Brown, R., C.B. Cazden and U. Bellugi (1969). The child's grammar from I to III. In J. P. Hill (ed.), *1967 Minnesota Symposium on Child Psychology* (pp. 28-73). Minneapolis: University of Minnesota Press.

Bruner, J. (1978). Learning how to do things with words. In J. Bruner and A. Garton (eds.), *Human Growth and Development* (pp.62-84). Oxford: Oxford University Press.

Bruner, J. (1981). The pragmatics of acquisition. In W. Deutsch (ed.), *The Child's Construction of Language* (pp. 39-56). London: Academic.

Cazden, C. (1972). *Child Language and Education*. New York: Holt, Rinehart and Winston.

Crowhurst, M. (1990). The development of persuasive/argumentative writing. In R. Beach and S. Hynds (eds.), *Becoming Readers and Writers During Adolescence and Adulthood* (pp. 200-223). Norwood, NJ: Ablex.

Crowhurst, M. (1992). Some effects of corresponding with an older audience. *Language Arts*, 69, 268-273.

Cummins, J. (1979). Linguistic interdependence and educational development in bilingual children. *Review of Educational Research*, 49, 222-251.

deVilliers, J.G., and P.A. deVilliers (1978). *Language Acquisition*. Cambridge, MA: Harvard University Press.

Dunn, J., and C. Kendrick C. (1982). The speech of speech of two-and three-year-olds to infant siblings: "Baby talk" and the context of communication. *Journal of Child Language*, 9, 579-595.

Eimas, P.D., E.R. Siqueland, P. Jusczyk and J. Vigorito (1971). Speech perception in infants. *Science*, 171, 303-306.

Gleason, J. B. (1989). Studying language development. In J.B. Gleason (ed.), *The Development of Language*, 2nd ed. (pp. 1-34). Columbus, Ohio: Merrill.

Glucksberg, S., and R. Krauss (1967). What do people say after they have learned how to talk? Studies of the development of referential communication. *Merrill-Palmer Quarterly*, 13, 309-316.

Greenlee, M., E. Hiebert, C. Bridge and P. Winograd (1986). The effects of different audiences on young writers' letter writing. In J. Niles and R. Lalik (eds.), *Solving Problems in Literacy: Learners, Teachers, and Researchers, 35th yearbook* (pp.281-289). Rochester, NY: National Reading Conference.

Gunderson, L., and J. Shapiro (1988). Whole language instruction: Writing in first grade. *The Reading Teacher*, 41, 430-439.

Halliday, (1973). *Explorations in the Functions of Language*. London: Edward Arnold.

Hudson, S. (1986). Context and children's writing. *Research in the Teaching of English*, 20, 294-316.

Hunt, K.W. (1965). *Grammatical structures written at three grade levels* (Research Report No. 3). Champaign, IL: National Council of Teachers of English.

Krashen, S.D. (1985). *The Input Hypothesis: Issues and Implications.* New York: Longman.

Langer, J. A. (1986). *Children Reading and Writing: Structures and Strategies.* Norwood, NJ: Ablex.

Long, M.H. (1988). Instructed interlanguage development. In Beebe (ed.), *Issues in Second Language Acquisition* (pp. 113-142). New York: Harper and Row.

McNeill, D. (1966). Developmental psycholinguistics. In F. Smith and G.A. Miller (eds.), *The Genesis of Language: A Psycholinguistic Approach* (pp. 15-84). Cambridge, MA: M.I.T. Press.

Miller, G.A., and P.M. Gildea (1987). How children learn words. *Scientific American,* 257, 94-99.

Mueller, E. (1972). The maintenance of verbal exchange between young children. *Child Development,* 43, 930-938.

Nagy, W., and R. Anderson (1984). The number of words in printed school English. *Reading Research Quarterly,* 19, 304-330.

Newkirk, T. (1987). The non-narrative writing of young children. *Research in the Teaching of English,* 21, 121-144.

Nippold, M.A. (1988). The literate lexicon. In M. A. Nippold (ed.), *Later Language Development: Ages 9 through 19* (pp.29-48). Boston, MA: Little, Brown and Company.

Pease, D.M., J.B. Gleason and B.A. Pan (1989). Gaining meaning: Semantic development. In J.B. Gleason (ed.), *The Development of Language,* 2nd ed. (pp. 101-134). Columbus, OH: Merrill.

Perera, K. (1984). *Children's Writing and Reading: Analysing Classroom Language.* Oxford: Basil Blackwell.

Piper, T. (1993). *Language for All Our Children.* Columbus, OH: Merrill.

Scarcella, R. (1990). *Teaching Language Minority Students in the Multicultural Classroom.* Englewood Cliffs, NJ: Prentice Hall.

Shatz, M. (1978). On the development of communicative understandings: An early strategy for interpreting and responding to messages. *Cognitive Psychology,* 10, 271-301.

Shatz, M., and R. Gelman (1973). The development of communication skills: Modifications in the speech of young children as a function of listener. *Monographs of the Society for Research in Child Development,* 35, (Serial No. 152).

Squire, J.R. (1964). *The responses of adolescents while reading four short stories.* Urbana, IL: National Council of Teachers of English.

Tierney, R.J. (1982). Learning from text. In A. Berger and H.A. Robinson (eds.), *Secondary School Reading* (pp. 97-110). Urbana IL: ERIC Clearinghouse on Reading and Communication Skills.

Warren-Leubecker, A., and J.N. Bohannon (1989). Pragmatics: Language in social contexts. In J.B. Gleason (ed.), *The Development of Language, 2nd ed.* (pp. 327-368). Columbus, OH: Merrill.

Wells, G. (1986). *The Meaning Makers: Children Learning Language and Using Language to Learn.* Portsmouth, NH: Portsmouth.

Wong-Fillmore, L.W. (1976). *The second time around: Cognitive and social strategies in second language acquisition.* Ph.D. Dissertation. Stanford University.

Wong-Fillmore, L.W. (1983). The language learner as an individual: Implications of individual differences for the ESL teacher. In J. Handscombe and M. Clarke (eds.), *On TESOL '82: Pacific perspectives on language learning and teaching* (pp. 157-173). Washington, DC: TESOL.

Chapter 4
LANGUAGE IN THE CLASSROOM

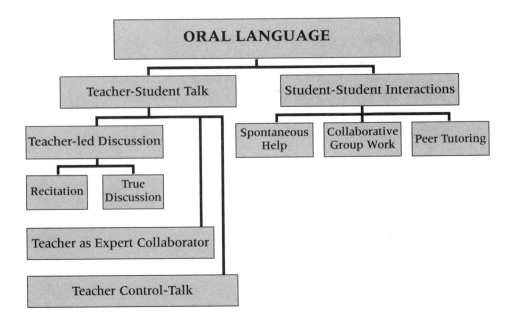

ORAL LANGUAGE

Teacher-Student Talk

Student-Student Interactions

Teacher-led Discussion

Spontaneous Help

Collaborative Group Work

Peer Tutoring

Recitation

True Discussion

Teacher as Expert Collaborator

Teacher Control-Talk

WRITTEN LANGUAGE

Language is the currency of the classroom. Talking, listening, reading, writing are the staple activities by means of which teachers teach and students learn. Like most human behaviour, classroom language use is governed by "rules" — by expectations about who will talk (or write, or read) to whom for what purpose. Sometimes the expectations for behaviour are explicitly articulated. For the most part, however, they are picked up by experience and could not easily be articulated by either teacher or students. We recognize the unspoken social rules of the classroom, however, and smile when we hear imagined violations. We cannot imagine, as Barnes (1976) points out, a student marking out errors in red pencil on a teacher's writing, or asking the teacher a question and replying, when he cannot answer, "Come now, Mr. Makin, think! I have told you that a dozen times!"

The purpose of this chapter is to describe classroom language — oral language and written language. Oral language consists, primarily, of teacher talk and student talk. Written language has two aspects, receptive and productive. Children must learn both to read and to produce written language.

ORAL LANGUAGE

Talk is the most common kind of language activity in the classroom. Flanders (1970), who devised a well-known system for coding classroom talk, found that, in the average classroom, someone was talking two-thirds of the time and that two-thirds of the talk was teacher talk. Staab's (1991) findings twenty years later were very similar. Classroom talk is dominated by the teacher. Students also talk. Some of that talk is illicit. Much of it is constrained by the teacher, particularly by the teacher's questions. Some of it serves important academic purposes. Both teacher talk and student talk are examined in this section.

TEACHER-STUDENT TALK

Teacher talk serves the following main purposes: to inform, to control behaviour by directives, by rebukes, and by praise and encouragement, and to promote and test the acquisition of knowledge and understanding by asking questions. The teacher speaks many times in a day to individual students. However, the focus in this section is the interactions that occur when the teacher deals with the class as a whole. It is this aspect of classroom talk that has been most widely studied by researchers. Three kinds of teacher-student talk are discussed: discussion (which, in fact, consists of two very different kinds of interaction patterns); talk by the teacher in the role of expert collaborator; and control talk.

Teacher-Led Discussion: Recitation

When teachers or students talk about classroom discussion, they are usually referring to the familiar classroom activity known as **recitation**. Recitation is a three-part turn-taking sequence consisting of a teacher initiation (usually a question) followed by a student response and a teacher evaluation. It is the most common discourse structure in classroom lessons. Recitation is to be distinguished from true discussion which occurs much less frequently.

Recitation covers a variety of activities called review, drill, quiz, guided discovery, and inquiry teaching. Its most common manifestation is in the review that follows the reading of textual material. The students read and the teacher quizzes them to see what they remember. Recitation is used by teachers to achieve three major purposes: to "cover" the content; to make sure their students

---

Figure 4.1
A Recitation Episode from a Primary Class

Teacher:	In my letter this morning I asked a question. Who remembers it? Daniel?
Daniel:	What changes have happened.
Teacher:	What changes have happened in our community since it became autumn. What happens to the trees in the summer time? What do they look like? Monique?
Monique:	They're all green.
Teacher:	Yes, they are. But what's happened to the trees now?
Prasad:	Yellow.
Teacher:	Yes. So we get yellow, or brown, red, green, all those neat colours that we have in the autumn. The leaves do something else. What else happens?
Annie:	They fall on the ground.
Teacher:	Good. What happens to the weather.
Stephen:	It changes. It starts to get cold.
Teacher:	It starts to get colder.
Sara:	It gets raining.
Teacher:	It starts to rain. Hamish?
Hamish:	It starts to get nice and muddy.
Teacher:	What gets muddy, Hamish?
Hamish:	The mud.
Teacher:	What changes to mud?
Hamish:	The soil.
Teacher:	Good for you … because it mixes with water. Usually if you go visiting the pumpkin patch you have to wear pretty big boots because it is all muddy.

Figure 4.2
A Recitation Episode from an Eighth-Grade Class

Teacher:	How does pregnancy occur, Carl?
Carl:	With uh, the sperm enters the female body and it travels through the uterus down the fallopian tube and then one sperm unites with the ovum.
Teacher:	Okay. When the sperm unites and joins with the female's ovum, it's called what, Danny?
Danny:	Conception.
Teacher:	It's called conception. *(Long pause.)* Okay. At the point of conception, the male's sperm and the female's ovum unite. How many chromosomes does a male's sperm cell have, Leon?
Leon:	23?
Teacher:	23 chromosomes. How many chromosomes does a female's ovum have, Kenneth?
Kenneth:	23.
Teacher:	23. Combine them: They become 46 chromosomes to start a pregnancy. Okay, the male and female both have 2 types of cells. What are those 2 types of cells called, Jim?
Jim:	Body cells and sex cells.
Teacher:	Okay. Body cells and sex cells. What's the difference between a body cell and a sex cell, Michael?
Michael:	A body, a body cell sends out directions for—(*inaudible*), and a sex cell turns out, uh, sexual directions.
Teacher:	All right—that's true. What makes them different as far as chromosomes are concerned, Buddy?
Buddy:	The sex cell unites with the egg cell.
Teacher:	Okay. It does unite with the egg cell.

---

master the facts, the information that the discipline consists of; and to retain control of the class.

The excerpts presented in Figures 4.1 and 4.2 illustrate the pattern well. The excerpt in Figure 4.1 is from a primary classroom where the teacher is introducing a lesson on the fall. The excerpt in Figure 4.2 is from an eighth-grade human development class; the class had read about pregnancy in their texts the previous day (Alvermann and Hayes, 1989, p.313).

The excerpt illustrates several points about the kind of interaction that occurs in recitation episodes. Teacher and students take turns in speaking, one teacher turn for every student turn. Turn-taking is controlled by the teacher. Students speak when they are invited to do so. Students speak only to the teacher and only to answer the questions asked by the teacher. They are expected to volunteer no more than is required to answer the question. Their responses are usually one of the following: an affirmative, a negative, a list-like answer given in very few words or, occasionally, an elaborated response in which the answer is developed beyond a word or two. Teacher evaluations may be a simple acknowledgement (e.g., a nod, "Okay", "Good"), a repetition, a paraphrase, an elaboration of the student's response, or a rejection. This question-response-evaluation sequence has been observed across age levels and across subject areas throughout the English speaking world (Duffy, 1983) and has persisted for well over half a century (Hoetker and Ahlbrandt, 1969; O'Flahavan, Harman, and Pearson, 1988).

Of the three components of the basic question-response-evaluation sequence, teacher questions have been most studied. Their importance is due to "...their frequency, the pedagogical work they are intended to do, and the obvious control they exert over the talk and thereby over the enacted curriculum" (Cazden, 1986, p. 440). Teacher questions have several characteristic features. For one thing, teacher questions do not fulfil the usual pre-conditions for questions. In the world outside the classroom, we ask questions when we want to know something. We ask because we do not know. Teachers, however, usually know the answers to the questions they ask. We occasionally come across this kind of question-asking outside the classroom, but it is a behaviour that seems decidedly odd in everyday life. A second difference is that, when we ask a question in everyday life, we address it to someone we think will be able to answer it. Teacher questions often violate this condition as well. Teachers may address questions to students they think will *not* know the answer to put them on the spot for some reason — for not attending or not participating, for example. Teachers' known-answer questions are not real questions at all. They have the form of questions but they do not serve the function that questions serve in everyday life. Rather, they serve the function of testing, or, if addressed to an inattentive student, of controlling.

Teacher questions are *who, what, how* or *when* questions that ask students to give back factual information. If *why* questions are asked, they usually require students to supply reasons given in the text or covered in lectures. It is much less common for the teacher to ask students to express opinions, to draw inferences or conclusions, or to make evaluations. In other words, teachers' questions are predominantly "lower-level" questions rather than "higher-level" questions. The pace is rapid. Answers are expected within a second or two, and the average pause between an answer and the next question is less than a second (Rowe, 1986).

Teachers commonly have particular answers in mind for the questions they ask. If they do not get the answer they want, they rephrase the question and supply hints as necessary until they get the answer they seek and perhaps even the form of answer they require. The following excerpt (Torbe and Shuard, 1982, pp. 5-6) occurred in a mathematics class in the United Kingdom with thirteen to fourteen-year-olds. The recitation sequence is being used to revise the procedure for solving simultaneous equations:

Teacher: OK then; $3x - y = 5$ ... $2x + 3y = 7$. Who can remember what we call this kind of problem? Gail?

Student 1:   Equations.

Teacher: Oh, we know they're equations—but what kind? Who can remember their special name? Yes?

Student 2:   Simultaneous.

Teacher: Yes. "Simultaneous equations" (*writing on board*). Right. Now, what do we have to do with these? What do I do first? Yes?

Student 3:   Solve them, sir.

Teacher: Well of course we have to solve them, but what do I do first? Come on, I've told you often enough.

Student 4:   Write them down under each other.

Teacher: Good—write them down under each other, like this (*writes on board*). Were you talking, Dean?

Student 5:   No, sir.

Teacher: Oh, yes, you were. Pay attention; I'll only show you this once today—shouldn't even have to do that—I've shown you often enough before. Right, then, what do we have to do now?

Student 4:   Find x and y.

Teacher: Ye...es.

Student 4:   Find x first and then y?

Teacher: Well — yes, but I'm thinking of something else first. Who can tell me what it is?

Teachers have a variety of strategies for indicating that an answer is less than satisfactory. They may say straight out that the answer is wrong or inadequate. They may react disparagingly towards the answer and rephrase the question more precisely, as the teacher above does to Student 1 and Student 3. They may answer with a long-drawn-out, unenthusiastic "ye...es" as the teacher does to Student 4 causing the student to try again. They may utter a non-committal "Uh-huh," and ask another student what she thinks. They may come right out and say, as does the teacher in the excerpt quoted, that the student is supposed to try to guess what he is thinking. Whether teachers say so outright, or indicate in more subtle ways that they have particular answers that they want, students quickly become adept at the game. Their task is to memorize the material or the interpretations that the teacher prefers and to provide answers that prove they have done so. If they are uncertain that their answer is the expected one, they answer with a rising inflection that turns it into a question, as Student 4 above does in his third utterance.

The teacher's rebuke delivered to the student, Dean, underlines another feature of the question/response/evaluation pattern. Students are not expected to speak unless they are invited to do so. Both they and the teacher understand this rule. This feature of the interaction pattern ensures that the teacher remains in control. Students are sometimes invited to make comments or to ask questions. However, questions or comments, even if invited, may not be answered by the teacher if they do not suit his purpose. In the lesson on simultaneous equations mentioned above, only one question was asked by a student as recorded in the following excerpt (Torbe and Shuard, 1982, p. 9):

Teacher: Any questions before you begin — No? — right then…

Student: Sir, why are they called 'simultaneous'?

Teacher: What?

Student: Why are they 'simultaneous'?

Teacher: Oh — well — it's a bit hard to explain quickly. See me after the lesson and I'll tell you then…

Questions, comments, or answers that do not suit the teacher's purposes are likely to be ignored or deflected.

True Discussion

Though students and teachers tend to refer to any kind of teacher-student talk as *discussion*, most classroom interaction between teacher and students is recitation. Discussion and recitation differ in important ways. Both involve teacher and students in talking back and forth, and both involve questioning and answering. But the purpose and interaction patterns are markedly different. Recitation is teacher-controlled. Students speak only to the teacher. They give short answers to questions that require recall of curriculum material. The purpose of discussion is the *construction* of knowledge or the *use* of knowledge. It involves questions that ask for student opinions and thoughts, not merely right answers. It involves student-student exchanges as well as student-teacher exchanges. Students as well as teachers may ask questions. Responses are longer than in recitation.

Table 4.1 (Dillon, 1990, p. 11) compares a recitation class with a discussion class. Both classes were history classes in the same school taught by equally competent teachers to students aged 16-17 of approximately the same verbal ability.

Table 4.1
Questions in Classroom Processes

Aspect of questioning	Recitation class (%)	Discussion class (%)
Teacher talk (vs student talk)	69	22
Question turns	78	11
Teacher-student turns (vs student-student)	88	6
'Higher-cognitive' questions (vs 'lower-cognitive')	29	87
Students participating	41	77
Rate of exchanges	6 per minute	1 per minute
Average student response	4 seconds	25 seconds

Source: Dillon, 1990, p.11.

In the discussion class, the students talked more than the teacher whereas the opposite was true in the recitation class. Responses were, on average, six times longer in the discussion class than in the recitation class. More students participated in the discussion class. The focus in the discussion class was on higher cognitive questions rather than lower as in the recitation class.

Discussion occurs infrequently in schools, estimates varying from less than 1 percent to 8 percent of the time across various grade levels (Dillon, 1984; Staab, 1991). It is not easy for teachers to learn to conduct discussions. Alvermann and Hayes (1989), together with two research assistants, worked with five volunteer secondary teachers from a variety of different subject areas for a period of six months trying to improve classroom discussion in a number of ways: by involving more students; by increasing the number of student-to-student exchanges; and by increasing the number of longer, elaborated student responses. Their efforts were largely unsuccessful. Two of the five teachers were able to increase the *number* of students participating in the discussion. However, students' responses remained brief and unelaborated. They continued to address the teacher rather than their peers. The authors point out that "given that it is oral language that weaves the fabric of classroom culture, attempts to modify classroom discussion amount to nothing less than attempts to modify the very culture of the classroom" (p. 307).

The kinds of interactions between teacher and students greatly influence the kinds of thinking and learning that occur. The functions of students' contributions to classroom discussions are largely determined by teachers' questions. Questions that call for the recitation of memorized material promote memorization; they do not promote higher-level thinking. Given the prevalence of recitation as a classroom strategy, the limited kinds of thinking that it promotes, and the persistence of the strategy even in the face of attempts to change, it is worth examining two excerpts that illustrate different kinds of interactions between students and teacher.

The first excerpt comes from a grade 9 science class on heat and temperature (MacKinnon, 1989, pp. 54-56). The thermal expansion of solids was about to be demonstrated using a brass ball and ring apparatus. The excerpt is taken from the introductory part of the lesson where the teacher's purpose was to elicit students' prior conceptions about the expansion of solids. He did this by asking students to suggest some possible tests that might be made using the ball and ring and to predict the outcomes of those tests.

Teacher: Okay, what kind of tests can you think of that we might have? (S1)?

Student 1: You could heat them up and then the ball will expand because of the heat, and then you won't be able to pull it out.

Teacher: Okay, and so you're saying you'll heat them both up?

Student 1: Yeah, one inside the other. Put the ball inside it …

Teacher: Yes (*puts the ball inside the ring*) Like that?

Student 1: … and then heat it up.

Teacher: Yeah.

Student 1: And then you won't be able to pull the ball out.

Teacher: I see … okay. Why do you think that might be?

Student 1: I think that the metal inside the ball is going to expand.

Teacher: Okay, good.

Student 1: (*Softly*) … and so will the metal in the ring.

Teacher: Okay. (S2), what would you test?

Student 2: But that wouldn't work because if you did that, then the ring would expand too, and they probably both would expand at the same rate, so then you'd still be able to move it.

Teacher: I see. Okay. So you suggest the same test, but you predict a different result.

Student 2: Yeah.

Teacher: Interesting. Okay. (S3)?

Student 3: Uhm … (*inaudible*) …

Teacher: Sorry … a nice loud voice so that everyone can hear you.

Student 3: If you heat up the ring, then the ring will expand, and when you put the ball inside the ring, there'll be much more room?

Teacher: Okay, so you're suggesting a second test where I heat up the ring but not the ball?

Student 3: Yeah.

Teacher: You think, then, that it will fit much better (*puts the ball through the ring*)?

Student 3: Yeah.

Teacher: Okay. (S4)?

Student 4: If you heated up the ball. If you put the ring inside, or around the ball, then heat it up, you wouldn't be able to get it off. Or, either way.

Teacher: Okay. (S5)?

Student 5: Uh, to the thing that (S1) said, with the ball inside the ring, well, I think that would work because the ball has more or less mass than the ring has. So I think it would heat up differently because one has more mass than the other ... (*inaudible*)

Teacher: Okay, do I hear you saying, then, that the rate at which they expand or contract depends on how much of the stuff there is?

Student 5: Yeah.

Teacher: Okay. (S6)?

Student 6: I just think you should heat up the ball and then see if it'll fit through the ring or not ...

Teacher: Okay. What do you think would happen, (S6), if I heated up the ball without the ring?

Student 6: Well, the ball would expand, and then it wouldn't fit through.

Teacher: Okay. Can anyone think of any other tests? Yeah?

Student 7: I think both (S2) and (S3) are wrong ... even though ...

(*Students all laugh.*)

Student 7: If you put the ball inside the ring, they both expand. But the ring doesn't just expand out, it also expands inward.

Teacher: Yeah?

Student 7: So it would be tight, you wouldn't be able to get it out.

Teacher: Okay, let's try all of these things. I'll just heat the ball up first, but we'll try each one of them (*Begins heating the ball*). What I hear a couple of you saying is that the ball will no longer fit. Any other variations on that? Do I hear a no?

Student 8: Sure ... no.

Teacher: (S8), what do you think (*continues to heat the ball*)?

Student 8: Well, I think that if you heat up either, both of them will expand anyways.

Student 9: The ball's not in (the flame).

Student 8: So if you heat up the ring, the ball won't fit through. If you heat up the ball, it won't fit through. And if you heat up both, it won't fit through either.

Teacher: Okay, so whatever I do, I can never get it through there. All right. Yes?

Student 5: Well, if you just heat up the ring, the ring will expand. It'll also expand inward and outward.

Teacher: I'm keeping this one (the ring) cold.

Student 5: Oh.

Teacher: I'm just heating up the ball now. Yeah?

Student 3: I was just stretching.

Teacher: All right. Well, let's try it then. Okay? Watch carefully.

This excerpt differs in several ways from the kind of interactions that occur during recitation. The students' turns are longer. In fact, the students speak more, in total, than the teacher. They are producing not memorized materials but predictions and the reasons for their predictions. They address the teacher, but often make contributions that address a point made by a peer. The teacher's questions are real questions, not known-answer questions. He uses questions to invite contributions ("What kinds of tests can you think of?" "Any other variations on that?"); to ask for explanations ("Why do you think that might be?"); and to check that he understands what the students mean ("So you suggest the same test, but you predict a different result?"). He acknowledges responses with neutral comments like "okay," "yeah," and "interesting," but makes no attempt to resolve the contradictions in the suggestions made by different students. He offers no explanation of his own: he is not playing the teacher-as-expert role. Though it is not evident in the typed transcript, he allowed ample "wait time" to give students time to think and to formulate their answers.

The second excerpt is a segment of a discussion by a heterogenous class of 23 seventh graders who were discussing *The Girl Who Owned a City* by O.T. Nelson (1975) (Roberts and Langer, 1991, pp 26-28). The novel is about a city ruled by children after all those over the age of 12 have mysteriously died. Students had spent several class periods responding to the novel in small groups prior to this whole-class discussion. For the discussion, students and teacher were seated on chairs in a circle. The excerpt is taken from about halfway through the class and illustrates the kind of discussion that went on throughout the class. The question under discussion is raised by Conrad who questions whether the last part of the story is needed.

Speaker

Teacher: Conrad? Conrad wanted confirmation of something at the ending of the story a few minutes back, so ...

Conrad: Okay, the only thing that he (the author) really said in the last part, was that Lisa gets better, and then she talks to Tom. And they really, the author just kept going. He really didn't need the part about the ... where she goes around to the other people, and talks about the Chicago gang, they really didn't need that. I think he was just writing for the sake of writing.

Teacher: So you don't think there was any reason for any of that in there, when she went around?

Conrad: No. The reason they make her better, and then talk to Tom, but most of the last part wasn't really needed.

Teacher: Okay, anybody want to respond to *that* particular issue? Let's respond to him, his need about what is in the end of the story. Gerrick?

Gerrick: I think, like that sort of loop around, when she went around and just checked all the places, that was sort of like make you think about Craig, when he decided to start his own farm, like the Chicago Gang and stuff like that. When I heard about that I started to think about Craig, well wait a minute, he's got no sort of defense system, he's just living on a farm now. It sort of made me think of *all* the possibilities that could happen. That it opened the door up, so like, at the end of the story, if you wanted to carry on, you think you could.

Teacher: You think that the loop was there to provide you with some things to think about when the story ended?

Gerrick: Yeah.

Conrad: But you really didn't need to think about those things. You really had enough danger from Tom Logan's gang, and the gangs around there. They didn't really need to put the part about the gang from Chicago and stuff. I don't think, it really wasn't needed. And it was like he just put that in there for, something to do with the sequel or something.

Teacher: All right, some of you are not trusting the author. You think it is something for the sequel. Okay, Jimmy?

Jimmy: When you said about the other gangs, they might need Tom Logan in the next book though. That's maybe why they didn't shoot Tom Logan. Or why she didn't pick up the gun. Because if she had picked up the gun, and shot Tom Logan, that means in the next book, ... if the other gangs *had* come, and had blown away the other gang, and they had kids left, that other gang comes and wipes them out, and all that's left is like 20 kids from this building, and they're just there. And, then they wouldn't be able to do anything, because if they did have Tom Logan's gang, it would be a lot easier for them.

Teacher: Ann?

This excerpt illustrates what was true for the lesson as a whole. It presents a very different picture from the interaction in a recitation episode. Most of the talking was done by the students. Seventeen out of 23 students participated in the lesson of which the excerpt is part. The students took 56 percent of the total turns and spoke 79 percent of the words; they had more turns than the teacher, and their turns were appreciably longer. Students' contributions were not controlled by the teacher. The teacher's most frequent contribution was orchestrating the discussion by regulating turn-taking (54 percent of her turns). She clarified students' meanings by restating their ideas (29 percent of her turns) but did not put forward ideas of her own. She occasionally offered help by focusing what a student had said or by modifying a student's language to tighten the argument the student was making (16.5 percent of turns). She made no evaluations of students' contributions. She did not introduce topics for discussion. She did not give overt reinforcement or reassurance. She did not call upon students unless they had first indicated that they wanted to participate.

Students spoke for a wide range of purposes. They introduced topics, expanded ideas, clarified ideas, and challenged ideas. They paid close attention to each other's ideas, affirming, confronting and questioning each other. They spoke to each other rather than to the teacher.

The teacher's purpose was to produce active thinkers — students who could develop and support their own interpretations of what they read. The social organization and interaction within the class supported student thinking.

Teacher-led discussion is a very common classroom activity. Usually, the activity is not true discussion but recitation. The three-part recitation sequence is so common that it has been called "… the criterial or 'unmarked' discourse structure" in lessons (Cazden, 1986, p. 436). Recitation is the "'default' pattern — what happens unless deliberate action is taken to achieve some alternative" (Cazden, 1988, p. 53). It focuses on the memorization of facts and procedures. True discussion is less common and harder for teachers to master. It has considerable potential for promoting higher-level thinking.

The Teacher as Expert Collaborator

The role of teacher as expert collaborator is an important one not much practised in most classrooms. The importance of the role is suggested by Vygotsky who believed that learners are helped to higher levels of understanding and performance through collaborative interaction with an adult or more capable peers. The teacher, as expert guide, interacts collaboratively with a learner or groups of learners. She models behaviours and supports students as they learn the behaviours. In teacher-led discussion, as described above, the teacher acts collaboratively with students to facilitate the expression of their observations and opinions; the teacher is a facilitator rather than an active participant in the discussion. The teacher as expert collaborator takes a more direct role while still working in a collaborative, interactive mode.

One example of the teacher as expert collaborator comes from the writing class. The teacher engages in writing along with the students, and models many aspects of composing with the goal of helping students develop understanding and skill in writing processes. He also models responding to his students' writing so that students also learn to respond to their peers. A second example is reciprocal teaching devised by Brown and her colleagues (e.g., Brown and Palinscar, 1987; Campione, Brown, and Connell, 1988) and applied to helping students learn the kinds of skills that experts use in reading and in mathematical problem solving.

Teacher Control Talk

A considerable percentage of what teachers say to their students is control talk — talk that has as its purpose the management of student behaviour. Teachers give many directives about things students are to do. They control not only classroom behaviour but also classroom discourse. They call the class to attention in preparation for information to come ("Everybody paying attention, please"). They nominate those who are to speak. They rebuke — gently or more firmly, as needed — those who "call out" or those who volunteer for too many turns ("Okay, Wendy, I think we'll let Jason have a turn"). They control the amount of talk that is permitted with statements like, "Some people are speaking instead of working." They determine the topics for discussion and decide whether or not contributions are relevant ("Well, right now we are talking about St. John's, not about Saskatoon").

When teachers make a comment like: "Some people are speaking instead of working," it has the form of a statement. It sounds as if the intention is to inform. Those of us acquainted with classrooms, however, recognize immediately that the intent of the speaker is not to inform but to request or command. The students who are speaking are being told to be quiet and get on with their work. Such *indirect commands* are very common in classrooms. They may be confusing to young children or those whose cultural background leads them to expect more direct expressions (Cazden, 1986). Sometimes control language is even more complex. Cazden (1986) cites the instance of a secondary science teacher who said, "I can't hear you, Ian," after Rosie called out an answer when Ian had been nominated to speak. The teacher's comment carries a double directive: for Ian to repeat his answer and for Rosie to refrain from calling out.

Three points are to be made about teacher control talk. The first is that the language of control is pervasive in the classroom. The second is that understanding the precise intent of specific instances of control language requires some experience of the culture of the classroom. Children who come from cultures very different from the dominant culture of the classroom may take longer to adapt to the form of control language used in the classroom than those whose home backgrounds match the classroom culture more closely. (See Chapter 11 for a fuller discussion.) Thirdly, it is essential for teachers to be able to control their classes. Students are not well served by teachers who cannot exercise appropriate control. However it is questionable whether teachers need to exercise the close control of classroom behaviour and interactions that is commonly practised. Experienced teachers can afford to give up some of the control they exercise in order to achieve valuable pedagogical ends.

STUDENT-STUDENT INTERACTIONS

Students also speak in classrooms. They speak to teachers when nominated to make contributions, and occasionally to ask questions or to make requests. In some classrooms they interact individually with teachers in interviews and conferences; conferences can be highly beneficial both for students and for teachers who have the opportunity to find out what a student is thinking that is not easily available otherwise. In true discussions — a fairly rare type of classroom discourse — they make contributions of varying kinds for a variety purposes.

Students also speak to their peers. A certain amount of unsanctioned talk between students occurs in the classroom. Such talk is tolerated to a minor extent but is usually seen as a nuisance. Talk between students, however, may serve useful academic purposes. Cazden (1986) identifies three kinds of talk for academic purposes: talk that gives spontaneous help to an individual peer; collaborative talk for the purpose of completing a group task; and peer tutoring where a student is asked to teach one or more peers.

Spontaneous Help

Traditional classrooms have commonly operated on a transmission and testing model. The teacher's job is to know what needs to be taught, to pass on the requisite knowledge and skills to her students, and to test in order to determine whether students have learned. In traditional, transmission-oriented classrooms of this kind, help given by one student to another is not usually regarded favourably. It is often seen as a kind of cheating. However, in classrooms where more emphasis is placed on students' construction of meaning rather than on teachers' transmission of knowledge, talk among peers is not negatively viewed. Collaboration is often encouraged. In such classrooms — most likely to be primary classrooms and least likely to be high school classes — interesting examples are often seen where students give spontaneous help to their peers: with the spelling of a word; with a response to a piece of writing; with a suggestion for writing a number sentence; with a response to a piece of art in progress.

Studies show some interesting findings about those who give and those who receive spontaneous help. In a second-grade class, "the two children who received the most unsolicited information from their peers were also the ones most frequently sought as consultants" (Cooper et al., 1982, p.76) Thus they received a double benefit: the benefit of explaining to others and the benefit of receiving instruction from their peers. In a kindergarten class (Garnica, 1981), the six children who ranked lowest on the sociometric scale were least spoken to by others and made least attempt to speak to others. They neither gave nor received help from their peers. If spontaneous interactions among students are educationally beneficial, as seems likely, it is important to know how to bring about the inclusion of isolated children who are often those most in need of help.

Collaborative Group Work

Collaboration among students has not often been encouraged in schools. Rather, the emphasis has usually been on individual effort with strong overtones of competitiveness. Learning has usually been defined as the ability to memorize and produce transmitted information. Since collaboration has not been much practised, it is not surprising that there has been less analysis of peer interaction than analysis of teacher-student interaction.

Nonetheless, there is emerging research support for the cognitive value of collaboration among peers. A group of Swiss psychologists conducted a series of experiments to examine the effect of peer collaboration on logical reasoning skills of children aged 4 to 7. The problems were Piagetian tasks involving perspective-taking, conservation, and so on. They found that peer interaction enhanced logical reasoning (Cazden, 1986).

Forman (Forman and Cazden, 1985) examined the effect of collaboration in the solution of a series of chemical reaction tasks. Her eight 9 year-old subjects worked in pairs. Their performance was compared with that of 15 students who had worked individually. The students who worked collaboratively solved many more problems than those who worked individually. Moreover, the pair that had the largest number of cooperative interactions solved the most problems. These two students assumed complementary roles, and gave each other support, correction, and guidance. In this way they were able to do what neither could do alone.

Bereiter and Scardamalia (1987) describe an example in which a group of four sixth-graders engaged in planning a story that was to end with the sentence,

"And so, after considering the reasons for it and the reasons against it, the duke decided to rent his castle to the vampire after all, in spite of the rumour he had heard." Though they did not find it easy to compose a story that met all the constraints imposed by the ending, the students engaged in high level planning of a kind rarely observed in individual students working alone, even as high as the grade 8 level.

Forman and Cazden (1985, p.344) suggest that peer interaction is especially important in schools because teacher-student interactions are limited and rigid:

> In school lessons, teachers give directions and children nonverbally carry them out; teachers ask questions and children answer them, frequently with only a word or a phrase. Most importantly, these roles are not reversible, at least not within the context of teacher-child interactions. Children never give directions to teachers, and questions addressed to teachers are rare except for asking permission. The only context in which children can reverse interactional roles with the same intellectual content, giving directions as well as following them, and asking questions as well as answering them, is with their peers.

Collaboration enables students to do together what they could not do as individuals. Over time, they internalize the thinking that enabled them, collaboratively, to solve problems and thus develop higher-level thinking processes.

Peer Tutoring

Peer tutoring usually involves the teacher modelling a procedure until students have learned it. Students then use the procedure to tutor their peers. One example of peer tutoring is Brown and Palincsar's (1987) reciprocal teaching procedure, which is designed to help novice readers learn to use the kinds of strategies that expert readers use. (For a description of reciprocal teaching, see Chapter 8.) Numerous examples of peer tutoring come from writing classrooms where students hold "peer conferences" about their writing with one another. The values of peer tutoring are not only for the recipients of the tutoring but also for the tutors who benefit from having to put words to what they know. Which of us has not found that we learn very well what we have to teach?

SUMMARY

The oral language of the classroom is usually dominated by the teacher. The teacher has the right to speak to any person at any time. The teacher also exercises major control over much student talk, determining who says what to whom. The most common pattern of teacher-student interaction is the three-part recitation sequence. Recitation is used by teachers, more or less successfully, to achieve the following purposes: to cover course content, to maintain control over the class, and to test students' knowledge. Discussion by the class as a whole with the teacher as moderator, collaborative interaction between the teacher-as-expert and students, and interactions among students in pairs and small groups are much less common. These kinds of oral language offer important potential cognitive and affective benefits. Though teachers must expend time and energy to master the necessary skills and to develop them in their students, the rewards are well worth the effort.

Written language

Children come to school with well developed skills in oral language. One of the major tasks they face in school is learning to deal with written language. They must learn to read and to write.

Written language is sometimes described as speech written down. In actual fact, however, written language is very different from spoken language. There are several major differences. One is a set of linguistic differences between the two — linguistic differences that affect vocabulary, sentence structure and the organization of discourse. A second difference is that written language is largely independent of the non-linguistic context whereas speech is embedded in the context in which it occurs. Thirdly, written language is relatively permanent whereas spoken language is gone as soon as it is uttered.

Linguistic Differences   The organizational unit is different for written language than for spoken language. Spoken language is organized by means of intonation patterns into intonation units. Written language is organized into sentences. The concept of a sentence is a concept related to written language, not to the spoken language that children bring with them to school.

Written language favours economy. It is much less redundant than speech. Many syntactic constructions that are uncommon in spoken language occur commonly in written language — constructions that facilitate more compressed, more economical expression, and constructions that produce stylistic effect are important in written language but not in spoken language. These constructions were discussed in greater detail in Chapter 2.

A further linguistic difference is that written discourse is structured differently from spoken discourse. Spoken language deals with topics sequentially. A topic may be dropped temporarily and taken up again for further discussion and elaboration five or fifteen minutes later. Written language demands very different patterns of organization.

In learning to read, children must learn to process sentences that are structured differently from the units of spoken language, and must learn to recognize patterns of organization in order to understand whole texts. In learning to write, children must learn to write sentences, and to use the more economical, more varied sentence structures of written langauge; they must learn, also, to structure their writing in ways appropriate to written language. Capable readers and writers commonly take many years to develop high levels of skill in reading and writing.

Written Language Is Decontextualized   The oral language that children meet first is embedded in an ongoing flow of events. Children do not interpret words or sentences in isolation. They interpret situations. Language occurs in a context which supports it. Children figure out the meaning of what is said by reading the context as much as by understanding the words and sentences they hear. When mother holds out a banana to her infant daughter and says, "Would you like a banana?" the child does not need to understand all the words in order to understand the offer that is being made. Writing, however — at least, the kind of writing that comes in books — is decontextualized language. There is nothing to help the reader except the text itself. Learning to read and write places different demands on children's linguistic skills than is made by oral language, especially the oral language that they have been exposed to before they come to school.

Written Language Is Relatively Permanent   Margaret Donaldson (1978) points out that dealing with written language both requires and enables children to become aware of language as an object. The fact that written language endures on the page gives the child time to consider the words as words, and to read them again in another place at another time, if he wishes. Many children come to school with little understanding of what a word is. Young children rarely ask what a word means even though they listen to stories with words that must be unfamiliar to them. They have little awareness of language as a system separate from the meanings that are conveyed by language. Learning to read brings an awareness of language as object.

The permanence of language on the page makes it possible for the child to consider possibilities, as Donaldson says. Since written language is decontextualized, free of the non-linguistic context, its meaning is not determined by the context as is usually the case with spoken language. This quality of written language, Donaldson believes, encourages awareness of one's own thinking and, ultimately, facilitates "the development of the kinds of thinking which are characteristic of logic, mathematics and the sciences" (p. 95).

Written language is an essential aspect of classroom language. Learning to deal with written language is a demanding task with important consequences for thinking and learning. It is a task that will engage students all their school years and beyond, if their education continues.

CONCLUSION

Language is central to learning and teaching. The classroom is a special speech situation. Like all speech situations, there are particular forms of oral language and oral language behaviour that are typical, and that are well understood by participants. The unspoken rules of classroom discourse assign major speaking rights to the teacher; students' speaking rights are much more limited. There are good reasons for believing that learning will be facilitated if teachers work to encourage more interactive patterns of oral language in the classroom, both in the large group setting and in small cooperative groups.

Mastering written language is one of the main tasks that students face when they come to school. Written language is different from spoken language in ways that teachers need to understand. It is important to understand both the demands that written language places upon students, and the important consequences of both reading and writing for thinking and learning.

EXERCISES

1. The following transcript is taken from an early primary class of children aged 6 and 7.

   a. Categorize the teacher's utterances according to the *function* of the utterance, e.g., informing, questioning, testing.

   b. Are there any utterances that are *indirect speech acts*, that is, the literal meaning is different from its intended meaning?

   c. Identify those of the teacher's utterances that you think invite "higher-level" thinking from her students. What kinds of thinking are evidenced by students as a result of such utterances?

Teacher: Someone give me a number story for what we just did (*They had checked to see how many out of 24 were absent*).

Mark: 24 take away 1.

Teacher: Who's away?

Mark: Oh, no. 24 plus zero equals 24.

Teacher: Good. Give me a number story using the take-away sign, Robin.

Robin: 24 take away ....

Teacher: (*prompting*) How many are away?

Robin: Zero.

Teacher: (*continuing the number story*) ... zero equals?

Robin: 24.

Teacher: Let's see if she's right. She says there's 24 people here. You be 1. (*pointing to child. Children count around to 24.*)

Teacher: 24 students here. Was she right?

Chorus of voices: Yes.

Teacher: Who is the person who left this folder? Harold, you are. (*Hands it to him.*) Thank you. I don't want to have to put any more folders away.

Gerald: I'll help Harold.

Teacher: Gerald, Harold knows where it goes. He's been doing it all the week.

Teacher: (*Takes a number and holds it hidden in her hand.*) You know, what is interesting is that our date today is the same as the number of people who are here. What number have I got in my hand?

Beatrice: 24

Teacher: Tell me something about 24. Anything at all.

Cindy: 24 equals two 10s and four 1s.

Teacher: Thank you. Two 10s and four 1s. Let's see if he's right. How do we draw 10s?

Teacher: Somebody else give me a number story.

2. The following transcript is taken from a grade 7 class. List the ways in which the exchanges illustrate characteristics of teacher talk and characteristics of student talk.

Teacher: Eyes to the front. Drop everything and eyes to the front. I'm still waiting for a couple of people to look here. Today we are going to be looking at the development of cities a little bit more. We have looked at villages and we have looked at societies and how they started to form and now we are going to be looking at cities. In the handout I gave you, there was a lot of information about what was happening with the changes in society and why cities were coming about. Let's think about some of the words that were in the reading. For example, the word, *urban*. What does *urban* mean. Jane?

Jane: Sort of city, a big town.

Teacher: Right. A city or a big town with lots of people. What about *fertile*. What is fertile land? Is it good land or bad land? Allan?

Allan: It is good land, useful land, good for farming.

Teacher: Good and useful land for farming. Exactly. Very good. What about *irrigation*? We've heard that word a few times now. What does it mean to irrigate something or to have irrigation? Kate?

Kate: You get like water from a ditch or something like that.

Teacher: Okay. Would you use irrigation in a place like Vancouver or would you use irrigation in a place like a desert? Where do you think you would use more irrigation systems?

Sally: Vancouver?

Teacher: How many of you would say Vancouver? (*A few hands go up.*) How many of you would say a desert? (*Many hands.*) Yes. Why is that, Walter?

Walter: There's not much water in a desert so you need to transport it.

Teacher: Because there's not a lot of water in a desert. You might have to bring water to the plants because you're not going to get a lot of rain. In Vancouver … just look outside now, how rainy it is and you can see that we do not need a lot of irrigation systems. Now how did irrigations help the farmers back then? Alex?

Alex: Took water to the plants.

Teacher: Okay. To take water to the plants to help the plants grow. How else?

Sally: To prevent too much water running away in the ditches.

Teacher: Great. What else did the people use on their land to help them with their crops? Harold?

Harold: The plough.

Dennis:. Yes. The plough and the plough was an ox-drawn plough and they also had irrigation. Those were the two main things that helped them with their farming needs around the city.

———————   ▬▬▬▬▬▬   ———————

REFERENCES

Alvermann, E.E., and D.W. Hayes (1989). Classroom discussion of content area reading assignments: An intervention study. *Reading Research Quarterly*, 24(3), 305-335.

Barnes, D. (1976). *From Communication to Curriculum*. Harmondsworth:Penguin.

Bereiter, C., and M. Scardamalia (1987). *The Psychology of Written Composition*. Hillsdale, NJ: Lawrence Erlbaum.

Brown, A.L., and A.S. Palincsar (1987). Reciprocal teaching of comprehension strategies: A natural history of one program for enhancing learning. In J.D. Day and J. Borkowski (eds.), *Intelligence and Exceptionality: New Directions for Theory, Assessment and Instructional Practice* (pp. 81-132). Norwood, NJ: Ablex.

Campione, J.C., A.L. Brown and M.L. Connell (1988). Metacognition: On the importance of understanding what you are doing. In L.R.Charles and E. Silver (eds.), *The Teaching and Assessing of Mathematical Problem* Solving (pp.93-114). Reston, VA: National Council of Teachers of Mathematics.

Cazden, C.B. (1988). *Classroom Discourse: The Language of Teaching and Learning.* Portsmouth, NH: Heinemann.

Cazden, C.B. (1986). Classroom discourse. In M.C. Witrock (ed.), *Handbook of Research on Teaching,* 3rd ed., (pp. 432-463). New York: MacMillan.

Cooper, C.R., A. Marquis and S. Ayers-Lopez (1982). Peer learning in the classroom: Tracing developmental patterns and consequences of children's spontaneous interactions. In L. C. Wilkinson (ed.), *Communicating in the Classroom* (pp. 69-84). New York: Academic Press.

Dillon, J. T. (1990). *The Practice of Questioning.* London: Routledge.

Dillon, J.T. (1984). Research on questioning and discussion. *Educational Leadership,* 42 (3), 50-56.

Donaldson, M. (1978). *Children's Minds.* Glasgow: Collins (Fontana).

Duffy, G.G. (1983). From turn taking to sense making: Broadening the concept of reading teacher effectiveness. *Journal of Educational Research,* 76, 134-139.

Flanders, N.A. (1970). *Analyzing Teaching Behaviour.* Reading, MA: Addison-Wesley.

Forman, E.A., and C.B. Cazden (1985). Exploring Vygotskian perspectives in education: the cognitive value of peer interaction. In J.V. Wertsch (ed.), *Culture, Communication, and Cognition: Vygotskian Perspectives,* (pp. 323-347). Cambridge: Cambridge University Press.

Garnica, O.K. (1981). Social dominance and classroom interaction—The omega child in the classroom. In J. Green and C. Wallat (eds.), *Ethnography and Language in Educational Settings,* (pp. 229-252). Norwood, NJ: Ablex.

Hoetker, J., and W.P Ahlbrandt (1969). The persistence of recitation. *American Educational Research Journal,* 6, 145-167.

MacKinnon, A. (1989). Conceptualizing a hall of mirrors in a science teaching practicum. *Journal of Curriculum and Supervision,* 5 (1), 41-59.

O'Flahavan, J.R., D.K. Hartman and P.D. Pearson (1988). Teacher questioning and feedback practices: A twenty-year retrospective. In J. E. Readance and R.S. Baldwin (eds.), *Dialogues in Literacy Research. Thirty-seventh Yearbook of the National Reading Conference* (pp. 185-191). Rochester, NY: National Reading Conference.

Roberts, D.R., and J.A. Langer (1991). *Supporting the process of literary understanding: Analysis of a classroom discussion,* Report Series 2.15. Albany, NY: Center for the Learning and Teaching of Literature, State University of New York.

Rowe, M.B. (1986). Wait time: Slowing down may be a way of speeding up! *Journal of Teacher Education*, 37, 43-50.

Staab, C.F. (1991). Teachers' practices with regard to oral language. *The Alberta Journal of Educational Research*, 37 (1), 31-48.

Stubbs, M. (1983). *Language, Schools and Classrooms*, 2nd ed. London: Methuen.

Torbe, M., and H. Shuard (1982). Mathematics and language. In R. R.Harvey et al. *Mathematics*, Language Teaching and Learning Series (pp. 1-21). London: Ward Lock Educational.

Chapter 5
THE LANGUAGE OF SPECIFIC DISCIPLINES

CHAPTER OVERVIEW

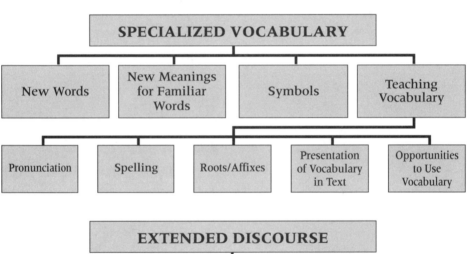

SPECIALIZED VOCABULARY

- New Words
- New Meanings for Familiar Words
- Symbols
- Teaching Vocabulary
  - Pronunciation
  - Spelling
  - Roots/Affixes
  - Presentation of Vocabulary in Text
  - Opportunities to Use Vocabulary

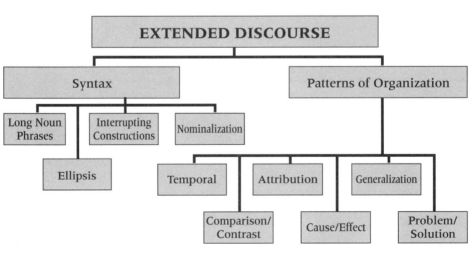

EXTENDED DISCOURSE

- Syntax
  - Long Noun Phrases
  - Interrupting Constructions
  - Nominalization
  - Ellipsis
- Patterns of Organization
  - Temporal
  - Attribution
  - Generalization
  - Comparison/Contrast
  - Cause/Effect
  - Problem/Solution

When students study a particular discipline, one of their tasks is to learn the register of the discipline. They must learn to understand and to use the particular forms of language that are either essential to the discipline, or, if not essential, common or customary.

Vocabulary is an obvious way in which the languages of various disciplines differ. Each discipline has its own specialized terms to express important concepts. We are not surprised that the vocabulary of the physical education class is different from that of the art class. However, the languages of disciplines differ in more than vocabulary. As well as technical terms, the register of a discipline includes customary grammatical structures, characteristic modes of arguing, and ways of organizing text.

The language of a discipline, like language in general, occurs in both spoken and written forms. Some aspects of the language are evident in both forms. Specialized vocabulary, for example, occurs in both speech and writing. However, some aspects of the language of a discipline are especially associated with written language. Written texts in various disciplines tend to have their own characteristic ways of organizing material; and special forms of notation, like those used in music and mathematics, occur, of course, only in written forms.

For convenience, the discussion of the language of specialized disciplines is treated under two headings: specialized vocabulary; and extended discourse.

SPECIALIZED VOCABULARY

Learning the specialized vocabulary of a discipline means learning: (a) words not previously known; (b) new, specialized meanings for words that are already known in some other context; and (c) in some subject areas, like mathematics and music, a symbol system.

NEW WORDS

You easily understand the terms from your own discipline in the following list: *asymptote, isosceles, byte, pixel, mesa, wadi, hegemony, plebiscite, toccata, a cappella, loge, proscenium, ode, hyperbole, osmosis, exospore, ohm, shim, mortise, aquarelle, aspic, canapes, chattel.* On the other hand, some terms on the list from other disciplines may be either unknown to you or only vaguely understood.

Every discipline has specialized vocabulary that students must learn if they are to understand spoken language in the classroom and the written language of texts. In some subject areas — like biology, for example — the burden of new words to be learned is enormous.

Sometimes specialized terms are also used technically in other related fields. For example, *protozoa* and *transpiration* are used in both geography and biology.

When a word is adopted from another field, it acquires a meaning that is specific to the discipline it is adopted into. Specialized terminology that occurs with different specialized meanings in more than one discipline deserves special attention.

NEW MEANINGS FOR FAMILIAR WORDS

A second aspect of specialized vocabulary is the use of everyday words with specialized meanings. Examples are *dredge, render*, and *coddle* from home economics; and *jig, frog*, and *throat* from woodworking. *Gross* has two common meanings in accounting but neither is the meaning most likely to occur first to students.

Sometimes the specialized meaning has little or no connection with the everyday meaning. The meanings of *product, odd*, and *difference* in mathematical language are so far removed from the everyday meaning that most students would not readily see the connection. For other words, the specialized meaning is more closely related to everyday use — for example, *remainder, average* and *similar* (triangles) in mathematics, and *animal* in science. Note, however, that the technical term usually has a more refined or specialized meaning than the everyday usage.

Everyday words used with specialized meanings are very likely to cause misunderstanding. The teacher, hearing students use the correct word, is likely to assume that they understand, and not be aware that they are using the word in its everyday sense and lack an understanding of the specialized meaning.

Otterburn and Nicholson (1976) examined 16-year-old students' understanding of common mathematical words and found that some words were poorly understood by many students. *Product*, for example, was clearly understood by only 21 percent of the students. Many interpreted the word in its everyday sense as something that has been produced so that *product* could refer to the result of adding or subtracting, as well as to the result of multiplying. The word *integer* was clearly understood by only 15 per cent.

Even such a common word as *multiply* may cause difficulty for younger students. In everyday English, if things multiply, they become more numerous. But multiplication in mathematics does not always result in a bigger number. Pimm (1987, p.9) cites the following excerpt from an interview with a 14-year-old boy.

Teacher: How about if I did one like this: 6.23 × 0.48? What do you think the answer to this would be?

Student: Um. About twelve. Yes.

Teacher: How did you get that?

Student: It's about half of a whole number. Halfs into six equals twelve.

Teacher: In this case the answer is twelve. You've divided, but the answer is bigger. What if you multiply? Can you make the answer smaller?

Student: No, it won't work out smaller.

Teacher: Do you want to work it out? (*Hands him a calculator*)

(Student laughs)

Teacher: What's happened?

Student: It's got smaller. It's 2.9904.

Teacher: How do you explain that then?

Student: I don't know. I thought maybe if you … Oh, is it one of those funny numbers? But multiplication still makes it bigger.

Other interesting examples of misunderstanding are cited by Pimm (p. 8). A 9-year-old, when asked, "What is the difference between 24 and 9?" replied that one number was even and the other was odd. A second 9 year-old replied that 24 has two numbers in it whereas 9 has only one. Sensible answers for the everyday meaning of the term but not what the teacher was expecting!

The following anecdote (Pimm, 1987, pp. 83-85) illustrates a 13-year-old's misunderstanding of the word *diagonal*. She was shown the following problem and said she understood it:

PROBLEM

Here are some polygons.

a. How many diagonals does each one have?

b. If you knew the number of sides of any polygon, could you work out the number of diagonals?

The student's answers were as follows:

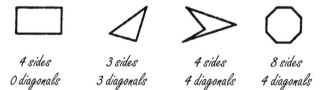

4 sides   *3 sides*   *4 sides*   *8 sides*
0 diagonals   *3 diagonals*   *4 diagonals*   *4 diagonals*

The researcher made no comment on her answer, but asked her to answer the second part of the problem, that is: If you knew the number of sides of any polygon, could you work out the number of diagonals? His discussion with her went as follows:

Student: No, you can't, 'cause if you turn it round you get more diagonals.

Teacher: Could you show me?

Student: (*Draws Fig. i*) This has four diagonals.

Teacher: Oh, I see. Could you show me a triangle which has one diagonal?

Student: Sure (*Draws Fig. ii, crosses it out and draws Fig. iii*).

Teacher: And a four-sided figure with less than four diagonals?

Student: (*Draws Fig. iv*)

Teacher: Yes I see. What about an eight-sided one? Could it have eight diagonals?

Student: (*Draws Fig. v*)

Teacher: Could you write down for me what you have found out?

Student: (*Writes*) It depends on what the shape is and which way you place it.

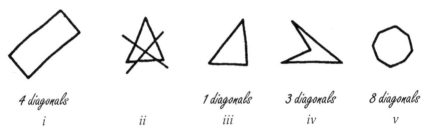

4 diagonals		1 diagonals	3 diagonals	8 diagonals
i	*ii*	*iii*	*iv*	*v*

Her problem was caused by the fact that she understood *diagonal* in its adjectival sense as it occurs in everyday use as in: *The pedestrian crosswalk is marked by diagonal yellow stripes.* She assumed that when *diagonal* was used as a noun in the assigned problem, it had the same meaning.

Even very common words like *some*, *any*, and *all* have different meanings in the mathematics register from that of everyday English. *Any*, for example, tends to mean "every" to the mathematician. The sentence

Is any even number prime?

has the following meaning to the mathematician:

Is any (i.e., every) even number prime?

And the answer is:

No. Most even numbers are not prime.

In everyday English, the meaning is:

Is any (i.e, one single) even number prime?

And the answer is:

Yes, 2 is. (Pimm, 1987, p. 79)

Even university graduates who are not mathematicians are sometimes unaware of the mathematical usage, and are surprised when presented with the mathematician's answer to the above question.

Bell and Freyberg (1985) studied students' understanding of everyday words that are used by scientists with specialized meanings. They found, for example, that many students, at every level, used *animal* with a meaning different from the biologist's meaning. Only 37 percent of 11 year-olds and 86 percent of experienced elementary teachers identified a worm as an animal. For *boy*, the percentages were 57 percent and 96 percent. (Even university biology students were not unanimous in agreeing that a worm and a spider were animals!)

Even very common words like *make* may be used with a specialized meaning. A 13-year-old was asked to comment on the sentence *Plants can make their own food using the sun's energy but animals are unable to make their own food*. The student explained that animals cannot make their own food because they have only legs, not hands and fingers as humans do. Her explanation revealed that she was using both *animal* and *make* in their everyday senses and not in the scientific sense intended by the author (Bell and Freyberg, 1985, p. 36).

SYMBOLS

Mathematics, music, and science are subjects where symbols are extensively used. Reading music is a matter, entirely, of reading non-alphabetic symbols. The meanings of the symbols must be learned in order for scores to be understood and translated into the appropriate sounds.

In mathematics, symbols of many kinds are used. Talking about mathematics must include the verbalization of symbols, and reading mathematics texts involves being able to recognize symbols and understand their meaning. Even the commonest of mathematical symbols are often misunderstood. This is partially because students do not know how to verbalize symbols. For example, the expression $15 \div 3$ could be read as "15 divided by 3," "fifteen shared between 3 (people)", or "3 into 15," but is sometimes translated "share 15 by 3" or "share 3 into 15," neither of which makes sense (Kerslake, 1985). Kerslake (1985, p. 47) reports that 194 students aged twelve to fourteen from a London school were asked to write what they thought $3 \div 4$ meant. Only 28.8 percent of them thought that it meant 3 divided by 4. More than 50 percent of them read it as 4 divided by 3.

Another very common symbol that is misunderstood is the equals sign, =. Many students oversimplify the meaning and translate the symbol as "makes." The oversimplification works well enough in an example like 3 + 4 = 7. However, it is not easy for children to understand 7 = 3 + 4, as illustrated by the following conversation between a teacher and a first grade child reported by Ginsberg (1977):

Teacher: How do you think you would read this ($\Box$ = 3 + 4)?

Student: ... Blank equals 3 plus 4.

Teacher: Okay What can you say about that, anything?

Student: It's backwards! (*He changed it to* 4 + 3 = $\Box$) You can't go, 7 equals 3 plus 4.

TEACHING VOCABULARY

Given the importance of vocabulary in learning in various disciplines, teachers need to take conscious, specific action to ensure that students both know and accept the meanings of words critical in the discipline. As Bell and Freyberg (1985, p. 35) point out, students may hold to their own meaning even when they clearly know that the teacher is using a word in a different way. As one 13-year-old said: "I still think spiders are insects, not animals. Don't know why. I just don't feel a spider's an animal." Students may use the teacher's meaning to enable them to get the right answer on a test, but their pre-existing beliefs and understanding are sometimes untouched by what they have been taught.

Students may "know" vocabulary in several different ways. To be able to pick out the meaning of a word from a set of suggested meanings in a multiple-choice format is one way of knowing. To recognize the word and understand it when it is heard or seen in a text is a second kind of knowledge. To be able to use the word correctly in speech or writing is a another kind of knowledge. To be able to recite a definition is yet another kind of knowledge. To be able to give appropriate examples is another. The aim should be for students to have a thorough knowledge of critical vocabulary so that they not only understand words when they hear them or see them in print, but can also use them comfortably in both speech and writing.

Teachers cannot assume that, because a term has been introduced and explained, students necessarily understand it. Even the ability to repeat a memorized definition does not necessarily mean that a student clearly understands the term. Kerslake (1982, pp. 42-43), cites the following instructive conversation between a teacher and a child as the teacher helps the child make sense of a question beginning: "A point where 2 sides meet is called a vertex."

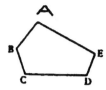

Student:	A point where 2 points meet is called a vertex. What does it mean, that?
Teacher:	A point where …?
Student:	Two points meet
Teacher:	Read it again carefully
Student:	A point where two sides meet …
Teacher:	Well, where do these sides meet? Show me 2 sides next to each other
Student:	B and A
Teacher:	B and A are what?
Student:	Vertexes
Teacher:	Yes
Student:	How?
Teacher:	BA is a side
Student:	Oh, yes
Teacher:	And AE is a side
Student:	BC, CD, DE
Teacher:	They are all sides, aren't they?
Student:	So they are all vertex?
Teacher:	No. Well, what do you mean — are they all vertex?
Student:	That's vertex — DB is vertex, CD is vertex …
Teacher:	How many sides has that figure?
Student:	Five
Teacher:	Now point to one of the five sides … what's its name?
Student:	AB
Teacher:	Tell me the name of the sides next to that one
Student:	CB
Teacher:	Yes, CB. Now, where do CB and AB meet?
Student:	There (*pointing to the diagram*)
Teacher:	At?

Student: B

Teacher: So B is the point where sides AB and BC meet. So what do we call B?

Student: A vertex … So they are all vertex, then. A's a vertex, B, C … Oh, that's what they put it in for!

Teacher: So how many vertices has a 5-sided figure?

Student: Five.

Despite the seemingly clear definition of *vertex* at the beginning of the question, it required a good deal of talking through before the student was able to make sense of the new word. Definitions, as Kerslake (p.44) points out, are usually the result of much careful thought. They are precisely and economically stated in a way that gives no indication of the effort that has contributed to their formulation. They are often not easy to understand. Students need to be helped to "unpack" the meaning contained in the economically stated definition. One way of unpacking the meaning is to give many different examples. Right-angled triangles, for example, should be shown as *a* and *b* below, as well as *c*, lest the child assume that *c* is the prototype. Pimm (1987, p. 87) cites one child who called a triangle like *a* a "left-angled triangle." The student had noted that it was oriented to the left rather than to the right as had been all previous examples of right-angled triangles that he had seen.

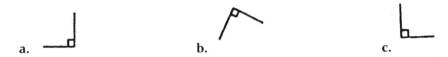

a.   b.   c.

It is important, then, to remember that teaching vocabulary is not a once-and-for-all activity. It is a task that requires consistent, continuous attention. The following are some important aspects of teaching vocabulary.

Pronunciation   When presenting new vocabulary, make sure that students can pronounce the word. If they do not know how to say it, they are not likely to use the word in their own talk. If they do not use it, they are less likely to make the word their own.

Spelling   Spelling and pronunciation are closely related. Make sure that students are helped to recognize the various parts of the word.

Roots and Affixes   Consider teaching common roots, prefixes and suffixes, especially in subject areas, like sciences, where these are commonly used. Piercey (1982) suggests that students be encouraged to set up a glossary of scientific word parts after the pattern shown in Table 5.1. Such a table will help students to learn common roots and affixes, and will encourage them to recognize other words they come across that use the same roots.

Table 5.1
The Language of Science:
Some Common Word Roots and Affixes

Root/Affix	Meaning	Example	Your Word
a-/an-	without	anaerobic	
astro-/aster-	star	astronomy	
cardi(o)-	heart	cardiogram	
chrono-	time	chronology	
hyper-	over, excess	hyperactive	
hypo-	under, less	hypodermic	
pedi/pod	foot, footed	anthropod	
tele-	far, distant	telescope	

Presentation of Vocabulary in the Text   Help students to understand and use the methods used in the text to present vocabulary. The first introduction of an important term in a text is usually marked typographically. The most common ways of signalling new terminology are by the use of: italics, boldface, capitals, quotation marks, or by marking it off by parentheses or commas. You need to make sure that the text uses a consistent system and that students understand the system. Usually when an important term is presented for the first time, the term will be defined or explained. Definitions and explanations take many different forms. Students must be able to recognize the various forms of definitions, and to use context clues of various kinds that help to explain new terms. (See Chapter 8 on strategies for teaching reading for further discussion.) The subject area specialist should be familiar with the textbook and the method used to present technical terminology. You need, especially, to be aware of instances where key terms are not defined or explained, or where explanations are incorrect, incomplete, or confusing. In such instances, you should be ready to offer clear definitions and explanations.

Opportunities To Use Vocabulary   Give students many opportunities to use new vocabulary in their own speech and writing. It is through using new words that students make the words their own. When students work in small groups or engage in individual conferences with the teacher, they have opportunities for using vocabulary in speech. A novel idea for using vocabulary in writing is suggested by Johnston (1985). At the end of a unit or chapter in biology, she gives her students a list of fifty or sixty recently used terms and has them do a writing assignment called "Use as Many as You Can Correctly." Students must use as many words from the list as they can. They may write fact or fiction, but what they say must be biologically correct. Students must have repeated opportunities to use the terminology of a given discipline in speech and writing in order to make it their own.

SUMMARY

Learning vocabulary is a critical part of learning in a content area. The methods teachers adopt to teach vocabulary will vary somewhat with the grade level. Certainly, in upper grades, specific attention must be given to helping students with the sometimes burdensome task of learning the terminology essential for understanding the discipline. At all grade levels, teachers need to be aware that the meanings students bring with them to school are likely to get in the way of their learning unless particular care is taken to teach them the specialized meanings the words have in the register of the discipline.

Extended discourse

Extended discourse occurs in both spoken language and written language. However, it is extended discourse in the written mode that is likely to present most problems for students. The two major areas of difficulty in written prose are syntax, and the organization of discourse.

SYNTAX

Syntax refers to sentence structure. As was noted in chapter 2, written language favours economy of expression; written sentences use the kinds of constructions that favour economy, such as nominalizations, prepositional phrases, non-finite subordinate clauses, long noun phrases, and ellipsis. These constructions are especially common in content area texts and make for prose that is hard to understand. The following examples of potentially difficult constructions are illustrated, in most instances, by sentences taken from textbooks commonly used in Canadian schools.

Long Noun Phrases   Long noun phrases are especially difficult if they are in subject position. The reason is that, to understand a sentence, a reader must connect subject and verb correctly. Long, complex subjects strain short-term memory; readers have to keep the long, developing subject in mind while they search for the main verb. The following sentences are the same length:

The weary guard clubbed the hoodlums who attacked him in the dark alley.

The weary guard clubbed by hoodlums who attacked him fell down the stairs. (Isakson, 1979, p. 161)

But the second takes longer to process because of the long subject (*The weary guard clubbed by hoodlums who attacked him*) which must be held in short-term memory until the verb (*fell*) is reached. Long noun phrases are very common in texts prescribed for school subjects:

— *Mineral deposits that are known but cannot be economically mined or are thought to exist but have not been discovered,* are described as *resources.* (Grade 12 Geography)

— *A regular pyramid* is *a three-dimensional figure formed by joining the vertices of a regular polygon to a point (vertex) that is not in the same plane as the base and that lies directly above the center of the base.* (Grade 12 Geometry)

— *The pressure on less developed countries to grow cash crops and sell their minerals at low prices to industrialized countries* would be reduced as a result. (Grade 11 History)

— *Insertion of cloned genes into human reproductive cells, where they would be passed on to all the cells of a resulting embryo,* might be possible within the next ten years. (Grade 11 Biology)

The examples cited above from senior high school texts are most likely to illustrate for an educated adult reader the kind of difficulty posed by long noun phrases. But the same kinds of constructions, in simpler sentences, occur in texts for lower grades and cause the same kinds of difficulties for younger students:

— *Still another way to be sure your body is working properly* is to visit a doctor for a checkup at least once a year. (Grade 5 Science)

— *One builder who signed a contract to build a section of the Cariboo Road* was Joseph Trutch. (Grade 5 Social Studies)

— *The things that hunters or trappers thought most important to them, like their spears or harpoons or pipes,* were lovingly decorated. (Grade 5 Social Studies)

Long noun phrases are potentially difficult not only because of their length, but because they include difficult structures like interrupting constructions and nominalizations.

Interrupting Constructions   A construction much used by text-book writers is the interrupting construction — something that intervenes between the subject and the verb. Perera (1984) cites the following examples taken from texts used in the junior school:

> Meanwhile, the Normans, *who, early in the Confessor's reign, had narrowly failed to gain a commanding position in the kingdom,* were now preparing a landing somewhere along the south coast.

> Because plastics need heat to soften them the barrel (*that is the part of an extruder between the hopper and the hole at the end, which is called a die*) must be made so that it can be heated and controlled at a steady temperature (p. 291).

In the first sentence, the subject (*the Normans*) is lengthened by a 17-word interrupting construction which hinders the reader from connecting subject and verb (*... the Normans ... were ... preparing*). In the second sentence, the interrupting construction is 21 words long. Note the strain imposed on short-term memory by the long interruption. Examples of interrupting constructions are plentiful in Canadian textbooks:

> — The art of tailoring clothes — *carefully cutting and sewing skins together* — was highly developed by the Inuit. (Grade 5 Social Studies)

Nominalizations As noted in Chapter 2, nominalization occurs when verbs or adjectives are turned into nouns. Compare, for example, the following (Martin, 1986, p. 95):

> In order for us to plan intelligently to defend ourselves we must recognize that war at any level can be won or lost, and that whether we win or lose will be significant.

> Recognition that war at any level can be won or lost, and that the distinction between winning and losing would not be trivial, is essential for intelligent defense planning.

The verbs *plan, defend, recognize, win* and *lose* in the first sentence have been nominalized in the second sentence (*recognition, winning, losing, defense, planning*). The second sentence is shorter than the first (29 words versus 33) but more difficult to process. Nominalizations are common in school texts. They increase the burden of processing a text's meaning.

> — *Information* on *registrations* is also available from registrations for Social Insurance numbers, driver license *applications*, and family allowance *payments*. (Grade 11 History)

> — *Noticing regularities* across observed events helps in *communicating* just as *classification* does. (Grade 11 Biology)

> — Methods for *extracting* metals like copper, iron, and lead from their ores may differ in detail, but all involve the same three essential steps:

concentration of the ore to produce an in-between material with a higher percentage of the metal compound; *smelting* of the ore to break the bonds between the metal and the other elements in the compound; and *refining* the metal produced by *smelting* to increase its purity, usually by electrolysis. (Grade 12 chemistry)

— Along with *eating* properly and *getting* enough rest, *getting* enough exercise is a way to help your body work properly. (Grade 5 Science)

— *Learning* about nutrients and the four food groups may help you eat properly. (Grade 5 Science)

Ellipsis Ellipsis involves the omission of words or phrases that are repeated in a clause. It occurs in textbooks of various subject areas. It is very common in math texts in questions where the "stem" is to be read as if it were repeated as in the following example intended for twelve-year-olds (cited by Shuard, 1982, p.90):

— If a straight line measures 12 cm, how long would one quarter of the line be? one-third? one-half? one-sixth? one-eighth? two-thirds? five-sixths? one tenth?

The constructions listed and illustrated above are not the only constructions that are hard to understand. But they are important because they are very common in texts.

A final point to note in this brief discussion of syntax is that the syntax of mathematics texts is particularly demanding. It is highly condensed (the more so because symbols are often used in a sentence along with conventionally written words); it makes frequent use of passive verbs, which are harder to understand than active verbs; and it uses various specialized forms of sentences that are often very formal and sometimes somewhat archaic — including "if" clauses, and frequent use of *let*, and *suppose*. Note the following examples:

— Let n, p, q be integers with p, q prime, such that q divides $n^p - 1$ but not $n - 1$. Let a relation $\sim$ on the set $\{1, 2, 3 \ldots q - 1\}$ be defined by writing $x \sim y$ if q divides $y - n^r x$ for some r. Prove that ... (Kerslake, 1982, p. 41).

— By finding for what value of x the derivative is zero, and then looking at the sign of the derivative, determine the *maximum* or *minimum* value of $f(x)$ where:

   1. $f(x) = 3x - x^2$

   2. $f(x) = x^2 + 4x$ (Shuard, 1982, p. 89).

The difficulty of understanding the language of mathematics is illustrated by a study conducted by Elliott and Wiles (1980). They gave a cloze test — a kind of readability test — to a group of well-qualified secondary mathematics teachers.

The cloze test was from a well-known mathematics text for eighth graders. About 25 percent of the teachers received scores that suggested that they would not be able to read and understand the text without assistance.

The constructions described above are not the only ones likely to cause difficulty. Perera (1984) lists sixteen constructions that make for comprehension difficulty. The constructions discussed were selected because they illustrate the point and because they are common in school texts.

THE ORGANIZATION OF EXTENDED DISCOURSE

In extended discourse, sentences are organized into paragraphs and paragraphs into longer structures. There are many ways of organizing paragraphs and longer pieces of discourse. Some of those ways are more difficult than others.

The study of patterns of text organization is quite recent. No exhaustive, agreed upon list of text patterns exists. However, six patterns commonly used in school texts are: **temporal order** (time order); **attribution** (list structure); **generalization**; **compare-contrast**; **cause-effect**; **problem-solution**. Temporal and attribution structures are easy to recognize. Problem-solution, cause-effect, and compare-contrast are more difficult. To identify the structures used in a reading, it is useful to examine key words and phrases used, and the kinds of questions answered in the text.

Temporal   Time-ordered discourse is used to describe continuous and connected events or the steps in a process. It is characteristic of narrative and is also common in history texts and in science texts that describe processes. Common key words are *first, then, next, a second ..., finally*. Some examples of temporal order are:

(a) A maple tree is one kind of tree that changes with each season. A maple tree is bare during the winter. But if you look closely, you can find tiny buds on the tree. These buds begin to grow in the spring. They slowly open up to become broad green leaves. During the summer the maple tree is covered with green leaves. Late in the summer some of the green leaves turn bright red and orange. By autumn the whole tree is covered with brightly coloured leaves. As winter approaches, all the leaves fall off the tree.

(b) The lytic cycle begins as a phage, tail down, attaches to the bacterial cell wall. The wall is opened as a hole is dissolved in it by a phage enzyme. The phage tail then contracts, forcing the DNA core into the cell. The protein coat does not enter the cell itself. Next, the phage DNA alters the DNA of the bacterial host. This change causes the bacterial host cell to make more phage DNA and protein. Soon the host cell is filled with phages.

Attribution   This pattern uses listing as the pattern of organization. The text may list the attributes or characteristics of an item; it may enumerate a series of points; or it may list classes or categories. Other names sometimes used for an attribution pattern are *description, enumeration, classification*. This pattern of organization is common in many subject areas. Some examples are:

(a) Most flowers have the same basic parts. These parts can be seen in the drawing. The petals are usually the most colourful part of the flower. Surrounded by the petals are the pistil and the stamens. The stamen is the male part of the flower. The pistil is the female part. The pistil and the stamens are the parts of the flower that produce seeds. The seeds develop inside the base of the pistil. This part is called the ovary.

(b) There are two main varieties of the tea plant. That in China usually grows only 3 or 4 feet high. The Indian plant reaches a height of over 20 feet, if allowed to do so.

Generalization   This pattern consists of a main idea followed by evidence for the main idea. Some sentences *clarify* the main idea by using examples, others *extend* the main idea by providing more details. This pattern, also, is common in many subject areas. Some examples are:

(a) Energy can be transformed from one form to another, and we have already encountered several examples of this. A stone held high in the air has potential energy; as it falls, it looses potential energy, since its height above the ground decreases. At the same time, it gains kinetic energy, since its velocity is increasing. Potential energy is being transformed into kinetic energy.

(b) Only humans have the biological ability to produce a large number of different sounds and to put them together in many different ways. Nonhuman primates have at most 40 different vocalizations, each one having a definite meaning, such as one that means "baby on the ground," which is uttered by a baboon when a baby falls out of a tree. Investigators have overcome the biological inability of chimpanzees to articulate many sounds by having them learn a sign language. Chimpanzees have learned as many as 400 signs of an artificial visual; however, thus far it has not been possible to demonstrate unequivocally that they are capable of putting the signs together to create new sentences and meanings. It still seems as if humans may possess a communication ability unparalleled by other animals.

Comparison-Contrast   In this pattern of text organization, likenesses or differences between events or objects are described. A comparison structure analyzes both similarities and differences. A contrast structure focuses on differences only. This text pattern is commonly used to organize information in a variety of subject areas: science, mathematics, and social studies, for example. Common key words are *different, similar, in contrast, on the other hand, whereas*. The kinds of questions answered in this kind of structure include: What is being compared? On what basis are they being compared? How are they alike? How are they different? Examples are:

(a) Conifers are like flowering plants in that they both use seeds to reproduce. However, conifers are different from flowering plants in several ways. For one thing, flowering plants produce seeds in flowers, while conifers produce seeds in cones. The seeds in flowering plants are protected in an ovary. The seeds of conifers are protected by the scales of the cone. Most flowering plants have broad leaves. Conifers either have needle-shaped leaves or scalelike leaves.

(b) Copper wires use electricity to carry signals, but optical fibres use beams of light instead. Optical fibres can carry many more signals at once than copper wires can. For example, if 24 people are making phone calls at the same time, four copper wires are normally needed to handle those conversations. By contrast, one single optical fibre might carry up to 12 000 phone conversations. There would still be room left over for television or radio signals to travel the same fibre. So it is cheaper to use cables with optical fibres than cables with copper wires because one cable can carry more signals.

Cause-Effect   This pattern is important in reading science texts, history texts and narratives. Cause-effect relationships are difficult for unskilled readers at all levels. Example are:

(a) The coffee plant thrives in almost any tropical climate, but it grows best on fairly high ground with good drainage. This kind of soil and climate is found in the foothills of Brazil. That's why today three-fourths of the world's coffee is produced in Brazil.

(b) When a continent that is at the edge of a plate collides with an ocean floor plate, the ocean floor plate plunges beneath the plate of which the continent is a part. This happens because, as you have read, continents are made of lighter rock than the ocean floor. When collisions occur, the rock layers at the edge of continents may change shape by folding or faulting, but remain on the surface of the plate.

Problem-Solution   This pattern of organization presents a problem and, usually, several possible solutions. It is common in economics, social studies, geography, and psychology. In order to understand this kind of text, readers must be able to identify the problem and recognize the solutions offered. A text may present various solutions before the problem is fully explained; it may present the problem followed by suggested solutions; it may present various problems before a full solution is given. Key words that may cue a problem/solution pattern of organization are *question, solution, solve,* and *answer*. Examples are:

(a) Victoria City Council wanted to improve Chinatown. For 15 years, the council studied the problem. The council tried several plans for improving the community. Nothing seemed to work because the council had not involved the people of Chinatown. Finally, the council decided to get some help.

In 1979, the Victoria City Council asked a university professor, David Chuen-yan Lai, to get ideas from Chinese Canadians and other people in the community. He met people who lived in Chinatown or who owned property or businesses there. He asked them what they did not like about Chinatown and what changes they wanted. Lai found people to work on committees to improve Chinatown.

(b) There are many ideas about where viruses came from. One idea is that viruses represent a link in the origin of life. Perhaps they are the non-cellular ancestors of cells. On the other hand, some scientists feel that viruses had cellular ancestors who became adapted to a parasitic way of life. Selection would have favoured the loss of many of the characteristics of cells. Viruses as we know them today would be the result. Another view is that viruses are simply fragments of other cells.

A given text — a chapter, say — will commonly use several different patterns of organization. The chapter, overall, will probably have one type of organization. Each section will have its own pattern of organization. A single paragraph may also have its own pattern of organization.

Chapters of texts are commonly organized by an attribution pattern. The chapter is divided into a list of logical subcategories. Sometimes the subcategories will be ordered chronologically; sometimes, the order is unimportant. In science texts, chapters are often organized into subcategories ordered from simpler to more complex concepts (Catterson, 1990).

A useful discussion of the organization of mathematics texts is offered by Shuard (1982, p. 98-99). She points out that math texts have the following types of writing serving varying purposes:

1. *Exposition* of concepts and methods; this may include explanations of vocabulary and notation, and the statement of principles or rules. Exposition may be done by means of prose passages, worked examples, or structured sequences of exercises designed to enable students to acquire an idea as they work through them.

2. *Instructions* to the student to write, draw, calculate or   undertake some practical activity.

3. *Exercises* Many exercises are fairly routine tasks designed to give practice in what has been learned. Problems may ask for a more demanding application of the learning in new situations.

4. *Peripheral writing* includes introductory remarks, summaries, and comments that are not actually part of the exposition, but intended to help the reader to understand the exposition better. Other comments may "jolly the reader along" through an especially dense passage, or give clues to the method to be used in solving a problem.

5. *Signals* Because mathematical writing often has a very complicated structure and layout, signals such as headings, exercise numbers, coloured boxes to indicate important formulae, and pictorial "logos" are often used to steer the reader around the page.

6. *Diagrams and graphs* which may be (a) an *essential* part of the text; (b) not essential, but *related* to the material in the text; or (c) purely *decorative*.

Students need to be able to recognize these various types of text so that they can respond appropriately and so that they do not miss vital information.

CONCLUSION

Every discipline has its own register. The register consists of specialized vocabulary, characteristic expressions and sentence patterns, and ways of organizing text. Vocabulary is acquired over time as students meet words in different contexts and use the words frequently in their own speech and writing. Words that have one meaning in everyday use and another specialized technical meaning present a particular problem since misunderstandings are hard to detect. Written language holds many pitfalls for students who are trying to make sense of the densely loaded, unfamiliar sentences and text structures that characterize written texts. You will be wise to note that your students need assistance of varying kinds in learning the language of the discipline you are teaching. Specific strategies are suggested in later chapters, especially Chapter 8.

EXERCISES

1. a. Make a list of words in a content area you teach that have one meaning in everyday use and a different meaning in the content area.

   b. Compare your list with two or three other people interested in the same content area.

2. a. Identify the text pattern(s) used in the following reading. (You will probably find it useful to re-read the section on text patterns under the heading *The Organization of Extended Discourse* in Chapter 5.)

   b. When you have finished, summarize the reading in graphic or diagrammatic form.

   c. Find two sentences that contain "difficult" syntactic structures.

   The problem of what to do with these wastes needs a reliable solution. Many nuclear wastes have half-lives of thousands of years and must be placed where they will not endanger life. Consider some suggestions for waste disposal that have been rejected. Ocean dumping is not a viable solution because of the danger of canisters corroding and releasing their contents. Incineration produces gaseous radioactive products that would be released into the air. Sending the wastes into outer space to burn up near the sun is possible but expensive, and nobody can guarantee that the vehicle will successfully clear Earth's atmosphere without a mishap. The issue is not an easy one to resolve.

   A promising solution to the growing nuclear waste disposal problem is to bury the material in canisters deep underground in beds of salt or in the bedrock of the Canadian Shield. Several problems need to be overcome in order for such disposal to prove safe. Will the canisters be able to maintain their integrity over many hundreds or thousands of years? Is the site for storage geologically stable? Can the risk of accident in transporting dangerous materials to the storage sites be minimized? What about future generations that may uncover these sites accidentally?

   A possible solution to the problem of disposal of spent nuclear fuel rods is reprocessing. The used rods are chemically dissolved in an aqueous solution, and the long-lived alpha emitters (nuclides of uranium, plutonium, and americium) are extracted and made into new fuel rods. The remaining radioactive wastes are then converted into a solid, usually glass, by a process known as vitrification. The glass is stored underground. France has had some success with *vitrification*, but at this time, the rate of waste production exceeds the rate at which the materials can be reprocessed, and the cost is high.

REFERENCES

Bell, B., and P. Freyberg (1985). Language in the science classroom. In R. Osborne and P. Freyberg (eds.), *Learning in Science: The Implications of Children's Science* (pp. 29-40). Auckland, NZ: Heinemann Education.

Catterson, J. (1990). Discourse forms in content texts. *Journal of Reading*, 33, 556-558.

Elliott, P.G., and C.A. Wiles (1980). The print is part of the problem. *School Science and Mathematics*, 80 (1), 37-42.

Ginsberg, H. (1977). *Children's Arithmetic: The Learning Process*. London: Van Nostrand.

Isakson, R. L. (1979). Cognitive processing in sentence comprehension. *Journal of Educational Research*, 72, 160-165.

Johnston, P. (1985). Writing to learn science. In A. Gere (ed.). *Roots in the Sawdust* (pp. 92-103). Urbana, IL: National Council of Teachers of English.

Kerslake, D. (1982). Talking about mathematics. In R. Harvey, D. Kerslake, H. Shuard, and M. Torbe. *Mathematics* (pp. 41-83). London: Ward Lock Educational.

Martin, J.R. (1986). Systemic functional linguistics and an understanding of written text. In J.R. Martin and J. Rothery (eds.), *Working Papers in Linguistics No. 4. Writing project report* (pp. 91-110). Sydney, Australia: University of Sydney.

Otterburn, M.K., and A.R. Nicholson 1976. The language of (C.S.E.) Mathematics. *Maths in School*, 5(5), 18-21.

Perera, K. (1984). *Children's Writing and Reading: Analysing Classroom Language*. Oxford: Basil Blackwell

Piercey, D. (1982). *Reading Activities in Content Areas: An Ideabook for Middle and Secondary Schools*, 2nd ed. Boston, MA: Allyn and Bacon.

Pimm, D. 1987. *Speaking Mathematically: Communication in Mathematics Classrooms*. London: Routledge.

Shuard, H. (1982). Reading and learning in mathematics. In R. Harvey, D. Kerslake, H. Shuard, and M. Torbe. *Mathematics* (pp. 84-121). London: Ward Lock Educational.

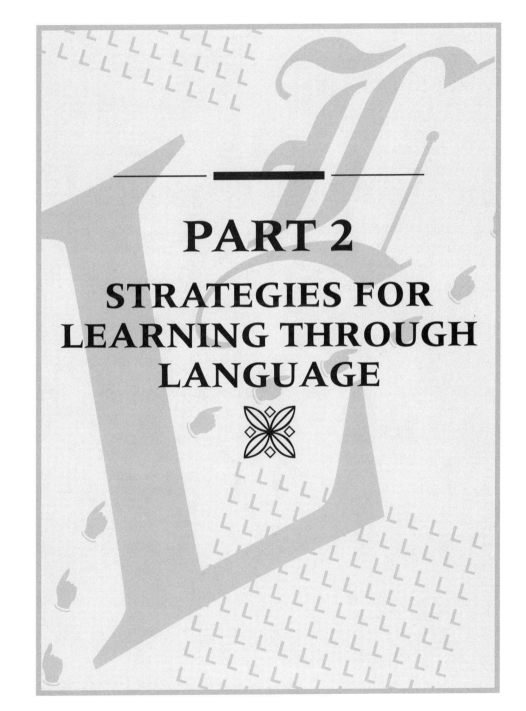

PART 2
STRATEGIES FOR LEARNING THROUGH LANGUAGE

Chapter 6
COOPERATIVE LEARNING: THE ROLE OF INTERACTIVE TALK

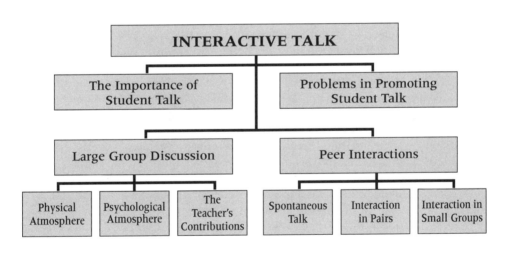

Talking by students has not, traditionally, been a highly prized activity in classrooms. Most of us can probably remember being rebuked by teachers for speaking — even in the quietest of whispers — when we were supposed to be working silently at our desks in the customary way. A great deal of talk goes on in the classroom, but most of it is teacher talk. The teacher talks more than all students put together. Moreover, when students *do* speak, what they say is usually determined by the teacher — and especially by the teacher's questions. When teachers are tape-recorded, they are often surprised to find how much they talk and how little scope they give their students to contribute original ideas or even to ask questions.

Yet there are important reasons why students should be encouraged to speak a great deal in class. A major reason is that talk is an important means of coming to know. When students put into words what they vaguely understand, they raise into consciousness what is only dimly grasped. Through talk they can clarify and develop those vaguely understood concepts.

Knowledge cannot be transmitted to learners. It must be constructed by individuals on the basis of their past experience and past learning. Talking is an important means by which students can engage in exploration and knowledge construction. Talk plays a critical role in knowledge construction during the pre-school years (Wells, 1986), but in school students' talk is greatly limited, its form usually determined by the teacher. The central importance of talking has received gradually increasing attention in the past twenty years (e.g., Barnes and Todd, 1977; Moffett, 1968; Wells, 1986), yet talk by students is still little encouraged by teachers. Staab (1991) found that, while more than 90 percent of the teachers in her study thought that talking was important for learning in all content areas, only 1 percent of class time was spent on activities like group discussion, brainstorming, and problem solving — that is, on activities that permitted students to talk in ways not constrained by teachers' questions.

There are many kinds of interaction patterns in the classroom: teacher to the whole class; teacher and a small group; teacher and individual student; student to student; student to small group; student to large group. In all these situations talk may contribute to learning. Two kinds of talk are especially important for learning: talk with peers, and discussions where teachers act as facilitators of student talk rather than dominating exchanges with their questions and expert knowledge. These two kinds of interaction permit and encourage students to engage in the kinds of talk that lead to understanding. Students may ask questions, clarify ideas, formulate opinions, evaluate the ideas of others. These kinds of interaction, though potentially of great value, are not easily established in classrooms.

In this chapter, five topics are addressed. The first section discusses the importance of interactive talk. The second section describes some of the problems and hindrances associated with establishing productive student talk in the classroom. The next two sections address procedures for establishing (a) productive teacher-facilitated discussion and (b) productive peer interactions. The final section gives examples of tasks in various subject areas that encourage productive student talk.

THE IMPORTANCE OF STUDENT TALK

Student talk is important for many reasons. Some of the most important are as follows:

1. The act of verbalizing helps students to come to know. (Talking and writing, it is to be noted, are two sides of the same coin. Both involve putting thoughts into words.)

> The most important reason for encouraging pupil talk is that it will increase the pupils' understanding of . . . concepts. Concepts are embodied in language, even in our thoughts. Our ideas are built up of words and phrases that make sense to us; other people's words and phrases may be remembered, but rarely, and it is our own reworking and collecting together of words and examples that help us define and therefore understand concepts ... for most pupils most of the time this exploration will be done only through talk. If we do not provide the opportunity for our pupils to talk through concepts then the chances of them thinking them through at all, never mind successfully, is remote (Bulman, 1985, p.115).

2. The ability to speak effectively in large and small groups is an important life skill for students to acquire.

> The primacy of the spoken word in human intercourse cannot be too strongly emphasised. Important though the written word is, most communication takes place in speech; and those who do not listen with attention and cannot speak with clarity, articulateness and confidence are at a disadvantage in almost every aspect of their personal, social and working lives (DES, 1982, p.5).

3. Through listening and talking in groups children are enabled to explore other people's experiences and to modify and extend their own ... All pupils need to be given ample opportunity for discussion of a wide range of experiences ... Pupils should be encouraged to explore ideas which are new to them in their own words before being introduced to the technical terms for those ideas (DES, 1989, p.21-23).

4. Talking helps students make the technical vocabulary of a discipline their own as they use that vocabulary in a variety of contexts.

5. Cooperative work in groups increases motivation and positive attitudes towards work.

6. Cooperative groupwork leads to increased time on task because it produces more active, task-oriented behaviour than individual seatwork.

7. Cooperative groupwork promotes student decision making. Students learn to take responsibility for their own learning.

8. Students who participate in discussion in large and small groups engage in more higher-level thinking than those who work alone. They also retain information longer.

9. Student talk can inform the teacher. When small groups of children discuss and solve mathematical problems, for example, the teacher is able to observe individual students, ask probing questions, and note any conceptual difficulties individual students might be experiencing (National Council of Teachers of Mathematics, 1989, p.27).

The importance of student talk in large and small groups is emphasized by leading curriculum specialists in virtually every subject area. Note, for example, the statement of the National Research Council (1989, p. 59) in their report on the future of mathematics education: students are most likely to engage in the important activities of examining, representing, transforming, solving, applying, proving, and communicating if they "work in groups, engage in discussion, make presentations, and in other ways take charge of their own learning." Sutton (1980, p. 55) urges the need for a wider range of small group discussion tasks following or preceding practical work in science, tasks "which require the statement of similarities, differences and connections, of instances and explanations." Talk is an invaluable means of coming to know in all subject areas.

PROBLEMS IN PROMOTING STUDENT TALK

Social interaction is of critical importance in the development of language and thinking (Bruner, 1966, 1975; Vygotsky 1962; 1978; Wells, 1986). Its importance has been increasingly recognized in recent decades. Nonetheless, interaction in most classrooms is strictly controlled and constrained, as noted in Chapter 4. There are a number of reasons for this.

Talk Is not Valued   In predominant views of teaching and learning, student talk is not valued as a productive activity. The traditional view is that of the teacher-expert transmitting knowledge to novice students. The two pictures of the typical classroom that spring most readily to mind are: (1) the teacher standing at the front of the class talking while students listen or answer questions; and (2) students, individually, working quietly at their desks. Emig (1981, p.22) relates an instructive anecdote. An administrator came to a classroom to evaluate a teacher's performance. He found the teacher "helping small groups of writers actively construct their reality through imaginative sequences of experiences and activities." He slipped the teacher a note that read: "I'll come back when you're teaching." The implication is clear: if students are talking, teachers are not teaching.

There is abundant evidence that student talk is not a valued learning activity. In more than two decades as a teacher educator, I have repeatedly had teachers express reluctance to let students talk except, perhaps, on Friday afternoon when students are tired and restless and deserve a break from serious work. Talk is associated with socializing; it is not seen as real work that leads to learning. Staab's (1991) teachers believed that talk was important for learning in all content areas, but little student talk occurred except during art, free time, and physical education. Teachers believe that if they let students talk they are not doing their job.

Teachers Worry About Loss of Control   The traditional class consists of teacher lecture or teacher-led recitation (described in Chapter 4) followed by seatwork (writing answers to questions, working mathematical problems, etc.). In such classes it is fairly easy for the teacher to maintain control. Students who talk while the teacher is lecturing or during seatwork are quickly called to order; during recitation, students are expected to speak only to provide short answers to the teacher's questions. Once the class is opened up to true discussion, however, the teacher has much less control over what is said. It is not as easy to be sure that the desired material will be covered. The problem of control is even greater if students work in small groups. Teachers often feel anxious that students will get off task and waste time. They also worry about discipline problems if they allow students to work in groups. The noise level in the class is likely to rise if they let students work in small groups. If the noise level rises, administrators, they are sure, will think that productive learning is not occurring.

Teachers Worry About Covering Course Content   Covering content is a major teacher concern (e.g., see Langer and Applebee, 1987). Content is seen as skills or information to be mastered. The curriculum is best covered if the teacher keeps tight control of what is done. Discussion and group activities are time-consuming. If time is spent on these activities, teachers worry that they will not cover the course. Increasingly, however, course content is being defined in other ways than a set of skills or information to be learned. In mathematics, the goal is not merely to have students memorize procedures and work examples but to engage them in higher order thinking, in solving non-routine problems, and in developing metacognitive awareness. History is not a set of dates and events to be memorized, but a matter of learning to consider matters as a historian does. Such learning is not achieved by a transmission-plus-testing model of teaching.

Lack of Teacher Know-How   By the time teachers take up their first teaching position, they have spent a minimum of fifteen or sixteen years of formal education. The predominant model to which they have been exposed is lecture or demonstration or recitation followed by seatwork of some kind. The chances are that they have participated in comparatively few small groups and have witnessed little true discussion where students have been encouraged to question, to speculate, or to respond to the comments of their peers. In other words, they have probably not been much exposed to models of teaching and learning involving student talk.

Dillon (1984) points out that it is hard to conduct a discussion and it is hard to *learn how* to conduct a discussion. Most of us discovered, as student teachers, that learning how to ask questions is not as easy as it looks. But the questioning skills used in recitation — difficult as they are to master — are useless in discussion. A whole different set of skills must be developed. Even more difficult than learning the appropriate questioning techniques is acquiring the necessary attitudes and commitments to classroom discussion. The hardest thing of all for teachers to do is to lay down their accustomed didactic teaching style and to learn discussion leadership style. The question-answer-evaluation routine is so well established that it is hard for teachers to develop other ways of responding to students.

Teachers are equally uninformed, for the most part, about ways to develop students' group skills. Good things do not happen merely because we put students in a small group and give them a task to do or a question to discuss. It takes time for students to learn how to work effectively in small groups. Problems inevitably arise in at least some of the groups as students learn interpersonal skills. Some students try to dominate. Some are unwilling to participate. Cultural groups vary in the ease with which they participate in discussion. It requires knowledge and skill on the part of teachers to deal with difficulties that arise in groups.

Given these problems, it is not surprising that teachers opt for other methods than class discussion and small group activities. However, the values of talk for learning are so great that it is important for teachers to master necessary skills.

LARGE GROUP DISCUSSION

As mentioned in Chapter 4, large group discussion is different, in a variety of ways, from the much more common question-answer-evaluation sequence of recitation. Some differences are the amount of student participation; the length of student responses; the functions of students' contributions; and the different roles played by the teacher. Learning to lead discussion requires practice by the teacher. Following are some suggestions for establishing an appropriate atmosphere for discussion, and suggested techniques that may assist the teacher to learn facilitative skills.

The Physical Atmosphere

The way the classroom is organized physically conveys a message. If desks are lined up in rows facing the teacher, the implicit message is that the teacher is the main talker and that students are expected to speak only to the teacher. An ideal arrangement for whole-class discussion is an open square or an open circle with the teacher seated in an unmarked position in the circle or square. An alternative is a double circle with the teacher sitting or standing in an opening at the front. This arrangement places the teacher in a more dominant position. However, it accommodates a larger number of students than an open circle and still allows students to direct remarks to other students as well as to the teacher. In some classrooms, desks will be arranged in clusters of four or six to facilitate group activities. This arrangement can also work quite well for whole-class discussion since students are facing in many directions and will feel free to turn to listen or to respond to other contributors. In order for whole-class discussion to proceed in an orderly fashion, it will usually be necessary for the teacher to recognize the student who is to contribute next. It is important, also, for there to be well-understood rules about listening, about not interrupting, and about practising courteous ways of disagreeing or offering contrary opinions.

The Psychological Atmosphere

It is essential to establish a psychological climate that supports students' attempts to participate. The following characteristics help to provide the kind of support needed (Bridges, 1979; Roberts and Langer, 1991):

1. Students are treated as thinkers with useful contributions to make.

2. All are free to participate and to offer sincerely held opinions.

3. All participants are treated with respect.

4. Different points of view are welcomed and considered.

5. The learning outcomes are open rather than pre-determined or predictable.

6. The discussion is open-ended, without pressure to come to a single conclusion.

7. The teacher's role is to support or "scaffold" students' own attempts to understand.

The Teacher's Contributions

As has been mentioned, learning how to lead a discussion is not easily achieved. No set of rules will be sufficient to guide the novice. The most likely pitfall is that the teacher will fall into the long-practised habit of making an evaluative comment after a student response and then fill the silence that follows with another question. The class is now back into the familiar question-response-evaluation routine. If different patterns are to be established, you will need, consciously, to learn and practise different kinds of responses. Some suggested alternatives are as follows (Dillon, 1984):

1. ***Remain silent.*** Research shows that if teachers wait for a few seconds after asking a question or after a student response, the effect on discussion is very beneficial. Silence tends to make teachers and students anxious. Teachers expect an answer within a second. A wait of 2-3 seconds seems very long, at first. But a pause of that length after a question has been found to increase both the quantity and the quality of students' responses. They not only talk more, but their talk is more relevant and the content is at a higher cognitive level. Waiting after a student response is likely to lead to further comment by that student or to a contribution by another student.

2. ***Make a declarative statement.*** For example, express an opinion.

3. ***Reflect back what the student has said*** ("So you are saying that ..."). Sometimes the reflective statement may clarify or focus what he has said.

4. ***Ask the student to repeat and clarify what she has said.*** ("I am not quite sure what you are saying.")

5. ***Ask the student to elaborate.*** ("I'd like to hear more about that.")

6. ***Encourage other students to ask a question.***

7. ***Make a neutral, non-evaluative remark.*** ("Interesting," "Okay," or "Let's think about that.")

Some kinds of questions are useful for prompting thoughtful student contributions to classroom discussion. The National Council of Teachers of Mathematics (1991, pp. 3-4) provides a list of desirable student behaviours and suggests the kinds of questions a teacher might ask to encourage th behaviours:

To help students work together to make sense of mathematics

- What do others think about what Janine has said?
- Does anyone have the same answer but a different way to explain it?

To help students to rely more on themselves to determine whether something is mathematically correct

- How did you reach that conclusion?
- Can you make a model to show that?

To help students learn to reason mathematically

- Is that true for all cases?
- Can you think of a counter-example?
- What assumptions are you making?

To help students learn to conjecture, invent, and solve problems

- What would happen if. . .?
- Do you see a pattern?
- Can you predict the next one?

Helping students to connect mathematics, its ideas, and its application

- What ideas that we have learned before were useful in solving this problem?
- What uses of mathematics did you find in the newspaper last night?

You can probably draw parallels for other disciplines, both in the kinds of thinking you might want your students to engage in, and the kinds of questions you might ask to prompt such thinking.

To change well established patterns of behaviour like the question-answer-evaluation sequence requires determination and application. One useful strategy is to record classroom discussions. This will enable you to listen critically to your contributions and the effect of your contributions on students' responses.

PEER INTERACTIONS

Many kinds of peer interaction occur in a classroom. Students engage in informal, spontaneous talk, and they work in pairs and in small groups.

Spontaneous Talk

Students engage in spontaneous talk whenever they can. Much spontaneous talk is social in nature. However, in the free give and take of spontaneous talk, students both offer help and solicit help from their peers. Such help is often useful. Certainly students believe their peers are an important source of informal help for a variety of tasks.

Spontaneous talk will be permitted to a greater or lesser extent in classes depending on the task at hand, teacher inclinations, the time of day, and a host of other factors. The amount of spontaneous talk and the degree to which it is either tolerated or encouraged also tends to vary with grade level. Many secondary teachers want students to work independently and do not encourage a lot of spontaneous talk. Primary teachers, on the other hand, tend to be aware that much incidental teaching can go on when students interact spontaneously. Observing in a primary classroom for children aged 6 though 8, I was interested to note the number and variety of spontaneous interactions that were educationally useful. The following kinds of help were given: assistance with spelling; informative responses to drawings, constructions, and writing; helpful suggestions in problem solving activities. The teacher of that class not only permitted but encouraged spontaneous interactions during most of the school day. She was well aware that her older students could help the younger students in many ways.

Interaction in Pairs

Students sometimes work in pairs. The teacher may assign tasks to be done in pairs, or pairs may come together informally — for example, to confer together about drafts of their respective compositions.

When you pose questions or problems that require thought, you may find it useful to let students discuss the question briefly with a partner. They are likely to be more willing to share with the whole class if they can first try out their ideas with a peer. Moreover, the strategy of having them work in pairs increases the likelihood that all children will actually consider the problem and try for an answer. To pose a problem and then take an answer from a single student relieves other students of the need to think about the problem. Work in pairs does not require unusual skill and does not usually pose problems for the teacher.

Interaction in Small Groups

Interaction in small groups is a type of peer interaction that poses more problems but promises great potential dividends. Small group discussion and its value have been well described by Moffett (1968, p. 46):

The heart of discussing is *expatiation,* picking up ideas and developing them; corroborating, qualifying, and challenging; building on and varying each other's sentences, statements, and images ... Discussion is a process of amending, appending, diverging, converging, elaborating, summarizing, and many other things. Most of all, it is an external social process that each member gradually internalizes as a personal thought process: he begins to think in the ways his group talks. Not only does he take unto himself the vocabulary, usage, and syntax of others and synthesize new creations out of their various styles, points of view, and attitudes; he also structures his thinking into mental operations resembling the operations of the group interactions. If the group amends, challenges, elaborates, and qualifies together, each member begins to do so alone in his inner speech ... The teacher's job is to establish the forms of discussion that, when internalized by individuals, will most enhance the growth of thought and speech.

The potential of small group interaction is great. However, getting groups to work effectively in classes is not easy.

I remember well the first time I tried small group discussion in a class. I gave my seventh-grade students a poem to discuss, and provided questions which I expected would lead to rich insights. As I moved about listening in to the various groups, I heard little that was even modestly insightful. In one group, three conscientious students tried to do as I had asked while the other two yawned, and doodled on pieces of paper. In a second group, the discussion centred on how boring poetry was. A third group was intolerably rowdy and argumentative. In another group, two of the students were finishing their math homework while the others discussed a current movie. I did not try group work again with that class.

However, I was only temporarily discouraged, mainly because James Moffett (1968) had persuaded me that group work was invaluable in achieving the purposes of the English classroom. I made up my mind to find out more about it. I read a lot and took some courses. But, most important, I kept trying out ideas in my classes. As a result of my somewhat stumbling attempts to put into practice ideas gleaned from a number of sources, I compiled a list of *do's* and *don't's* for teachers who are enticed by the possibilities of peer-group discussion, but who are nervous about making a start. The following list of suggestions (Crowhurst, 1983) is intended for use when students are assigned to groups in which they work consistently for a period of weeks in order to develop particular group-interaction skills. They may work in other groups or in pairs for other purposes during the same time period.

1. *Set the development of group-interaction skills as one of your goals for the year.* Keep clearly in mind — and make clear to your students—that the development of group skills is an important objective. Group skills are important, first, because effective interaction by your students in cooperative, collaborative small groups will help you to achieve many learning objectives

throughout the rest of the year. Secondly, if students learn to interact courteously, confidently, and productively with others, the ability will be useful to them throughout their lives in both social and work situations. Teachers are always short of time. You will be reluctant to spend time on group skills unless you keep reminding yourself that it is critically important to do so. If you set group skills as a goal, you give yourself the right to work towards that goal as systematically as you work towards any other. You will be willing to spend time — especially during the critically important early weeks of the year — that you might otherwise begrudge.

2. *Arrange an appropriate physical environment.* Students should sit in a circle. Any person physically out of the group — because her chair is set back outside the circle, for example — is likely to be psychologically outside the group. Preferably, students should not sit around a rectangular table; those at the ends will be in a dominating position (i.e., at the "head" of the table) if they are strong, or, if they are weak, will be cut out of the discussion by the cross-fire of talk between more verbal members sitting across from each other.

3. *Take care in assigning students to groups.* Size will vary, somewhat, depending on grade level. Groups of six work well. This allows one student to be absent and another to act as "observer" (described below) without reducing the group to a size too small for useful interaction.

   Since one of the values of group discussion is to share ideas with different others, groups should be heterogeneous — boys and girls, native speakers and non-native speakers, the bright, the average, and the not-quite-average, all represented in each group. Insights about life and living are by no means limited to the brightest in the class. All students have unique experiences, significant insights about their experience, and varied talents to bring to the group.

   Since it is important for students to feel comfortable, try to let each student work in a group with at least one person of his or her choice. Ask students to write on a piece of paper the names of three students with whom they would like to work. You can then assign students to groups making sure that each person works with one person of his or her choice. On the other hand, it is not usually a good idea for a group of good friends to cluster together in one group. A benefit of group work is that students get to know and to appreciate others with whom they might not otherwise interact.

4. *Leave students in their original groups for a sustained period.* Good talk — exploratory, constructive talk — only happens among peers who know each other well and who feel relaxed enough to try out ideas and let them go easily if they are seen to be inadequate. Relaxed, comfortable feelings take

time to develop. Even students who have sat for years in the same class often do not know each other well. Students should work in the same groups for several weeks. When they have developed some skill, they can be reassigned to another group, again for a sustained period, to practice skills with a new group. Note, however, that in addition to working in this kind of group where membership of the groups is sustained for some weeks for the purpose of developing important skills, students will work in many other groups with different students, sometimes for the purpose of completing a single task in a short period of time. Sometimes students will self-select the other students they wish to work with for short, task-oriented groups.

5. ***Select group tasks carefully.*** Tasks in the early "training" period should be fairly brief — short enough to be completed in ten to twenty minutes, depending on the age of the class. Tasks should be open-ended — calling for expressions of opinions so that all can contribute, or having more than one answer or more than one way to solve the problem. Tasks with one correct answer should usually be avoided at first. You should also avoid tasks that lend themselves to polarized positions since they are likely to result in mindless argument rather than useful discussion.

   Initially, you should avoid questions about which you want students to reach particular conclusions. The best results come when students are free to explore a question by making tentative, slightly random, sometimes misguided stabs at it. If the topic is one you regard as important, you are likely to become anxious if a group discussion goes in an unexpected direction, or tends towards unwarranted conclusions. You will be less concerned about the outcome of the discussion if the task is to determine how many "lutts" there are in a "mipp". (Group problem-solving exercise, Myers and Myers, 1973, p. 337). For the first few discussions, then, you should avoid tasks involving content that you are anxious for students to master. Many books contain useful tasks which can be adapted for classroom use (e.g., Johnson and Johnson, 1982; Myers and Myers, 1973; Stanford and Roark, 1974; Stanford and Stanford, 1969). Some tasks are specially designed to develop specific skills, or to help deal with the problems that inevitably arise in groups (Stanford and Roark, 1974; Stanford and Stanford, 1969).

6. ***Specify group skills to be practised.*** You should tell students the specific behaviours that you want them to practise. I like to start with Whipple's (1975) set of five "grouptalk" rules. They are simple enough for primary children to understand, yet useful enough to be profitable in discussions by adults. They are:

 Understand   Everyone should think about what the question means before the group tries to answer it.

Contribute   Everyone should make an attempt to answer the question.

Be relevant   Everyone should keep to the point.

Listen   Everyone should try to understand what others say in order to respond.

Respond   Each speaker should try to respond to what the previous speaker said by asking for further explanation; agreeing with what was said; providing a relevant example; presenting an alternate point of view.

Sum up   Everyone should try to sum up the main points of the discussion.

Though these rules are simple, they are not usually understood and practised even by university students — or university faculty, for that matter. Many people imagine, for example, that the most useful group members are those who speak a lot and thus make a big contribution. However, people who speak a lot may preempt those who could make valuable contributions but who cannot get the floor. There is no one to one relationship between the ease with which a speaker gets the floor and the importance and value of what that speaker has to say. Those who speak too much may well be a hindrance to the most effective operation of the group. All group members need to realize this so that they can be alert to the need for all to be heard.

One of the rules most frequently violated is "Listen." Group members frequently use the time when another is speaking to practise in their heads what they are going to say when they get the floor. When I mention this — and confess that I have often erred in this way myself — there are usually a number of sheepish smiles of acknowledgement. You need to encourage students to listen to the contributions of others in their group and to respond to those contributions by agreeing, clarifying, adding an example, asking a question, and so on.

When students have spent time practising these basic skills, they can be introduced to the idea that people can make different kinds of contributions to the work of the group. Some ways are: contributing, clarifying, initiating, summarizing, encouraging, compromising. They may also be told that there are certain behaviours that prevent groups from getting their work done, for example: competing, being aggressive, withdrawing, seeking recognition (by smarting off or by dominating, for example). Students who contribute easily and fluently can be encouraged to diversify by practising new skills.

7. ***Encourage shared responsibility for the functioning of the group.*** I do not usually appoint a chair in a small group if discussion is the purpose. If strong group members are appointed as chair, they get more practice doing what they already do well. Moreover, some students become somewhat

overbearing in this situation. If weaker group members are appointed as chair, they are not likely to be able to wield the requisite influence to carry out the task.

Rather than appointing a single person to oversee the functioning of the group, I like to encourage shared responsibility. This means that if one person talks excessively and another person says nothing at all, the responsibility is shared by the excessive talker, the person who says nothing, and all the other members of the group who do nothing to rectify the imbalance. In the long run, shared responsibility makes for group effectiveness. However, you must be prepared to work patiently to achieve the goal of shared responsibility.

Sharing responsibility for group functioning is especially appropriate in discussion tasks. On the other hand students also need to learn how to chair a group, how to curb tendencies to be overbearing, and how to organize a group to accomplish a task efficiently. Moreover, some tasks will be accomplished more efficiently if a chair is either selected by group members of appointed by the teacher. This is especially true for tasks where a product is to be produced particularly if the group is to work over two or more meeting times.

8. **Arrange for feedback.** If students are to learn the skills of engaging in productive interaction with other students, they need to receive continuing feedback. Giving feedback emphasizes that groupwork is a serious activity. It also provides students with information about their performance as individuals and as a group — information they need if they are to improve. Feedback may be given in a variety of ways.

Self evaluation   Nothing is more useful than having individuals consider their own performance. The behaviour one can most easily modify is one's own. At any grade level, the two simple questions that follow can produce useful insight:

- List the useful things you did today to help your group.

- Write down one thing you could do next time that would improve the working of your group.

Students may be asked, informally, to respond in writing to such questions at any time. Alternatively, a self-report form such as that illustrated in Figure 6.1 may be used. Such self-reports help to give you insight into development over time. Note that you need not necessarily ask them to answer all questions on every occasion.

Individual evaluations of the group   The *Group Self-Report* Form illustrated in Figure 6.2 is an excellent means of encouraging all members of the group to consider how the group is doing and how it might be improved.

Figure 6.1

INDIVIDUAL SELF-REPORT

NAME_____ DATE_____

_____

What was the group's task?

_____

1.   In the following list, put a check mark against the things you did today to help your group:

    ☐ contributed
    ☐ stayed on task
    ☐ listened carefully
    ☐ responded to others
    ☐ summed up

2.   Did you speak too much? too little? or about the right amount?

3.   What was the most important thing you did to help your group today?

4.   Write down one thing you could do next time to help your group.

5.   What did you like best about your group today?

6.   What did you like least about your group today?

Source: Adapted by the author from S. Jeroski, A. Sharp, J. Craib and B. LeGear (1988). *Enhancing and evaluating oral communication in the intermediate grades: Teacher's resource package* (Victoria, BC: British Columbia. Ministry of Education).

Figure 6.2

GROUP SELF-REPORT

NAMES:

DATE:

What was the group's task?

---

1. Think of *one* problem the group had. What was it?

2. How did the group solve the problem?

3. What else could you have done to solve the problem?

4. Which group member helped the group most in today's task?

5. What did he or she do that was helpful?

6. Who is the most encouraging member of your group?

7. What does he or she do that encourages you to take part in the group?

Source: Adapted by the author from S. Jeroski, A. Sharp, J. Craib and B. LeGear (1988). *Enhancing and evaluating oral communication in the intermediate grades: Teacher's resource package* (Victoria, BC: British Columbia Ministry of Education).

It may be useful to share with class members, sometimes, the varied responses that are made by their fellow group members. It is useful for students to realize that everyone does not see things the same way. On a day when I reassigned a class of grade 12 students to new groups, I asked them to respond to the following question: "How did you feel about being moved to a new group?" The selection of answers shown in Figure 6.3 indicates the range and variety of opinions:

Figure 6.3
Student Responses to Assignment to New Groups

— Didn't mind being moved as much as I thought I would, possibly because I knew slightly the persons in the group.

— It was interesting to move because then you get to speak to people that you might not have ever talked to.

— It was a good idea because once you know how to participate it is easy to go into another group.

— !!!&*@#*!

— Sort of uncomfortable because I was used to discussing with other people.

— I felt more comfortable in the old group and was starting to voice my opinions freely. Now it will take a while for it to happen again.

— Allows for better class communication being exposed to everyone.

One member as observer   One group member — a different member each time — is assigned to sit outside the group and act as an observer. Observers are asked to count certain behaviours, or to describe instances of particular behaviours, but to avoid making value judgments. On the first occasion, for example, the observer is simply told to count the number of times each person speaks and to report the number to each individual, without further comment, at the end of the group activity. The purpose is to emphasize that all are expected to contribute more or less equally. In later sessions, the observer might list and describe clarifying behaviours, compromising behaviours, or encouraging behaviours (for example, "Susan looked at whoever was speaking, and often smiled and nodded encouragingly." "Bill made three encouraging comments like: 'I thought so-and-so made an important point when he said such-and-such.'"). In addition to providing feedback to the group, observers learn a good deal about group interaction when they are specifically observing rather than engaging in the group task.

Group on group observation   The observing group sits in a circle around the group being observed; every member of the observing group takes responsibility for giving feedback to one member of the group being observed. Observing another group can be a very instructive experience for the observer who sees different things when not involved in participating as a group member.

Teacher feedback I myself constantly observe and write notes to students with comments such as:

— You are an excellent contributor to the group. You offer information and opinions frequently and fluently. If I were you, I would start concentrating on developing other skills, for example, helping others to clarify what they are saying, encouraging those who find it hard to contribute.

— I think you made a valuable contribution when you said such-and-such. It opened a whole new line of discussion in the group.

You may find the rating scale illustrated in Figure 6.4 useful for recording observations on individuals in a given group on a given occasion. The form illustrated in Figure 6.5 may be used to construct a profile of participation for each student in the class. Records of this kind will give you the kind of information you need to help students to develop the skills they need.

Invaluable though it is, effective peer-group interaction does not come about merely because students are placed in groups and assigned a topic for discussion. Most students, whatever their age, need practice and instruction in order to be effective contributors. You will find the suggestions listed above a useful guide in beginning such groupwork with your classes. As noted, these suggestions apply particularly for learning the skills of groups discussion. You will doubtless have students working in other kinds of groups for many purposes. The skills described above can be expected to carry over to all their work in groups.

Examples of Tasks Involving Peer Interaction

Talk is central to the model of teaching and learning on which this book is based. Student talk will occur for many purposes in virtually every class. Students will talk in pairs or in small groups or in a whole-class brainstorming session to identify what they know about Sweden or about electricity before beginning a unit on Sweden or on electricity. They will talk *before* reading a poem or a chapter to predict what will be in the poem or the chapter. They will talk after reading to share ideas about what they thought the reading was about. They will talk in small groups to solve math problems and science problems, to plan a menu in home economics, to write an advertisement in business education, to create a skit or a dialogue in social studies or English, to respond to a peer's painting in art, to discuss their initial responses to a piece of music, or the techniques that they noted were used by a composer to create certain effects. They will talk, not for the sake of talking, but for the sake of learning through talk.

Since talk is envisaged as such a pervasive feature of the classroom, it may be superfluous to describe particular group tasks. However, the following examples

Figure 6.4

RATING SCALE: BEHAVIOUR IN A SMALL-GROUP SETTING					
	Student's Names				
Recording 1 Needs improvement 2 Average 3 Above average					
1. Speaks clearly and audibly					
2. Listens attentively and follows along					
3. Initiates ideas					
4. Add productively to others' ideas					
5. Stays on topic (task)					
6. Disagres tactfully					
7. Accepts criticism well					
8. Summarizes group's activity upon request					

Source: S. Jeroski, A. Sharp, J. Craib and B. LeGear (1988). *Enhancing and evaluating oral communication in the intermediate grades: Teacher's resource package* (Victoria, BC: British Columbia Ministry of Education.), p. 9:1.

Figure 6.5

STUDENT PROFILE FOR BEHAVIOUR IN SMALL-GROUP SETTINGS

NAME: DATE:

A. INTERPERSONAL STRATEGIES	**Weak**	**Developing**	**Strong**
– Communicates feelings	☐	☐	☐
– Shares ideas	☐	☐	☐
– Supports and encourages others	☐	☐	☐
– Listens attentively, courteously	☐	☐	☐

B. TASK-RELATED CONTRIBUTIONS	**Weak**	**Developing**	**Strong**
– Generates ideas	☐	☐	☐
– Formulates questions to clarify or elaborate	☐	☐	☐
– Offers information clearly and concisely	☐	☐	☐
– Stays on task			
– Works towards a solution	☐	☐	☐
– Takes responsibility	☐	☐	☐

OVERALL RATING

INTERPERSONAL STRATEGIES	1	2	3	4	5
TASK -RELATED CONTRIBUTIONS	1	2	3	4	5

Source: S. Jeroski, A. Sharp, J.Craib and B. LeGear (1988). *Enhancing and evaluating oral communication in the intermediate grades: Teacher's resource package* (Victoria, BC: British Columbia Ministry of Education.), pp. 9-23.

may assist you in thinking of many examples to suit your particular age group or the content areas you teach. Most of the tasks suggested are applicable — sometimes with slight modifications — across a wide variety of grade levels from primary through high school.

1. A useful group discussion task appropriate for use early in the history of the group and early in the school year is to have students rank order, individually, a set of characteristics of the ideal teacher or the ideal class. After individuals have completed ranking, the task for the group is to take twenty minutes to reach agreement as a group on the ranking of the words in the list. The task might read as follows:

    > What do you think are the most important qualities for a good teacher? Your task is to complete the following sentence using the words listed below:
    >
    > "A good teacher should be _____ "
    >
    > Read the list of words, and pick out the best word to complete the sentence. Put *1* in the space next to that word. Now pick out the second best word and put *2* next to it. Continue until you have a number next to every word. The number *8* should be next to the word that you think is the worst word to complete the sentence. (More words, fewer words, or different words may be used depending on the age of your class.)

kind _____	funny _____
well-organized _____	intelligent _____
strict _____	fair _____
good-looking _____	athletic _____

    > When you have finished, work with members in your group to reach agreement on a group ranking for the words in the list. You must *agree* on the ranking. Do not determine ranking by voting.

Note that this task serves not merely as a useful group task, but helps in establishing an open classroom climate by saying, in effect, "In this class, it is okay to let the teacher know the things about the class and the teacher that you think are important."

2. Topical issues in the school can be excellent tasks for group discussion.

    Primary grades: Moffett's (1968) cooperating teachers found that, for second and third graders, petty stealing in the classroom was a "burning issue" that got the children completely involved in group discussions when they were invited to try to solve the problem. The activity led to a proposal to prepare a publication about the problem of petty stealing. This project lasted more than two weeks. The children conducted a survey, wrote ads, lost-and-founds, tall-tales about what happens to stealers, what-to-do-when-you-find-something, and what-to-do-if-you-don't-want-something-stolen.

Upper elementary through high school: In my seventh-grade class, students were completely and immediately involved when they were asked to brainstorm ideas for writing group letters to the school principal, letters in which they would set out their suggestions for improving the school.

Useful discussion questions can also come from literature texts and from topical issues in the press.

3. Problems of the "speculate … explain" kind can be set on a variety of science topics. For example, grade 5 students might be asked to speculate in groups about what would happen if a large can with some water boiling in the bottom were taken off the boil and sealed. Later, they might be asked to try to account for what actually happened (Jones, 1988).

4. "What if …" questions may be posed for group discussion. What if we had no thumbs? What if there were no friction? Questions like these can be asked at any grade level.

5. A task for high school students that would invite integration of information from a variety of disciplines might be to prepare and present a television news item on a natural disaster. The task would involve detailed research, and collaboration in the preparation of visual material such as diagrams and maps, and in the preparation of the script (Jones, 1988). Appropriate topics might vary with the region. In British Columbia, for example, the topic of earthquakes is of continuing concern; on the prairies, tornadoes wreak havoc periodically; hurricanes occasionally threaten provinces in the eastern part of the country.

6. The following tasks provide excellent opportunities for mathematical thinking. These tasks are suggested by the National Council of Teachers of Mathematics (1989; 1991) for use across a wide variety of grade levels. Many of them can be used in primary grades, especially with the support of concrete materials to manipulate; the same tasks can be used for slightly different purposes in the junior high school.

    a. Students are given two sets of quadrilaterals, one set of parallelograms and one set of nonparallelograms, as shown in Figure 6.6. The students's task is to discover the teacher's rule for sorting the shapes (NCTM, 1989, p. 24).

    b. I have six coins worth 42 cents; what coins do you think I have? Is there more than one answer? (NCTM, 1989, p. 24).

Figure 6.6
Two Sets of Quadrilaterals

Source: Adapted from the National Council of Teachers of Mathematics (1989), *Curriculum and Evaluation Standards for School Mathematics* (Reston, VA: NCTM), p. 24.

c. With your group, use counters of different colours to model each of these problems and then discuss how the problems are alike or different.

- Maria had some pencils in her desk. She put 5 more in her desk. Then she had 14. How many pencils did she have in her desk to start with?

- Eddie had 14 helium balloons. Several of them floated away. He had 5 left. How many did he lose?

- Nina had 14 seashells. That was 5 more than Pedro had. How many seashells did Pedro have? (NCTM, 1989, p. 27).

d. Have students "decide whether to calculate means, medians, or modes as the best measures of central tendency, given particular sets of data and particular claims they would like to make about the data, then to calculate those statistics, and finally to explain and defend their decisions." The task, in addition to giving practice finding means, medians, and modes, asks students to speculate and to pursue alternatives (NCTM, 1991, p.26).

e. Have students try "to figure out how many ways 36 desks can be arranged in equal-sized groups — and whether there are more or fewer possible groupings with 36, 37, 38, 39, or 40 desks." The task gives practice in multiplication facts and in finding factors. It may also "provoke interesting questions: How many factors does a number have? Do larger numbers necessarily have more factors? Is there a number that has more factors than 36?" (NCTM, 1991, p.26).

The list of useful tasks is virtually endless. The most important thing to remember is that tasks to be used for the purpose of developing group skills should allow for contributions by all members. This is most likely to happen with brainstorming tasks, tasks that call for opinions, or tasks that have more than one answer or more than one way of solving a problem.

CONCLUSION

Talk is a critically important activity in the classroom if students are to be encouraged to engage in active construction of understanding and knowledge. Despite its importance, student talk is not much encouraged in a majority of classrooms beyond the primary level. Teachers, anxious about discipline and about covering course content, opt for direct ways of transmitting information rather than risking discussion and group work. Special skills are required by teachers who wish to become facilitators of true discussion. Skills must be developed also by students if they are to engage in productive work in small groups. The development of such skills takes time and conscious effort. Teachers who expect dramatic benefits from well-functioning groups within a few weeks are bound to be disappointed. Success requires long-term commitment. Primary and elementary teachers who have many hours a day with the same students have many opportunities to develop group interaction skills in a variety of situations. Secondary teachers who teach several classes may be well advised to start with one class, carefully monitoring student behaviour to diagnose successes and problems. It takes several years to become a first-rate teacher. New teachers with many skills to develop may be wise to hasten slowly, but yet to work consistently at developing necessary skills. Conscious effort over time is required. The benefits are likely to prove worth the cost.

EXERCISES

1. On a day when the instructor of your class has whole-class discussion, you might do the following, taking care to request your instructor's permission ahead of time:

    a. Count instances of the question-answer-evaluation sequence (often called the IRE sequence for initiation, response, evaluation), and note some specific examples.

    b. List any responses the instructor uses that serve to break out of the IRE sequence. For example, look for uses of the strategies suggested on pp. 137-138. Note, in particular, who makes the next contribution after the instructor uses one of these strategies, and what the *function* of that contribution is.

    c. If your instructor allows time for group work, share your observations with members of your group.

2. Examine the suggested group tasks on pp. 152-155. Work with a group of other people in a subject area of special interest to you and devise *five* group tasks that would be likely to encourage participation from all students in a group.

3. If you serve as observer in your small group, examine the behaviours of group members by using the following check list to record instances of the behaviours specified:

Names	Clarify	Initiate	Summarize	Encourage	Compromise

REFERENCES

Barnes, D., and F.Todd (1977). *Communication and Learning in Small Groups.* London: Routledge and Kegan Paul.

Bridges, D. (1979). *Education, Democracy and Discussion.* Windsor, England: NFER Publishing Company.

Bruner, J. (1966). *Toward a Theory of Instruction.* Cambridge: Mass: Harvard University Press.

Bruner, J. (1975). Early social interaction and language acquisition. In H.R.Schaffer (ed.), *Studies in Mother-Infant Interactions* (pp.271-291). London: Academic Press.

Bulman, L. (1985). *Teaching Language and Study Skills in Secondary Science.* London: Heinemann.

Crowhurst, M. (1983). Developing discussion skills: Eight classroom strategies. *Highway One,* 6 (2), 43-51.

DES. (1982). *Bullock Revisited.* London: MHSO.

DES. (1989). *The Curriculum 5-16,* 2nd ed. London: HMSO.

Dillon, J.T. (1984). Research on questioning and Discussion. *Educational Leadership,* 42 (3), 50-56.

Emig, J. (1981). Non-magical thinking: Presenting writing developmentally in schools. In C.H. Frederiksen and J.F. Dominic (eds.), *Writing: The Nature, Development and Teaching of Written Communication,* Volume 2, *Writing: Process, Development and Communication* (pp. 21-30). Hillsdale, NJ: Lawrence Erlbaum Associates.

Jeroski, S., A. Sharp J. Craib and B. LeGear (1988). *Enhancing and evaluating oral communication in the intermediate grades: Teacher's resource package.* Victoria, B.C.: British Columbia Ministry of Education.

Jones, P. (1988). *Lipservice: The Story of Talk in Schools.* Milton Keynes: Open University Press.

Johnson, D.W., and F.P. Johnson (1982). *Joining Together: Group Theory and Group* Skills. Englewood Cliffs, N.J.: Prentice Hall.

Langer, J.A., and A.N. Applebee (1987). *How Writing Shapes Thinking: A Study of Teaching and Learning.* Urbana, IL: National Council of Teachers of English.

Moffett, J. (1968). *A Student-Centered Language Arts Curriculum K-13: A Handbook for Teachers.* Boston: Houghton Mifflin.

Myers, G.E., and M.T. Myers (1973). *The Dynamics of Human Communication*. New York: McGraw Hill.

National Council of Teachers of Mathematics (1991). *Professional Standards for Teaching Mathematics*. Reston, VA: National Council of Teachers of Mathematics.

National Council of Teachers of Mathematics. (1989). *Curriculum and Evaluation Standards for School Mathematics*. Reston, VA: National Council of Teachers of Mathematics.

National Research Council. (1989). *Everybody counts: A report on the future of mathematics education*. Washington, DC: National Academy Press.

Roberts, D.R., and J.A. Langer (1991). *Supporting the process of literary understanding: Analysis of a classroom discussion*, Report Series 2.15. Albany, NY: Center for the Learning and Teaching of Literature, State University of New York.

Staab, C.F. (1991). Teachers' practices with regard to oral language. *The Alberta Journal of Educational Research*, 37(1), 31-48.

Stanford, G., and A.E. Roark (1974). *Human Interaction in Education*. Boston: Allyn and Bacon.

Stanford, G., and B.D. Stanford (1969). *Learning Discussion Skills through Games*. New York: Citation Press.

Sutton, C. (1980). Science, language and meaning. School *Science Review*, 62, 47-56.

Vygotsky, L.S. (1962). *Thought and Language*. Cambridge, MA: MIT.

Vygotsky, L.S. (1978). *Mind in Society*. Cambridge, MA: Harvard University Press.

Wells, G. (1986). *The Meaning Makers: Children Learning Language and Using Language to Learn*. Portsmouth, NH: Portsmouth.

Whipple, B. (1975). *Dynamics of Discussion: Grouptalk*. Belmont, MA: Porthole Press.

Chapter 7

READING IN THE CONTENT AREAS: THEORETICAL ISSUES

CHAPTER OVERVIEW

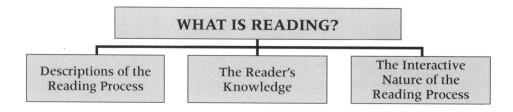

WHAT IS READING?

| Descriptions of the Reading Process | The Reader's Knowledge | The Interactive Nature of the Reading Process |

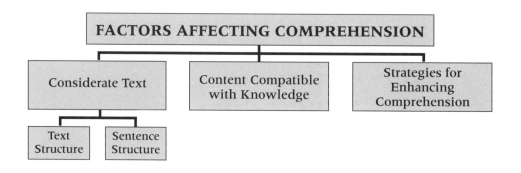

FACTORS AFFECTING COMPREHENSION

| Considerate Text | Content Compatible with Knowledge | Strategies for Enhancing Comprehension |

| Text Structure | Sentence Structure |

Most of you reading this book read so automatically that you never think about it. When you glance at advertisements on the highway, scan a phone directory, or skim a newspaper, you process information as routinely as you process oral language. When you face more difficult reading tasks — like reading a dense, expository text on an unfamiliar subject — you undoubtedly have a variety of skills at your disposal. Headings cue you about major divisions of the article or chapter. You have all kinds of knowledge about how texts are organized: if you see "In the first place. . .," you expect that, later in the text, there will be other related points. When you do not recognize a word, you can often figure out the meaning from the context; you know, for example, what a definition looks like. You know when you don't understand, and can take appropriate action — like rereading a sentence or a paragraph.

Experienced readers — university graduates, for example — take such knowledge for granted. They have acquired it over time, sometimes through instruction, but usually unconsciously, through experience. They are often unaware of the knowledge and skills they have developed and can easily assume that everyone reads the way they do.

But this is not the case. Inexperienced readers — many of those in high school classrooms and even some in college or university — lack the kinds of skills described above. They do not know how texts are structured; they do not realize they can figure out word meanings from context; sometimes they do not recognize definitions when they see them; they are not always aware when they do not understand, and if they are, they often lack strategies that can help them. For them, reading is a matter of starting with the first word and pressing on to the end of the passage. If they understand, well and good; if they do not, they do not know how to remedy the situation.

The purpose of this chapter is to describe the reading process. First, different models of reading are described. The second major section discusses factors that affect comprehension.

WHAT IS READING?

One problem in defining reading is that the term is used for a variety of very different activities. Reading the daily Ann Landers column is different from reading a text in an unfamiliar academic discipline. Reading a poem is different from reading a recipe, and scanning newspaper headlines is different again. Decades ago I learned French in high school; I can no longer understand much French because I have forgotten most of my French vocabulary, but I retain my knowledge of French pronunciation and can still read aloud with reasonable accuracy. If I read aloud a French text that I do not understand, can I be said to be reading? I can **decode** French text, that is to say, I can translate written symbols into words, but I cannot **comprehend** most French texts because my knowledge of French vocabulary and grammar is very limited. Any useful definition of reading must involve both decoding and comprehension. Comprehension cannot occur without decoding, but it involves much more than decoding; decoding is necessary but not sufficient for comprehension.

DESCRIPTIONS OF THE READING PROCESS

There is a variety of approaches in describing the reading process. One approach describes reading as a sequential process that begins with letter recognition. The reader sequentially perceives and identifies letters, words, and longer language segments. Comprehension is cumulative, built up bit by bit, a word at a time and then a sentence at a time. This kind of approach is described as **bottom-up** or **data-driven** (e.g., Gough, 1972; LaBerge and Samuels, 1974).

Another kind of approach describes reading as a **top-down** or **concept-driven** process. Top-down analyses emphasize that readers' conceptual knowledge causes them to have expectations about what the next word will be or what the text is likely to be about. Consider, for example, the following sentence:

Janet went to the library to borrow a …

The reader's world knowledge creates a strong presumption that the next word will be *book*. The hypothesis that the word will be book is confirmed as soon as the reader sees the letter *b*. Word recognition, then, does not always require letter-by-letter processing. Indeed, the following symbol, *event* is "recognized" in one way in the first sentence and another way in the second:

Harriet event to the store.
The event occurred at noon.

Recognition of the word was achieved not through letter-by-letter processing of the word but by other cues in the sentence. Indeed, proficient readers engage in letter-by-letter processing only when they come across unfamiliar words.

Current views of reading consider it to be an **interactive** process (Rummelhart, 1977). Bottom-up and top-down processes both contribute. The process is interactive and reciprocal rather than strictly sequential. That is to say, reading is a thinking process during which readers actively construct meaning using the text, background knowledge, and context. Reading is not to be thought of as the use of a set of skills to extract meaning from the printed page. Meaning is not on the page; meaning is in the reader's head. Meaning is constructed by readers who use various kinds of knowledge and information in order to comprehend.

THE READER'S KNOWLEDGE

One kind of knowledge used by readers is a knowledge of sound-letter correspondences. They need to know, for example, that *b* stands for the first sound in the word *bat*. Sometimes reading is understood as being primarily a matter of translating from written symbols to aural symbols. However, reading involves much more than such decoding. Proficient readers spend little cognitive energy on decoding. They do not need to look at words letter by letter or at sentences word by word. Indeed, on a first glance at the following, many readers fail to note the error precisely because they do not need to read word by word

A second kind of knowledge readers use is knowledge about texts. They have knowledge about sentence structure (syntactic knowledge) and knowledge about the way texts are structured.

When they read the subject of a sentence, their knowledge of sentence structure tells them to expect a finite verb. They may not know that the main verb in a clause is called a finite verb, but they certainly know if a clause does not have a finite verb when it is needed. At the end of the next sentence, proficient readers have a "Huh?" reaction:

> Informed guessing means by making the best use of nonvisual information, of what one already knows.

They assume they have misread, and go back to the beginning of the sentence to take a second run at it. Their knowledge of sentence structure leads them to expect a finite verb that is not there in this mal-formed sentence.

Sometimes difficult syntax contributes substantially to text difficulty. Certain syntactic constructions are difficult for well defined reasons. Some of these constructions are common in certain kinds of school texts.

Readers' knowledge about texts includes not only knowledge of sentence structure, but also knowledge about how various kinds of discourse are structured. Proficient readers know that headings and sub-headings can give the reader an overview of the content of an article or chapter. They know that if they read: "There were several major causes of World War I," the author is probably about to embark on a sequential discussion of the various causes of the war. Such knowledge of text structure plays an important role in helping the reader to predict what will come next.

The third kind of knowledge used by readers is their knowledge of the world, the background knowledge they bring with them to any text they read. Such knowledge plays a crucial role in meaning construction. If readers have little knowledge of the subject matter of a text, the task of reading the text is more difficult.

Knowledge is not stored in memory as a list of discrete items. It is organized into complex, interconnected structures. Organized knowledge structures are known as **schemata** (or **schemas**). We have schemata for objects (e.g., a schema for face, for school, for car), for events such as a hockey game, for situations like being in love. A schema is a large, densely interconnected network of information that has been constructed by an individual over time as a result of experience. For example, a term such as car would at first be a label for a single particular car. But over time, after experiences with many cars of different kinds, an individual abstracts and generalizes the common properties and relationships of cars. Eventually, knowledge about an object such as a car is organized into a semantic map or knowledge structure, as depicted in Figure 7.1.

The figure shows that a car has such properties or parts as an engine, a body, upholstery, wheels. Examples of cars are sedan, sports coupe, station wagon. Cars are related to trucks, buses, tractors, and motor cycles for which the individual also has schemata. A car is an example of a more abstract concept such as a motor vehicle which, in turn, is an example of the more general concept of a vehicle.

The semantic map, then, represents a hierarchical organization of information about a concept within long-term memory. At upper levels (e.g., vehicle), schemata are more abstract and inclusive; at lower levels (e.g., sports coupe) schemata are more particular and less inclusive. When an individual hears or reads the word *car*, the schema for car is activated and all the diverse, interconnected information stored in memory is available.

Researchers have illustrated the crucial role played by schema activization in comprehending text. Anderson, Reynolds, Schallert and Geotz (1977, p. 372) used the following text in an interesting experiment:

> Every Saturday night, four good friends get together. When Jerry, Mike, and Pat arrived, Karen was sitting in her living room writing some notes. She quickly gathered the cards and stood up to greet her friends at the door. They followed her into the living room but as usual they couldn't agree on exactly what to play. Jerry eventually took a stand and set things up. Finally, they began to play. Karen's recorder filled the room with soft and pleasant music. Early in the evening, Mike noticed Pat's hand and the many diamonds. As the night progressed the tempo of play increased. Finally, a lull in the activities occurred. Taking advantage of this, Jerry pondered the arrangement in front of him. Mike interrupted Jerry's reverie and said, "Let's hear the score." They listened carefully and commented on their performance. When the comments were all heard, exhausted but happy, Karen's friends went home.

Figure 7.1
Knowledge Structure for a Car

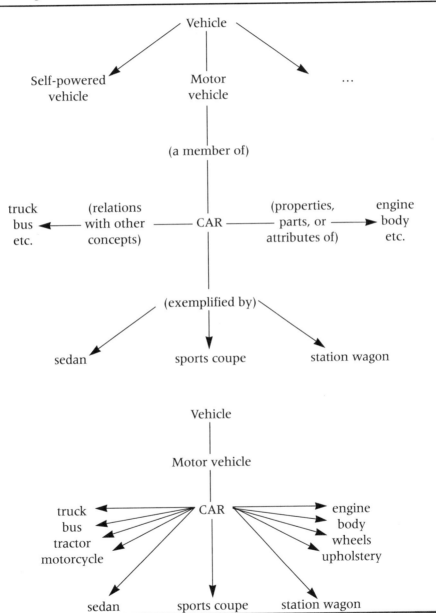

The above text is usually interpreted as a description of an evening of card playing; an alternate interpretation is that it describes a quartet of musicians engaging in a practice session. When the text was read by a class of thirty music education students, 70 percent of them made the practice-session interpretation; when the text was read by thirty students who were not music specialists, most of them made the card-game interpretation. In other words, the same text was understood differently depending on the particular schema that was activated.

THE INTERACTIVE NATURE OF THE READING PROCESS

Reading is an interactive process. Readers construct meaning using visual information from text and non-visual information which is stored in memory as a result of past experience. Meaning construction is a progressive activity. The first meaning constructed is likely to be partial. It is revised and filled out and sometimes changed as the reader reads, and as text and background knowledge interact. In the panel of sentences below (Trabasso, 1979, p.290), different meanings are constructed for "Mary had a little lamb" as different schemata are activated by succeeding sentences.

Mary had a little lamb. Its fleece was white as snow.

Mary had a little lamb. She spilled gravy and mint jelly on her dress.

Mary had a little lamb. The delivery was a difficult one, and afterwards the vet needed a drink.

In the following sentences (Sanford and Garrod, 1981, p.10), note how the first two trigger certain background knowledge and certain assumptions about the identity of John. Note, further, how successive meanings are constructed as information becomes available, progressively, in subsequent sentences.

John was on his way to school last Friday.

He was really worried about the math lesson.

Last week he had been unable to control the class.

It was unfair of the math teacher to leave him in charge.

After all, it is not a normal part of a janitor's duties.

Meaning construction occurs, progressively, as information in the text is interpreted in the light of the reader's knowledge.

Rereading of a text, in part or as a whole, also contributes to the construction of meaning. We perceive meanings in the second (or fifth) reading of a poem that eluded us in the first; after our second (or fifth) reading, the meaning we have constructed is richer and fuller than the meaning after the first reading. Points that were obscure in the first reading of a difficult chapter are more easily understood in a second reading when we bring to the text the richer knowledge base that has resulted from reading the chapter the first time. Successive meanings are constructed, then, as text is processed.

Factors Affecting Reading Comprehension

Given a reasonable degree of decoding ability, there are three main factors that affect reading comprehension: (1) the extent to which a text is "considerate"; (2) the extent to which text content is compatible with the reader's knowledge; and (3) the strategies used by the reader to enhance understanding and retention.

CONSIDERATE TEXT

A text is said to be considerate or reader-friendly (Armbruster, 1984) if it is written in such a way as to facilitate understanding. A number of factors contribute to the considerateness of a text, for example, familiar structure, clarity of presentation, coherence, and an acceptable level of syntactic difficulty. Two of these are discussed in detail, namely, text structure and sentence structure (or syntax).

Text Structure

Skilled readers have been likened to expert cab drivers (Horowitz, 1985). Cab drivers must know the layout of a city; they have an internalized mental map of main highways and side roads; they know how to read such cues as road signs and traffic lights.

In similar fashion, successful readers know how texts are patterned. They know about overall text design. They know how to determine the structure of individual chapters. They recognize the cues that tell them how smaller units of text such as paragraphs are structured.

Inexperienced readers, on the other hand, usually lack such knowledge. Most elementary students and many in high school can benefit from explicit instruction about the overall layout of texts and of chapters of texts — about the uses of tables of contents and indexes, and about chapter headings and subheadings. They also need to know how to recognize commonly used patterns and subpatterns used in structuring texts.

Patterns of text organization were discussed in some detail in Chapter 5. Some ways of organizing texts are easier to recognize and understand than others. The easiest patterns to recognize and follow are *temporal* (or chronological) order, and *attribution* (or listing). Other more difficult text patterns are *generalization, compare-contrast, cause-effect,* and *problem-solution.* Texts that have clear patterns of organization for chapters, subsections within a chapter, and paragraphs are easier to follow that those that are less clearly organized.

Sentence Structure

It is generally considered that long sentences are harder to process than shorter ones. There are a number of **readability formulae** that may be used to calculate the grade level of a text (e.g., Fry, 1977). Such formulae are based on two factors: a word-difficulty factor and a sentence-length factor.

However, length is only a rough measure of difficulty of sentence structure. Versions of text with shorter sentences are not always easier to understand. For example, 9-year-olds were asked to read sentences like the following:

John slept all day. He was lazy.

John slept all day because he was lazy.

They found the longer version easier to understand because the relationship between the two clauses is spelled out (Pearson, 1975).

In estimating readability, sentence length is one rough measure that may be used. As noted in Chapter 2, the sentences of written texts tend to be long, syntactically complex, and loaded with meaning — factors that tend to add to processing difficulty. In addition, however, it is important to note that some sentence structures are inherently difficult. Perera (1984) lists sixteen such constructions. Some of the most difficult sentence structures that occur commonly in school texts were discussed with illustrative examples in Chapter 5, namely, long noun phrases (especially in subject position), interrupting constructions, nominalizations, and ellipsis.

Writers of texts and teachers who prepare classroom materials can sometimes simplify sentence structure to some extent. Teachers working on textbook-selection committees can avoid selecting texts with excessively complex sentence structure. Nonetheless, school texts are bound to have a considerable number of sentences with complex structure. Many students will need help learning to process such material.

CONTENT COMPATIBLE WITH THE READER'S KNOWLEDGE

A book will have many readers all of whom will have their own individual knowledge bases. It is not possible, then, for a writer to accommodate all possible readers. Writers of school text books need to have in mind the likely level of knowledge of readers of a given age or grade level, and, when they write, they need to make links with likely stores of pre-existing knowledge. Teachers who introduce and use texts in the classroom can facilitate the use of background knowledge (See earlier section). They must also be aware that the limited knowledge base of many students will make a text difficult for them to understand. Teachers therefore need to give assistance with the reading of the text. Some suggestions for teaching strategies are given in the next chapter.

STRATEGIES FOR ENHANCING COMPREHENSION

Expert readers process text fairly automatically until something triggers their awareness that there has been a failure to comprehend. When there is a problem in understanding, proficient readers switch from the smooth-flowing "automatic" mode to a much slower processing mode. They allocate extra time and energy to resolving the problem. Expert readers have a variety of active strategies they can use to help them deal with comprehension failure.

A strategy may be as simple as rereading a sentence or a section. It may be as elaborate as constructing a detailed scenario to explain incompatible or problematic information. Many strategies are used by proficient readers. They hypothesize about the likely content of a text or segment; they question and elaborate both text content and their own knowledge; they compare their prior knowledge with information presented in the text; they think of counter examples and make additional applications; they summarize (Palincsar and Brown, 1984).

Palincsar and Brown (1984, p. 120) suggest that there are six major functions performed by proficient readers as they process demanding text:

- understanding the purposes of reading;

- activating relevant background knowledge;

- allocating attention so that concentration can be focused on major content at the expense of trivia;

- critical evaluation of content for internal consistency, and compatibility with prior knowledge;

- monitoring comprehension by periodic review and self-interrogation; and

- drawing and testing inferences of many kinds, including interpretations, predictions, and conclusions.

Proficient readers are guided in their reading by their **metacognitive knowledge**. They are able to assess the state of their understanding as they read and are able to take appropriate action if they do not comprehend.

In recent years, researchers have examined the mental processes of readers asking them to "think aloud" as they read. Transcripts of think-aloud sessions provide insight into the kind of thinking that goes on during demanding reading tasks. You may gain useful insight into the demands of reading texts in your subject area by listening to a fellow student doing a reading think-aloud. Business education majors listening to an English major do a think-aloud of a business education text were astonished to note that she did not refer to a graph presented in the text. (Indeed, she commented that she rarely consulted such graphic material to help her understand text — a comment that astonished her business education peers.) To listen to a competent reader reading in an unfamiliar area will give some understanding of the degree of processing and the kinds of skills required by the much less proficient readers who sit in high school classes.

Conclusion

Reading involves much more than the ability to decode print. It is a process during which a reader with certain kinds of knowledge interacts with a text and constructs a meaning that is, to some extent, an individual meaning. Reading tasks vary from very simple to very complex. The degree of difficulty of a reading task depends on a variety of factors having to do with both the text and the reader.

Readers deal with texts more or less easily depending on their background knowledge. Texts are said to be considerate if they are well structured and clearly written, if the sentence structure is not unduly complex, and if the conceptual burden is not unduly heavy for the intended readers. Proficient readers can comprehend even very demanding texts because they can call on a variety of thinking skills to help them deal with difficult passages.

Even well-written texts will be difficult for many students. Texts commonly deal with concepts that are unfamiliar to students; they use text structures like cause/effect, problem/solution, compare/contrast that tend to be difficult to recognize; and they use demanding syntactic structures. Most students will need help in order to use texts productively.

It is important for readers to know when they do not understand so that they can take remedial action. Unskilled readers often lack this kind of metacognitive awareness. They do not know what it is that they do not understand. They do not realize that failures to understand are common, even for the most experienced of readers. And they are unaware of the strategies that could help them. Some useful strategies to help students deal with the demands of printed text are described in the next chapter.

EXERCISES

1. Work with five or six people interested in a particular content area. Select a short text from the chosen content area and ask a friend who is not a specialist in the content area to do a reading think-aloud of the text. A suitable text should be difficult enough to require some processing but not so difficult as to be incomprehensible. A physics major, for example, might do a think-aloud while reading a poem; or an English major might read a book review from a science journal. The reader reads aloud stopping after every paragraph (or more frequently) to comment on what is being read. Observers should make a note of thinking strategies revealed by the think-aloud procedure. Look for such activities as:

    *   questioning

    *   predicting or hypothesizing

    *   calling on background knowledge

    *   evaluating

    *   summarizing

    After the reading, discuss: What did your reader do to make sense of difficult passages? What did you learn about reading from your observations?

2. Select a chapter from a text in a content area you teach.

    *   Identify the pattern of organization of the chapter as a whole.

    *   Identify the pattern (or subpatterns) used in each subsection of the chapter.

    *   When you have identified text structures in the chapter, prepare a visual representation of the chapter. You will probably need more than one visual—one for the chapter as a whole, and one for each subsection of the chapter.

    If you and a colleague work, independently, on the same chapter, you will find it useful to compare your visual representations.

3. The excerpt below presents the introductory section of a chapter from a history text followed by a list of the subheadings of the chapter.

    •   Scan the subheadings and decide what pattern of organization has been used.

    •   Read only the first two paragraphs of the introduction. Now predict what kind of structure is likely to follow in the rest of the introduction.

    •   The third paragraph of the introductory section starts with "One clear answer is..." This phrase flags the fact that the writer is giving an answer to his question. Skim the opening sentences in the remainder of the introduction and underline any word or phrase that flags the fact that another cause of the war is to be discussed.

    •   Read the introductory section beginning with paragraph 3, and

        i.   list the causes of the war;

        ii. make a note of anything about the text that causes you difficulty in comprehending.

THE SECOND WORLD WAR

When the Second World War began on 1 September 1939, Germany had already expanded to take in Austria and the whole of Czechoslovakia and she had reached an agreement with Russia by which she would share Poland with her. By 1942 German control reached from the Pyrenees to the towns of Leningrad, Moscow and Stalingrad and in the Far East Japan had destroyed the traditional empires of France, Holland and Britain; the whole pattern of the world had changed.

The German war which merged with the Japanese war did not arise from a German plan to create a world war. Initially the situation resembled that of 1914 in that a local war became a European war — the parallel was clear even in the German hope that Britain would stay neutral when she attacked Poland. Again there was a similarity in that to the outsider it would seem that Germany dominated the Continent in 1939 just as she had in 1914 and there was no clear need to fight a war to establish that dominance. Why then did the war come?

One clear answer is that the system of collective security based on the League of Nations had long since broken down. No effective action had been taken against Italy buccaneering in Ethiopia and against Japanese aggression in China. Hitler's technique of threat by propaganda, by a continually shifting series of demands, by the use of armour stationed on uncooperative frontiers had won for German a series of bloodless victories against Austria and Czechoslovakia. The German advance was made partly with the connivance of Western powers, like Britain, with a strongly developed sense of guilt about the 'injustices' of Versailles and a sneaking hope that Germany might be deflected to attack the Soviet Union, still seen as a potential political threat to the security of all Western states.

Anglo-French hopes for a permanent settlement with Hitler had been destroyed by the events of March 1939 when a Czechoslovakia, partly truncated by the Munich agreement of September 1938, was finally swallowed up by Germany. Hitler called the Czech President Hacha to his headquarters in the Bavarian mountains at Berchtesgaden, the Eagle's Eyrie, and threatened to order the immediate aerial bombardment of Prague, the Czech capital, unless Hacha signed a document calling on Germany for protection. Under this terrible threat President Hacha signed. Czechoslovakia was invaded and this new and hopeful state was taken over by Germany. From this point onwards Britain guaranteed states such as Poland, which looked as if they might be next on the German list and in this way Britain and France put themselves astride Hitler's path.

One other answer that might be made recalls 1914. To Hitler Britain was no immediate threat and it seemed unbelievable that she should want to go to war. Therefore if Britain was prepared to leave the rearrangement of the map of Europe to Germany, Germany on her side would guarantee the British empire. As the Germans saw it, there was no genuine clash of interests and this might be a sensible division of power. Britain's unwillingness to accept the rightness of Germany's role on the continent of Europe might be seen as a cause of the war.

Perhaps the fundamental answer to this question, 'why war in 1939', turns upon the nature of the Hitler regime. The tradition of militarism which marked Germany in former times was revived and the whole population in some sense was under arms. War had become the temper of the nation. Hitler as Leader (*Fuehrer*, a title made by merging the office of chancellor and president) in his semi-military uniform, his readiness to talk in warlike terms, his determination to unite all Germans in the Reich, even Germans in Danzig, the independent city established by the Treaty of Versailles; Hitler's aggressive policies can be seen as the root cause of the war.

And yet the question can be answered in a completely different way. It may be argued that the war was made inevitable by the signing of the Russo-German pact in August 1939 which protected Germany against a two-front war ... (I)n August Ribbentrop, the Nazi Foreign Minister, flew to Moscow and reached agreement with Russia which included a plan to divide conquered Poland between them. The Russo-German pact freed Hitler to deal with the Poles ...

As a warning to Hitler, Chamberlain, the British Prime Minister, had in March 1939 guaranteed help to Poland if she were attacked and soon after the same arrangements were made for Greece and Rumania. Without the help of the Red Army, the only large army in East Europe capable of holding the Germans, such guarantees were no more than futile propaganda gestures. British distrust of Russia made this impossible and therefore her Polish policy inept.

In Hitler's view the Russo-German pact had spiked the British guns and he fully expected that Britain would take the only reasonable course and remain neutral. Although his final plan for an attack on Poland was postponed in the hope that Britain would realise her true interests, he finally launched the attack on 1 September, claiming that Poles had first attacked, on the day before ...

On 3 September Britain, and then France, declared war on Germany ...

GERMAN CONQUESTS IN EUROPE

THE GERMAN INVASION OF RUSSIA

THE WAR IN THE MEDITERRANEAN

THE JAPANESE ATTACK

D-DAY AND THE DEFEAT OF GERMANY

THE WAR AGAINST JAPAN

Source: H. Browne (1970), *World History II: 1900-1965*, (New York: Cambridge University Press), pp. 108-110.

REFERENCES

Armbruster, B.B. (1984). The problems of "inconsiderate text." In G.G. Duffy, L.R. Roehler, and J. Mason (eds.), *Comprehension Instruction: Perspectives and Suggestions* (pp. 202-217). New York: Longman.

Anderson, R.C., R.E. Reynolds, D.L. Schallert and E.T. Goetz (1977). Frameworks for comprehending discourse. *American Educational Research Journal*, 14, 367-381.

Fry, E.B. (1977). Fry's readability graph: Clarifications, validity, and extension to level 17. *Journal of Reading*, 21, 242-252.

Gough, P.B. (1972). One second of reading. In J.F. Kavanagh and I.G. Mattingly (eds.), *Language by Ear and by Eye* (pp. 331-358). Cambridge, MA: MIT Press.

Horowitz, R. (1985). Text patterns: Part 1. *Journal of Reading*, 28, 448-454.

LaBerge, D., and S.J. Samuels (1974). Towards a theory of automatic information processing in reading. *Cognitive Psychology*, 5, 293-323.

Palincsar, A. S., and A.L. Brown (1984). Reciprocal teaching of comprehension-fostering and comprehension-monitoring activities. *Cognition and Instruction*, 1, 117-175.

Pearson, D. (1975) The effects of grammatical complexity on children's comprehension, recall and conception of certain semantic relations. *Reading Research Quarterly*, 10, 155-192.

Perera, K. (1984). *Children's Writing and Reading: Analysing Classroom Language*. Oxford, England: Basil Blackwell.

Rummelhart, D.E. (1977). Toward an interactive model of reading. In S. Dornic (ed.), *Attention and Performance VI* (pp. 573-603). Hillsdale, NJ: Erlbaum.

Sanford, A.J., and S.C. Garrod (1981). *Understanding Written Language*. New York: Wiley.

Trabasso, T. (1979). Reflections on reading about reading. In L.B. Resnick and P.A. Weaver (eds.), *Theory and Practice of Early Reading* (Vol. 2, pp. 271-284). Hillsdale, NJ: Erlbaum.

Chapter 8
STRATEGIES FOR TEACHING READING IN CONTENT AREAS

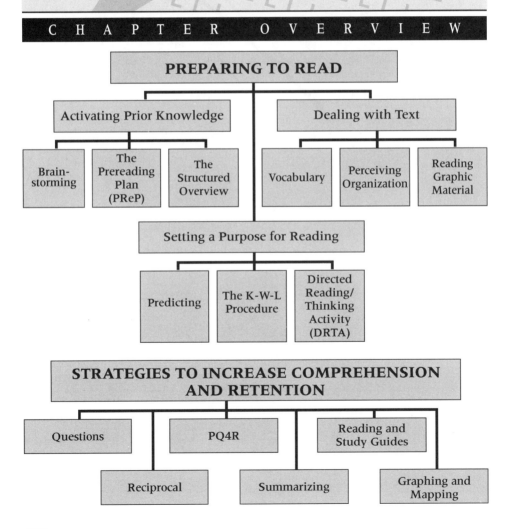

PREPARING TO READ

Activating Prior Knowledge

Dealing with Text

Brain-storming

The Prereading Plan (PReP)

The Structured Overview

Vocabulary

Perceiving Organization

Reading Graphic Material

Setting a Purpose for Reading

Predicting

The K-W-L Procedure

Directed Reading/Thinking Activity (DRTA)

STRATEGIES TO INCREASE COMPREHENSION AND RETENTION

Questions

PQ4R

Reading and Study Guides

Reciprocal

Summarizing

Graphing and Mapping

Reading is an important means of coming to know. You would expect it to be an important activity in content area classes. However, reading plays a minor role in many content classes. Teachers often rely on lecturing as the principal means of getting information across to their students and make little use of the assigned text. Even when reading from texts is assigned, it is not always usefully integrated with other learning activities. Teachers do not always assign a purpose for reading but merely indicate the number of pages to be read. Often, there is little in-class discussion of the reading. It is not uncommon for tests to be based on lectures and discussion but not on readings, even though readings have been assigned.

Reading can and should play an important role in content area learning. In order for that to happen, teachers need to be able to do two things: integrate reading into their teaching plans; and help students cope with the demanding task of reading content area texts. This chapter presents a variety of strategies that will help you to use reading productively in your content area classes. The strategies will help students to engage in the kinds of thinking that proficient readers engage in. Some of the strategies are aimed at promoting particular kinds of thinking like questioning, predicting or evaluating. Others are aimed at helping students to understand more about the ways texts are organized. Many involve a high level of teacher-student and student-student interaction. All are aimed at encouraging active engagement with the text.

As noted in the last chapter, proficient readers perform the following functions as they process demanding text: they have clear purposes in reading; they access relevant background knowledge; they concentrate on major content rather than on trivial details; they critically evaluate content; they monitor their comprehension by periodic review and self-interrogation; and they draw and test inferences (Palincsar and Brown, 1984). Each of the strategies described below is designed to engage students in one or more of these functions. The ultimate goal of reading instruction is to enable students to read and to learn from reading without teacher assistance. This means that they need to develop metacognitive awareness. They need to learn to monitor their understanding of what they read, and to regulate their reading behaviour in the light of their understanding.

For convenience, the activities are categorized as (a) prereading activities that prepare for reading, and (b) activities designed to increase understanding and retention of material by encouraging processing of text during the first and subsequent readings. These activities will help your students to read specific texts with greater understanding. Remember, however, that your ultimate goal is not merely to help them to read a specific text with understanding, but to help them to learn to use the kinds of strategies that expert readers use.

PREPARING TO READ

Reading should not be assigned without preparing students to engage productively with the text. Three important purposes of preparatory activities are: (a) activating relevant prior knowledge; (b) helping students to set purposes for reading; and (c) helping students recognize the way the text is structured. Prereading activities will usually serve one or more of these three purposes.

ACTIVATING PRIOR KNOWLEDGE

Prior knowledge consists of conceptual knowledge, vocabulary, and experiences. Background knowledge is crucial to comprehension. Ausubel wrote in 1968 (p. vi): "The most important single factor influencing learning is what the learner already knows. Ascertain this and teach him accordingly." Comprehending text involves making connections between what we already know and new information in the text. We understand and remember more of what we read when we have a rich store of background knowledge. High school students learning Spanish were tested on their comprehension of a text describing a baseball game. The researchers found that the students' background knowledge of the game was more important in determining their comprehension than was their ability in Spanish (Levine and Hause, 1985).

In some cases students may not know enough about a topic to enable them to read with understanding. In such cases, you may need to give them direct instruction about relevant concepts before they attempt to read the text. In some cases, students may have incorrect beliefs that will cause them to misunderstand or misinterpret the text. It is important for you to be aware of inaccuracies in background knowledge that may interfere with comprehension. Sometimes students may fail to make connections between their knowledge or experience and the topic of the reading. Prereading activities can help them to make important connections. The following are some useful strategies that teachers at all levels and in all subject areas may use to trigger prior knowledge.

Brainstorming

Before reading, students are asked to list everything they know about the topic. Brainstorming may be done by individuals, by groups, or by the whole class. If lists are made by individuals, they may then be encouraged to compare lists with one or two classmates. Comparing lists in this way should increase prior knowledge because it leads to sharing information and discussing differences in the information listed by different people. Note, especially, the usefulness of such writing and sharing for ESL students for whom these activities not only serve to call up relevant knowledge but also introduce them to some of the vocabulary they are likely to meet in the reading.

When a list has been made — either by individuals or by the class as a whole — students read the assigned selection. They are told to mark with a check the items on their list that are confirmed by the author; to mark with an *x* the items on the list not mentioned by the author; and to mark with a question mark items on the list about which the author gives information different from what they have listed.

This simple procedure can be used at any grade level and serves several useful purposes. It prompts students to activate background knowledge, prior experiences, and vocabulary related to the topic of the reading. It sets a purpose for reading and focuses attention. It raises questions for possible further study if information suggested by the students is not mentioned in the reading. If the activity includes small-group discussion, it promotes vocabulary development.

The Prereading Plan (PReP)

The prereading plan (Langer, 1981) is designed both to activate students' prior knowledge about key concepts and to allow the teacher to assess the level of student knowledge about those concepts. It involves both brainstorming and group discussion. The procedure has three phases.

The first phase involves students in making *initial associations*. The teacher decides on a key concept in the reading and selects a word, phrase, or picture to present to the class to start discussion of the topic. To begin the discussion, the teacher asks, "What do you think of when you hear or see the word, phrase, or picture …?" Students may answer orally or, better, they may answer in a free writing exercise and then share answers orally.

The second phase is designed to encourage students to *reflect on initial associations*. The teacher prompts reflection with such questions as, "What made you think of that?" During this phase, students interact in small groups and extend their background knowledge as they listen to and comment on the explanations of others. During this phase they may weigh, reject, accept, revise, and integrate ideas that are shared by group members.

The purpose of the third phase is to encourage students to *reformulate their knowledge* of the topic by responding to the question, "Based on your discussion, have you any new ideas about …?" Responses in the third phase often reveal a higher level of understanding than initial responses.

This procedure has several values. Students not only call up prior knowledge but explore and develop their conceptual knowledge in interaction with their peers. Oral exchanges allow vocabulary development. A further value is that the teacher is able to assess the level of students' knowledge and the language they use to express that knowledge. High-level responses are indicated, for example, by analogies and definitions; these responses indicate "much" knowledge. Responses that give examples and attributes indicate "some" knowledge. Low-level associations with parts of words or sound-alike words indicate "little" knowledge. Having assessed students' knowledge level, the teacher is able to plan instruction. Plans may differ for different groups of students depending on their level of prior knowledge. He may, for example, assign appropriate reading material for those with much or some knowledge. Those with little knowledge, however, may need instruction in relevant concepts prior to reading. Like brainstorming procedures described above, this procedure can be used at any grade level.

The Structured Overview

The structured overview (also known as the graphic organizer) is a graphic representation of concepts arranged in a hierarchy. This kind of presentation shows relationships among concepts. Thelen (1982) describes how structured overviews may be used in a systematic procedure for activating background knowledge, for developing aspects of relevant background knowledge that may be lacking, and for integrating background knowledge with new content. The activities associated with the structured overview are valuable also for developing vocabulary related to the concept to be studied. The procedure is as follows:

1. Prior to instruction, the teacher identifies and defines the concept to be taught (for example, mammals) and develops a hierarchy that includes the target concept. See the sample hierarchy in Figure 8.1 and note, in particular, that the hierarchy includes various levels of superordinate categories, categories that are coordinate with mammals (i.e., *birds, fish*, and *amphibians*), and categories that are subordinate to mammals (i.e., *bovines, canines,* etc.).

2. At the beginning of the class, the teacher names the target concept and invites students, working in small groups, to list all the examples they can think of.

3. Students read their lists and the teacher writes the examples on the board, organizing them into categories as she writes. If students suggest non-examples like the names of birds, for example, these are written under the slot that will later be labelled as *birds.*

4. After writing students' suggestions into the overview, the teacher completes the hierarchy as prepared ahead of time and explains the meanings of the terms.

5. The teacher guides students in discovering the characteristics that are common to all examples of the target concept. These are the *relevant attributes.* The teacher may clear up any misconceptions that become evident. Students might think, for example, that legs are a relevant attribute of mammals.

Figure 8.1
Hierarchy of Target Concept *mammals*

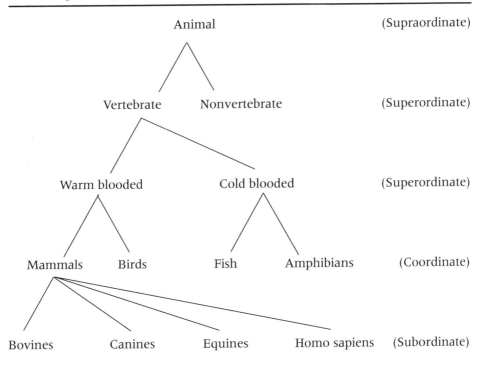

Animal	(Supraordinate)
Vertebrate Nonvertebrate	(Superordinate)
Warm blooded Cold blooded	(Superordinate)
Mammals Birds Fish Amphibians	(Coordinate)
Bovines Canines Equines Homo sapiens	(Subordinate)

1. **Examples:**
    dogs
    horses
    kangaroos
    whales
    humans

3. **Irrelevant attributes:**
    size
    weight
    habitat
    food

2. **Relevant attributes:**
    have vertebrae
    suckle their young
    air-breathing
    fur/hair covered

4. **Non-examples:**
    frogs
    ostriches
    hawks
    sharks

Source: Adapted from Thelen (1982) pp. 546-547.

6. The teacher guides the students in finding differences among members of the target concept; these are the *irrelevant attributes*. Mammals, for example, differ in habitat and size.

Structured overviews, used in the ways suggested, serve to activate prior knowledge, to organize that knowledge, and to develop it further prior to reading. Students, having completed preparatory work of this kind, are well placed to integrate new material from the reading with what they already know. Structured overviews may be used for many purposes. See below for suggestions for use in vocabulary development and in reading guides.

SETTING A PURPOSE FOR READING

Purpose is important because our purposes direct and focus our attention. Much reading of texts in content classes lacks purpose. Students are told merely to read the chapter or to read so many pages, or students, picked at random, read aloud in turn while the rest of the class is supposed to follow along. Purposeless reading leads to eyes sliding automatically across the page while the mind takes off on a journey of its own. Most of us have experienced such mind wandering when instructed to read — for no particular purpose — the close-packed print of a history or science text, or have sat in mind-boggling boredom as classmates stumble through the paragraphs they have been called on to read aloud. Reading assignments should always have a clearly stated purpose.

Predicting

Predicting the likely content of a reading is a simple and useful strategy for activating prior knowledge and establishing purposes for reading. Predicting is a useful strategy no matter what kind of material is involved — a poem, a story, or a chapter in a content area text.

The simplest procedure is to ask students, first, to list all they can remember about a topic. Students are then asked to use their lists to predict what they think they will find out from reading the text. Reading should be followed by discussion of the extent to which their predictions were confirmed by the text, and what new information they learned.

The K-W-L Procedure

Ogle's (1986) K-W-L procedure is a more structured procedure for setting a purpose for reading. It involves brainstorming, predicting, and summarizing or reviewing. Before reading, the teacher engages students in brainstorming about a key concept in the chapter to be read — the "what we *know*" part of the procedure. During brainstorming, points of uncertainty or ambiguity lead to questions — "what we *want* to find out." The students now list on individual worksheets (see Figure 8.2) things they know and things they want to learn. The teacher then prompts students to identify the categories of information that they expect the article to contain. For example, if a sixth-grade class is about to read a chapter on Japan in a social studies text, the teacher might ask, "What key categories of information do you expect to find in the chapter?" Key categories might include geography, climate, system of government, and industries. The key categories identified are listed on their worksheets. Students now read the chapter and make notes under the "what we *learned*" heading. In class discussion after the reading is completed, the teacher and students summarize what has been learned, what questions remain unanswered, and what new questions have emerged. Either the prereading brainstorming or the after-reading discussion or both activities might be conducted in small groups prior to whole-class discussion. The procedure models for students many of the strategies used by expert readers — activating prior knowledge, setting a purpose, asking questions, summarizing.

Figure 8.2
K-W-L Strategy Sheet

What We Know	What We Want to Find Out	What We Learned

Categories of Information We Expect to Use:

A.
B.
C.
D.
E.
F.

Source: Adapted from: D. Ogle, "The K-W-L: A teaching model that develops active reading of expository text," *The Reading Teacher*, February, 1986, 364-70.

Directed Reading-Thinking Activity (DRTA)

The directed reading-thinking activity (Stauffer, 1975) is a more elaborated prediction procedure. It was developed specifically to encourage active prediction not only before beginning but also throughout the reading.

Prior to introducing the DRTA, the teacher breaks the text into segments. A segment should end at a natural break in the story plot or in the expository material. The teacher begins with the title. Students keep the rest of the text covered with a sheet of paper or large index card. The teacher asks two questions:

What do you think the story (chapter) is about?

What makes you think so?

After many answers are given and accepted by the teacher, students uncover and read to the end of the first segment. After reading, it will usually be obvious whether or not predictions have been confirmed. Sometimes it may be useful to discuss how they fared with their predictions. After each segment, the same two questions are asked: What do you think will happen next? What makes you think so? This procedure is successful with students at every level from kindergarten through adults, with native-English-speaking students, and with those for whom English is a second language. Used by a skilful teacher, it can lead to high involvement with the reading.

The procedure may also be used by students working in small groups. Predictions about each segment are written down by a recorder. Students then read the segment individually and discuss what predictions were confirmed.

DEALING WITH TEXT

Experienced readers can recognize and use features of texts to help them extract information efficiently. They recognize definitions when they see them. They know how to use context clues to help them understand unfamiliar words. They can extract information from graphic material. They can use the organization of the text to get an overview of the content. Many of these skills are beyond the awareness of inexperienced readers. Teachers need to help them learn how to deal with text by helping them with vocabulary, with the organization of texts, and with graphic material.

Vocabulary

Success in learning a content area subject is heavily dependent on the student's success in understanding and learning the terminology of the subject. Many disciplines are heavily loaded with specialized terminology. Inevitably, content area textbooks are also heavily loaded with terminology. The following excerpt from a high school biology text illustrates the kind of specialized vocabulary that students are likely to encounter:

> A sperm unites with the egg to form a diploid zygote. The zygote becomes the sporophyte plant. As the sporophyte develops, it receives nourishment from the gametophyte tissue. The sporophyte develops an enlarged capsule, or sporangium, on top of a long stalk ... Inside the ... sporangium, meiosis gives rise to haploid spores.

Specialized terminology can be avoided, to some extent, in texts intended for lower grades but cannot always be eliminated from secondary texts because it is essential to the discipline. Since difficult vocabulary cannot be eliminated, you need to help students deal with it. Students will acquire some familiarity with terms over time as they hear and read them, but direct instruction is more effective than such incidental learning. You need to provide two kinds of help with vocabulary: sometimes you will need to help with vocabulary so that students can manage a given reading; secondly, you need to help students develop skills that will help them figure out the meanings of unfamiliar words independently.

Students can be helped in the following specific ways: (a) to recognize and use typographical devices; (b) to recognize and use linguistic devices, that is, the syntactic and semantic clues that are provided in the text; and (c) to use word structure clues in figuring out word meanings.

Typographical Devices   Textbook writers commonly indicate key terms when they are first introduced by marking them typographically. The most common means used are **boldface** print, *italics,* and "quotation marks." The typographic device should be drawn to students' attention. It is not to be assumed that they will notice and understand the reason for the typographical marking without explanation. Having explained the typographical device, you may ask students to skim the reading selection to pick out the words that are typographically marked, thus drawing their attention to key words to note as they read.

Examine the textbook to make sure that the system used to indicate key terms is dependable and adequate. Key questions to ask are:

a.   What typographic system is used?

b.   Is it used consistently? Some texts use more than one kind of marking. Note the two different kinds of marking in the following sentences that occur in the same chapter of a text:
- The British in India had only recently completely stamped out the practice of 'suttee'— widows burning themselves alive on their husbands' funeral pyres.

- That feeling or 'consciousness' of sharing a common past and the closeness of speaking the same language makes people into nations. We call the feeling itself *nationalism*.

c.   Are there key terms that are not explained?

d.   Are there explanations that are incorrect, incomplete, or confusing? If so, what alternative explanations can you give?

Linguistic Devices   When a vocabulary item is marked typographically as a key term, some kind of definition or explanation is provided. Definitions come in many different linguistic forms. In addition to items that are marked typographically, other vocabulary items will often have context clues that help with the meaning of difficult words. You need to help your students to recognize the different linguistic forms in which definitions and explanations appear, and to use context clues in general.

Some common forms in which definitions appear are as follows:

a.   *Ornithology* is the study of birds.

b.   *Ornithology* — the study of birds— ...

c.   *Ornithology* (the study of birds) ...

d.   The study of birds is called *ornithology*.

e.   *Precipitation* refers to all forms of water that fall from the sky.

Students must be able to recognize definitions no matter what syntactic form is used. Definitions are fairly easy to recognize. They say, in some way or another, X = Y. This fact should be pointed out to students.

Context clues come in a variety of forms. Some commonly used clues to word meaning are as follows:

Synonym   The key word is linked with a synonym or with closely related words:

- Marco was held in high *esteem* and respect by all.

- He conducted himself with so much wisdom and *prudence* ... that his services became highly acceptable.

Contrast   The key word is contrasted with an antonym or phrase that is opposite in meaning:

- Before the summer she would alternate between kindness and *malice*, with periods of indifference.

- Coming into the world was a *hazardous* business. It was much safer to be born in Sweden than in Russia …

Direct Description or Explanation   The key word is illustrated by examples or explained by a restatement:

- The lake is huge and cold and blue and *treacherous*. It can sink freighters, drown people.

- This suggests *isolation*, the separateness of peoples and countries.

Sometimes, two or more clues are given. The following example contains both a synonym for the key word *implode* and a cause-effect explanation:

- I will burst inward. I've read in the *National Geographic* about deepsea diving and why you have to wear a thick metal suit or the invisible pressure of the heavy undersea water will crush you like mud in a fist, until you *implode*.

Note that, in this case, the synonym (*burst inward*) occurs several lines before the key word. Students need to learn that synonyms, antonyms, or explanations may either precede or follow the key word; they may be in the same sentence, in a preceding sentence, or in a following sentence. Many of them will not realize this unless you point it out.

Sometimes context clues are much more subtle than the above examples and require the reader to draw more inferences. Consider the following sentence:

- I don't have the energy to be frightened. I lie in the snow, watching her with *lethargy*, and with a sluggish curiosity.

Hints as to the meaning of *lethargy* are provided in *don't have the energy* and *sluggish* but not every reader will easily recognize such subtle clues.

Context clues vary from the direct statements of definitions to subtle hints in surrounding text that suggest rather than explaining. Instruction should aim at helping students make full use of all kinds of context clues.

Word Structure   Students need to learn to analyze the structure of words so that they can recognize prefixes, suffixes, and common root words that give hints about a word's meaning.

Perceiving Organization

Helping students to recognize and use the organization of a text includes both introductory activities that acquaint them with the structure of the text as a whole and prereading activities for a specific reading assignment.

Structure of the Text as a Whole   Students should be introduced to the organization of the text by examining the table of contents and by learning to use such aids as the index and the glossary. An examination of the table of contents can give a general overview of the contents of the text. Students may be referred to the table of contents again before beginning a chapter or a unit. Sometimes the table of contents shows the major subsections of a chapter. By referring to it, students can get a quick overview of the chapter.

You might ask students to look up a particular term or set of terms in the index. They might then find the various references to the term in the text, and determine in what chapters the particular term occurs. The search for uses of the term may also cause them to discover the first instance of the use of the term where it is typographically marked and defined. This is a useful way of introducing them to the system used in the text to mark key words typographically.

The Structure of a Chapter   Much can be learned about the content of a chapter or article by skimming the introduction, the conclusion or summary, and the subheadings. Students should be introduced to these procedures for two reasons. A "walk through" a chapter by skimming these critical parts establishes expectations and makes reading easier. Secondly, the ability to skim a chapter in this way is an invaluable skill for students to acquire for use when they are trying to locate relevant information when they are reading independently or collecting data for a personal research project. It is important for them to learn that they do not need to read a chapter, word for word, in order to find out whether it has information relevant to their particular research needs.

You may find the following procedure useful:

1.   Ask students to note the title of the chapter and to predict what will be in the chapter.

2.   Ask students to skim the introduction and then ask whether their predictions have been either confirmed or changed in any way.

3.   Ask students to read the summary of the chapter and then to suggest what the author's main points seem to be. Are these the same or different from what the introduction led them to expect?

4.   Point out the typographical form used for the first main heading in the chapter. Ask students to locate other headings of the same kind, for example, those headings printed in capitals. Write these on the board, leaving room between headings for subheadings to be added.

5.   Ask students to surmise what will be discussed in the first major section. After accepting predictions, point out the typographical form of subheadings within the first major section. Ask students to locate the subheadings of the

first major section. Add these to the outline on the board. Check to see whether predictions were confirmed by the subheadings.

6. Repeat step 5 for each major heading.

This procedure will acquaint students with the structure of the text and break the back of the reading of the chapter. The procedure may be abbreviated or elaborated. An abbreviated form might simply note title, major headings and subheadings. For an elaborated procedure, see the description of PQ4R below.

Reading Graphic Material

Textbooks contain graphic material of many kinds. Pictures, charts, tables, graphs, cartoons, diagrams, and maps are the most common kinds of graphics. Graphic aids are included because of their potential to aid learning. Students, however, often pay scant attention to graphic material unless directed to do so. In addition to drawing graphics to their attention, you will need to help them to "read" graphic material.

Graphic material is useful to all students. Even capable readers will benefit from instruction designed to help them understand and interpret graphic aids. Graphic material can be quite demanding. Graphs and tables are often used to present information succinctly. Unless students are able to interpret them, important information will be lost.

Graphic material can be especially useful to students who, for some reason, have difficulty processing text. Students whose mother tongue is other than English, for example, take many years to learn to deal with the demanding task of processing academic texts. Graphic aids can be of great benefit to them. They need to be helped to extract available information from graphic materials which usually place less of a burden on the *language* expertise of the reader. Non-native speakers are not the only students who may have difficulty processing text. In any average classroom there will be a range of reading abilities. Those at the lower end of the scale need to be able to take full advantage of graphic aids to compensate for difficulty with text.

It is useful to plan one or more lessons that deal specifically with reading and interpreting graphic material. Lessons may be given during the early days of the course as part of familiarization with the text. Special attention should be paid to graphic material in dealing with particular readings. It is useful to lead students in interpreting illustrative material as part of prereading activities.

Charts, graphs and tables present information in highly condensed form. Sometimes texts include questions to help students extract information from graphic material. If they do not, you will need to formulate questions to help students unpack the information available. Interpretation of graphic material may be included as part of a study guide (described below).

Maps are a particular form of visual aid frequently used in certain kinds of texts. Students need help in learning to read them. Summers (1965) suggests that the following are the elements that need to be drawn to students' attention when reading a map:

1. *The title* provides a brief, succinct introduction to the map and its features and should be read carefully.

2. *Legend or key*, usually found in a separate box on the map, indicates what the symbols on the map stand for, the scale of the map, and other data. A symbol may be a drawing, pattern, or colour used to indicate map facts.

3. *Direction* — Cardinal direction is either indicated, or able to be inferred in some way. The top of the map usually indicates North.

4. *The scale* of a map indicates what a unit of distance on the map is equal to on the earth itself. Scale enables you to tell how far something is or how big something is.

5. *Location* — Grid systems are used to locate places on maps. Grids section maps into smaller segments by use of horizontal or vertical lines. A specific location is indicated by a pair of coordinates, one for the vertical axis and one for the horizontal.

6. *Types of maps* — The major map types are land, elevation, climate, natural vegetation and water features, political, economic, and population. Each type provides a different kind of information about an area. Often, combinations of several types appear on one map.

Students need assistance in learning to attend to these various elements in order to learn how to extract information and draw conclusions from maps.

STRATEGIES TO INCREASE COMPREHENSION AND RETENTION

Prereading activities prepare students for reading by activating prior knowledge, setting a purpose, and sometimes by doing necessary vocabulary development. The strategies suggested in this section are designed to help students with the actual reading of the text. Some activities encourage *close reading* of the text, some encourage *selective reading* of the text, some encourage *rereading* of the text — reading initially for one purpose and, subsequently, for another purpose. Strategies selected to help students process materials during reading of the text will often build on the preparatory activities of the prereading stage.

Students need to read first to comprehend at the *literal level.* They cannot make applications and evaluations unless they first understand what the text says, literally. Some activities are aimed at helping students comprehend at the literal level.

Students need to be able to go beyond literal understanding. They need to be able to *interpret* and to *apply* what they read. Activities aimed at literal comprehension enable them to get the facts from the reading. Activities designed to promote interpretive reading ask them to search for the author's implicit or intended meaning. They must go beyond what the author says by making inferences and drawing conclusions. Activities aimed at application ask them to go beyond the information in the text; they may be asked to analyze, synthesize, apply, or evaluate.

Students learn and remember material best when they reformulate the material in some way (Langer and Applebee, 1987). Reformulation requires them to think about the material in ways that help retention. Many of the activities suggested in this section encourage students to reformulate.

Questions

Questions are useful for prompting the kind of thinking that will increase comprehension. Questions may be used before reading, during reading, or after reading. Several of the procedures described above under *Preparing to Read* have questioning strategies built into the procedure. When students are asked whether or not their predictions have been fulfilled, they are being asked to discuss what the segment just completed said and how that related to the predictions they had made. Indeed, any kind of predicting as a prereading activity will be followed by questions that ask students to match the content of what they read with the predictions they made prior to reading.

Questions to be answered *during* reading should be formulated to prompt comprehension at each of the three levels of comprehension: literal, interpretive, and applied.

Niles (1985) suggests that *process* questions should be asked during reading as well as questions that deal with the *content*. Whereas content questions focus on the information in the text, process questions encourage students to think about strategies used in reading. They are designed to develop independent, strategic readers by helping students to observe and understand how meaning-making goes on during reading. Process questions might focus on the clarity of the text by asking for any words of sections that did not make sense. They might focus on the structure of the text. Proficient readers constantly ask themselves process questions as they read. The following illustrate the kinds of questions that flash through the minds of experienced readers as they read. (Of course, the questions that flash through our minds are not fully developed, syntactically, as I have developed these!)

- Here is a key word marked in italics. Now where is the definition of the term. Let's see. Can I think of an example of that?

- It says "secondly" but where is the *first* point the writer is making.

- This heading is in upper and lower case. What other headings in this section are in upper and lower case? How are all they related?

- I can't understand how this paragraph fits in with what the author is saying. Let's see. I'll have to go back and check on her line of argument.

By questions such as these, proficient readers constantly check on their comprehension and use text features to help them construct meaning. Process questions encourage students to engage in similar thinking activities.

Questions asked after reading have two kinds of main purposes: to help students review and consolidate what they have learned; and to prompt them to apply what they have read by making connections between what they have read and what they know from their own experience and previous learning. After-reading questions should ask students to make inferences, connections, evaluations, to go beyond the facts as stated in the text.

The sections that follow describe a variety of procedures that will encourage students to interact with the text during reading or after completing the first reading.

PQ4R

The PQ4R procedure (Thomas and Robinson, 1977; 1982) was developed to improve the reading of chapter-length assignments when thorough understanding of the material is required. The six steps in the procedure are: *preview, question, read, reflect, recite,* and *review.*

Preview   In the preview step, students examine the title, read the introductory statement carefully, glance over the subheadings, tables, captions, etc., and read the summary carefully. The preview step thus activates prior knowledge and establishes expectations about the content of the chapter. Students should be encouraged to preview all non-fiction material that they read. It will help them to read better and faster.

Question   The preview step will often produce questions that students want to answer during reading. A useful strategy is to formulate questions by turning headings into questions. For example, the heading "Hitler's Rise to Power" might produce the questions: Who was Hitler? How did he rise to power? When did he rise to power? This strategy may be applied to various levels of headings in the chapter.

Read   Students now read the chapter or text segment carefully to find answers to their questions. For students who are learning the procedure, it may be wise for you to lead them through a section at a time.

When teaching the procedure, you should lead students through the remaining steps of the procedure (reflect, recite, and review), helping them to think about and review what they have read. The six-step procedure emphasizes the kinds of strategies that proficient readers use, and helps students come to understand more fully the kind of effort required to read difficult texts.

Reading and Study Guides

Reading and study guides are aids prepared by teachers to assist students to process difficult text. Study guides present students with a variety of tasks to complete as they read the assigned text. The tasks are designed to engage students in active processing of text in such a way as to improve comprehension.

The kinds of activities suggested in study guides are varied. A study guide will always ask questions. Questions at all three comprehension levels should be included — some requiring literal comprehension, some requiring inferences and interpretations, and some requiring students to apply the information in the text.

Sometimes a study guide may provide a structured overview with some slots left empty. Students are required to fill in the empty slots and, sometimes, to provide other information. Some study guides may invite students to work in small groups to complete them. Figure 8.3 provides an example of a study guide for math.

Reciprocal Teaching

Reciprocal teaching (Palincsar and Brown, 1984) is a method devised to help novice readers learn to use the kinds of strategies that expert readers use. It involves four concrete strategies, namely, questioning, clarifying, summarizing, and predicting. These four activities were chosen because they require participants to engage in the major strategies used by expert readers. Instruction and practice take place in small cooperative learning groups. The teacher serves as the expert. She models the four strategies and provides support and guidance to novice readers as they learn the procedures. This kind of guided assistance is referred to as "scaffolding." The expert (i.e., the teacher) provides as much support as is needed — but no more than is needed — while the novice readers are learning the skills that experts use. The procedure is as follows:

1.   The teacher assigns a segment of text to be read. All read silently.

Figure 8.3
Math Study Guide

Directions
There are several important details in this section of Chapter 5. As you read, answer the questions assigned to you. Sometimes the page, column and paragraph are given to help you identify the place of the answer.

•••   1.   Is a carpenter's straight line the same as a geometric straight line?
••   2.   How should a line be correctly labeled? (p. 111)
•   3.   What are parallel lines? (p. 112 #5)
•••• 4.   What are oblique perpendicular lines?
••   5.   Why is a chalk board considered a plane surface? (p. 11)
•   6.   Name 3 plane figures. (p. 117, col. II)
•••   7.   How many planes can be drawn through a line?
••   8.   Which of the figures below are simple closed figures? (p. 129)

•   9.   Name 3 polygons. (p. 117, col. II)
•   10.   What is another name for five, six, or eight sided figures? (p. 117, col. II)
••• 11.   What are adjacent vertices?
••   12.   C   B
                 X   E   Are ∠ AED and ∠ BEC vertical? Why? (p. 120)
          A   D
•   13.   Name parts of a circle. (p. 126 #3)
••   14.   A cube has how many faces, vertices, and edges? (p. 138)
••• 15.   A cone and a cylinder have the same height and the same base diameter.
           What is the ratio of the Volume of the cone to the V of the cylinder?

Directions
For the statments listed below do the work assigned your group.
•   Tell whether the statement is True or False.
••   If the statement is false, write it correctly.
•••   If the statement is false, give the reason why you think it is so.
a. When we tell the features of anything such as size, shape, or color we are analyzing.
b. The edge of a book or paper is best described by the word plane.
c. If we do not know how many things belong in a group or their likeness, we say this is a set.
d. A part of a circle is called a segment.
e. Two lines that cross are said to intersect.
f. If we say that two lines cross we say they are parallel.
g. We call a geometric surface with length, width but no depth a plane.
h. Two lines which are not in the same plane but will intersect or are parallel are skew lines.
i. Lines which have no fixed limit or amount are said to be infinite or unlimited.
j. Lines which run parallel to the equator are said to be horizontal.

Source: H.L. Herber, *Teaching Reading in Content Areas.* Englewood Cliffs, NJ: Prentice Hall, 1970.

2. The teacher asks a question that a teacher or test might ask about the segment; summarizes the content; clarifies any points of difficulty; and makes a prediction about the next segment. Interaction between the teacher and groups members is encouraged during these procedures.

3. The teacher now calls on a group member to act as teacher for the next segment. The student nominated as teacher asks a question for the group to answer. Students clarify any points of disagreement or misunderstanding. The acting teacher summarizes and nominates the next teacher.

4. The role of teacher rotates around the group.

Initially, the teacher takes major responsibility for instruction. It may take some time before students are able to engage proficiently in the four key activities. The teacher may, for example, have to concentrate on one activity at a time — questioning, for example — until group members learn how to do it. If students have trouble formulating a question, the teacher suggests that they start a question with *why* or *how*. She similarly supports them as they learn to summarize. As students are able to take more responsibility, the teacher gradually relinquishes control. When students become proficient, they work in pairs or groups of three, taking turns at the teacher role.

The reciprocal teaching procedure may be used for whole class instruction. Students are assigned approximately four paragraphs of text to read silently and compose two questions and a summary. After several segments have been read in this way, the teacher writes sample questions and summary responses on the board for each segment. Students now work in groups to discuss the various responses and decide on the best one. Reciprocal teaching has produced dramatic improvements in reading comprehension for students of varying abilities and ages.

Summarizing

Students comprehend and remember material better when they engage in active processing of the text. Activities that require them to reformulate material in the text are very likely to increase retention. One activity that requires reformulating is summarizing. Recent research has shown that summary writing helps students to understand and retain information (Kintsch and vanDijk, 1978; Brown, Campione, and Day, 1981; Brown, Day, and Jones; 1983; Langer and Applebee, 1987).

Summaries may be either formal or informal. An informal summary of what has been read is part of the third step in Ogle's (1986) K-W-L procedure described above. As a cooperative group activity, students recall what has been learned from the assigned reading. This informal summary is written on a class version of the strategy sheet (see Figure 8.2 above). The items listed might then be organized by the class or by small groups into a written summary or a graphic representation.

The writing of a formal summary is a fairly demanding task that most students find somewhat difficult. Readers must be able to recognize text structure. They must be able to differentiate between the points of major importance and unimportant details that should be omitted from a summary. They must be able to delete material that is important but redundant. They must be able to supply superordinate terms for a list of items (e.g., furniture for table, chairs, beds, etc.). Since summary writing is a valuable study tool, it is worth your while spending time to develop your students' ability in this area. Summary writing is discussed in greater detail in the chapter on writing to learn.

Graphing and Mapping

The content of text may be summarized graphically instead of in words. Graphic representations of information are referred to in a variety of ways: creative graphing (Fry, 1981), graphic organizers (Barron and Stone, 1974), concept maps, semantic maps. Both verbal summaries and graphic representations are valuable in that they require students to reorganize material presented in the text. Research indicates that reorganizing complex material is an effective learning strategy (Shimmerlik, 1978). A major benefit of graphing is that, like writing, it requires more thorough processing of textual material than reading alone. Deeper processing results in increased comprehension and retention.

A second benefit of graphing is that it is spatial rather than linear as writing is. Graphing is likely to appeal to some students who find verbal material difficult. It is an especially useful aid for those whose mother tongue is not English and who have not yet mastered the demands of academic prose. A third value of graphic representations is that they are readily recalled and thus provide a useful study aid when work is being reviewed.

Table 8.1 presents five different types of graphs (star, tree, chart, chain and sketch) along with relationships that are appropriately shown by each type of graph and examples from a variety of content areas. Tree graphs have been illustrated and discussed above under *Structured Overviews*. The star graph shown in Figure 8.4 contains a shower of stars illustrating material from a grade 6 science text. Figure 8.5 summarizes six paragraphs from an article in *Scientific American* by means of a chain graph and a sketch. Figure 8.6 shows graphics that may be used to represent various kinds of text structures (See Chapter 5 for a description of various text structures.)

The kinds of graphics illustrated are some of the ways that can be used to represent textual material. Once you get them started, your students may think of others. You might consider breaking a chapter or reading into several segments and assigning each segment to two different groups to graph. Groups should make an overhead of their graph and prepare to explain it to the class. By the time the class has seen — and discussed — two different illustrated

Table 8.1
Graphing Various Types of Conceptual Relationships

Graph type	Appropriate relationships for graph type	Examples			
		in the humanities	in the social sciences	in the life sciences	in the physical sciences
Star (for a concept)	Definitions Attributes Examples	Characteristics of cubism in art	Attributes of the demand curve in economics	Examples of echinoderms in biology	Attributes of sunspots in astronomy
Tree (for hierarchies)	Classification Pedigree Analysis Structure Attributes Examples	Family tree of Ming Dynasty in China	Organization of the White House staff	Parts of the alimentary canal	Classes of isotopes in chemistry
Chart planets (for similar concepts)	Compare and Contrast Attributes	Comparison of imagery in poems by Anne Sexton	Comparison of Viet Nam war to the 1988 war in the Persian Gulf	Comparison of endocrine glands	Comparison of of the solar system
Chain (for changes over time)	Process Sequence Cause/Effect Chronology	Plot sequence of a particular novel	Stages of Piaget's theory of cognitive development in children	Process of cell division	Geological development of coal
Sketch (for visualizing a description)	Physical structures Descriptions of places Space relations Concrete objects Visual images	Description of a stage set in a drama	Description of a complex apparatus for studying eye movements in reading	The structure of the epidermis and dermis, the two layers of skin	Description of layers of ice that form a glacier

Source: L.L. Johnson, "Learning across the curriculum with creative graphing." *Journal of Reading*, March 1989, 509-519.

Figure 8.4
Shower of Stars from a Selection on Matter from a Grade 6 Science Text

Some Common Properties of Matter

Impenetrability – matter cannot penetrate other matter

Inertia – matter stays still or in motion until a force is exerted

Mass – the amount of matter

Volume – the space matter takes up

Density – the amount of mass in a certain volume

Some Special Properties of Matter

Colour

Brittleness – causes matter to break apart when hit

Elasticity – makes matter keep its shape

Conductivity – allows heat to pass through the matter

Matter Is Made Of

Molecules – smallest bit with the properties of the matter

Atoms – the building blocks of molecules

Atoms are made up of protons, neutrons and electrons

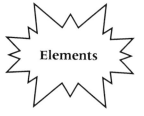

Elements

Made of only one kind of atom

More than 100 are known

Found in the air, in the ground, in water

Examples: oxygen, silver, mercury, chlorine

Symbols stand for elements, e.g., O for oxygen

Figure 8.5
Combination Sketch and Chain of Four Paragraphs
from a Magazine Article on a Thermonuclear Weapon

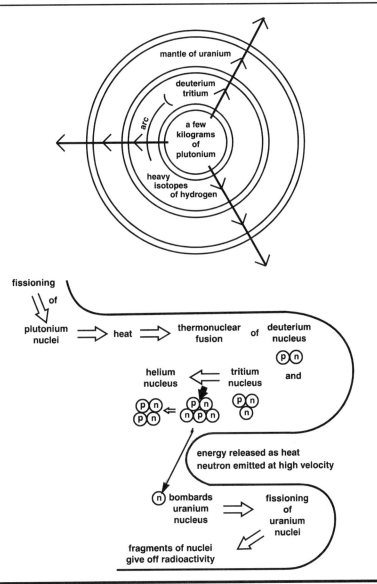

Source: L. L. Johnson, "Learning across the curriculum with creative graphing," *Journal of Reading,*
March 1989, 509-519.

Figure 8.6
Graphic Organizers for Common Text Structures

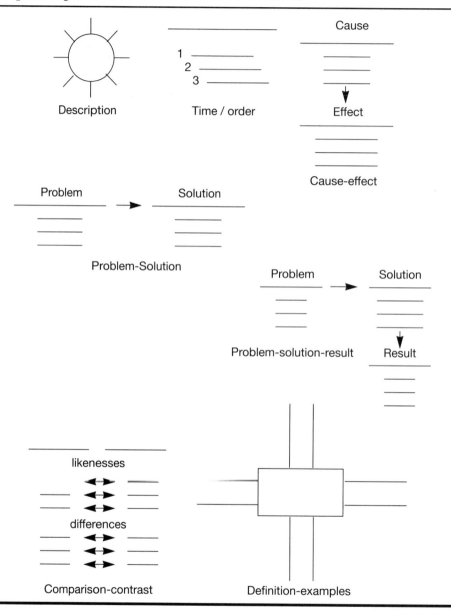

Source: P.L. Smith and G.E. Tomkins, "Structured notetaking: A new strategy for content area readers," *Journal of Reading,* October 1988, 46-52.

presentations on each segment of the chapter, the material will probably have been well covered.

Many of your students will need instruction and practice before they can create their own graphs. Johnson (1989) suggests the following steps to help students become aware of the uses of graphing.

1. Show transparencies of types of graphic aids from textbooks.

2. Have students, in pairs or groups, look through their textbook to list and categorize the graphic aids. This may be part of the initial process of familiarizing students with the text.

3. Set students a specific task based on a segment of text. For example, you may tell them to work in pairs to make a chart comparing similarities and differences between the United Nations and the League of Nations. Graphing is a useful alternative to answering questions or completing a worksheet after reading a chapter. The creation of a graph may be part of a reading guide.

4. Sometimes, for older, more able students in high school classes, distribute selections from a text and discuss with the class how the material might be graphed. Sometimes the content suggests an appropriate kind of graph (see Table 8.1). Sometimes, however, the most appropriate type of graph will not be obvious and you will need to supply a hint. Sometimes you will be pleased to discover one of your students come up with an idea you had not thought of.

5. You may then assign a passage and ask students to work in pairs or small groups to make a graph.

6. Compare the graphs for clarity and accuracy. Students will make different decisions about what should be included and how material should be organized. By the time students have worked to create a graph and have observed and discussed the graphs that their classmates have made, the material in the reading selection is likely to be very well known.

7. When students become adept at graphing, you may sometimes assign different sections of a chapter to different pairs of students so that each important section is graphed by two or three different pairs. Graphs should be made either on overhead transparencies or on large sheets of paper so that, when they are completed, they can be presented to the class. I have had great success with this technique. Students are motivated to make a graph that compares well with the graphs that other students have made on the same text section. They have the added benefit of making an oral presentation, and they listen to two or three brief presentations by classmates on each major section of the text.

Graphing has many benefits. The reorganization of text material requires active processing that results in improved comprehension. Graph making is especially useful for students with different learning styles who find verbal materials difficult. The graphs created are a valuable resource for reviewing for a test. Graph making is fun. It offers good opportunities for students to work cooperatively in pairs or small groups. Through making graphs, students become better able to interpret the graphic aids in their textbooks.

Summary

This chapter has presented a variety of strategies that will help teachers to use reading material as an integral part of the learning that goes on in content areas. Strategies are suggested for use in preparing students to read, and strategies to help them increase comprehension and retention of material. Many of the strategies involve the students in small group activities or in writing. Interaction among students and writing are both powerful means of learning, as stressed throughout the book. You will not, of course, use all the strategies for a given reading. Strategies should be selected and used to achieve your purposes.

EXERCISES

1. Select a concept that is important in a subject area you teach. Prepare a graphic organizer for that concept showing superordinate, coordinate and subordinate concepts. List examples, and non-examples, relevant attributes, and irrelevant attributes (see Figure 8.1).

2. Select a few paragraphs or a few pages from a text in a subject area you teach that deals with an important segment of a topic. Prepare a graph that presents the information in the text visually. Prepare copies of your graph for all members of a small group that consists, preferably, of people not expert in the subject area. Have members of your group translate your graph into words, either orally or in writing. After considering their responses, reconsider your graph to determine whether any aspects need revision or clarification. At the end of the exercise, consider what you learned.

3. Examine a chapter in a textbook in a content area you teach. Select ten words that are explained or clarified in some way in the text. Categorize them according to whether or not they are marked typographically. Categorize them further according to the type of aid used to explain the vocabulary item (synonym, antonym, direct explanation, example,

illustration, etc.). Mark any that you consider to be poorly explained or defined.

4. Select a chart, a graph, a table, or a map from a content area text that you may use and prepare a set of questions that will enable students to extract and use important information. You should include the following three kinds of questions: (1) literal level questions that ask for information; (2) interpretive questions; and (3) applied questions that ask them to evaluate or express opinions.

REFERENCES

Ausubel, D. (1968). *Educational Psychology: A Cognitive View*. New York, NY: Holt, Rinehart and Winston.

Barron, R.F., and V.F. Stone (1974). The effect of student-constructed graphic post organizers upon learning vocabulary. In P.L. Naeke and E. Nelli (eds.), *Interaction: Research and practice for college-adult reading*. Clemens, SC: National Reading Conference.

Brown, A.L., J.C. Campione and J.D. Day (1981). Learning to learn: On training students to learn from texts. *Education Researcher*, 10, 14-24.

Brown, A.L., J.D. Day and R. Jones (1983). The development of plans for summarizing texts. *Child Development*, 54, 968-979.

Fry, E. (1981). Graphical literacy. *Journal of Reading*, 24, 383-390.

Herber, H.L. (1970). *Teaching Reading in Content Areas*. Englewood Cliffs, N.J.: Prentice Hall.

Johnson, L.L. (1989). Learning across the curriculum with creative graphing. *Journal of Reading*, 32, 509-519.

Kintsch, W., and T. van Dijk (1978). Toward a model of text comprehension and production. *Psychological Review*, 85, 363-394.

Langer, J.A. (1981). From theory to practice: A prereading plan. *Journal of Reading*, 25, 152-156.

Langer, J. A., and A.N. Applebee (1987). *How writing shapes thinking: A study of teaching and learning*. Urbana, IL: National Council of Teachers of English.

Levine, M.G., and G.J. Haus (1985). Knowledge on the reading comprehension of second language learners. *Foreign Language Annals*, 18, 391-397.

Niles, O.S. (1985). Integration of content and skills instruction. In T.L. Harris and E.J. Cooper (eds.), *Reading, thinking, and concept development: Strategies for the classroom* (pp. 177-194). New York: College Entrance Examination Board.

Ogle, D. (1986). K-W-L: A teaching model that develops active reading of expository text. *The Reading Teacher*, 39, 564-570.

Palincsar A.S., and A.L. Brown (1984). Reciprocal teaching of comprehension-fostering and comprehension-monitoring activities. *Cognition and Instruction*, 1 (2), 117-175.

Shimmerlik, S.M. (1978). Organization theory and memory for prose: A review of the literature. *Review of Educational Research*, 48, 103-120.

Stauffer, R. (1975). *Directing the Reading-Thinking Process*. New York: Harper and Row.

Summers, E. (1965). Utilizing visual aids in reading material for effective learning. In H.L. Herber (ed.), *Developing Study Skills in Secondary Schools*. Newark, Del:International Reading Association.

Thelen, J. (1982). Preparing students for content reading assignments. *Journal of Reading*, 25, 544-549.

Thomas, E.L., and H.A. Robinson (1977). *Improving Reading in Every Class: A Sourcebook*. Boston, MA: Allyn and Bacon.

Thomas, E.L., and H.A. Robinson, H.A. (1982). *Improving Reading in Every Class: A Sourcebook*, 3rd ed.(abr.) Boston, MA: Allyn and Bacon.

Vacca, R. T., and J.L. Vacca (1989). *Content Area Reading*, 3rd ed. No city: HarperCollins.

Chapter 9
WRITING PROCESSES: THEORY AND PEDAGOGY[1]

C H A P T E R   O V E R V I E W

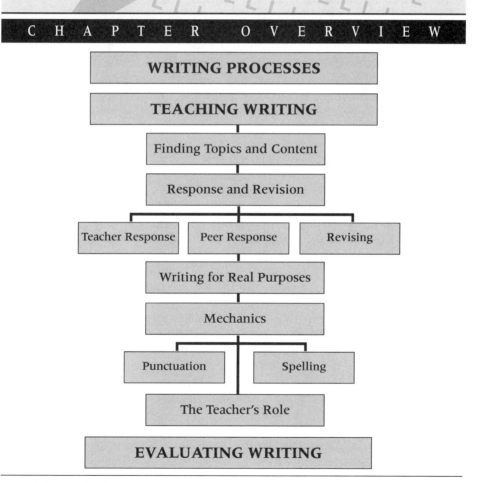

WRITING PROCESSES

TEACHING WRITING

Finding Topics and Content

Response and Revision

Teacher Response   Peer Response   Revising

Writing for Real Purposes

Mechanics

Punctuation   Spelling

The Teacher's Role

EVALUATING WRITING

---

[1] Some of the material in this chapter was previously published in: M. Crowhurst. *Writing in the Middle Years.* Markham, Ont. Pippin Publishing, 1993.

The argument made throughout this book is that language and learning are inextricably linked. Learning is mediated through the spoken and written word. It is important for learning that students put their thoughts into words. When we try to say what we know, we come to know in new and different ways. The two modes available to students for putting their thoughts into words are speech and writing. Both are important. Each mode has particular values. Speech allows the immediate response of others to help us as we shape and revise our thoughts. Writing, on the other hand, allows us to develop our thoughts by reconsidering, privately, what we have written. Because writing is relatively permanent, we can take as much time as we need to revise and develop our thinking.

We write for many different purposes and in many different forms. For purposes of the present discussion, however, it is convenient to make only a single distinction, dividing writing into two broad categories: writing to communicate, and writing to learn. If we write to communicate, the product that we are interested in is a product on paper — a written poem, essay, letter, or story. If we write to learn, the focus of interest is not a product on paper, but a product that is in the mind of the writer. The product of interest is insight or understanding.

This, then, is the first of two chapters on writing. It deals with writing in order to communicate. It has two major focuses: (1) the processes of writing, that is, the thinking activities that writers engage in as they produce pieces of writing; and (2) pedagogy — the ways in which teachers can organize classes and activities to help their students learn to compose. The next chapter deals with writing to learn, often a more informal kind of writing, where the aim is not necessarily to produce a piece of polished writing but to bring about insight and understanding.

You probably perceive at once that the dichotomy I have drawn between writing to communicate and writing to learn is an imperfect one. For when we work on an essay, an article, or a book, the struggle to be clear and coherent causes us to write and rewrite, and the process of producing a clear written product helps us learn. Nonetheless, the distinction is useful, even if imperfect.

For some teachers, teaching writing is a central aspect of their teaching responsibilities. This is especially true for elementary school teachers and for English teachers in the junior and senior high school. It is less central for some subject matter specialists in the high school — teachers of chemistry, home economics, and business education, for example. But even in these subjects, writing plays a part. Students write reports, business letters, resumes, and essays. This first chapter, then, is of central interest to English and language arts teachers, and of some interest to most other teachers. The following chapter that focuses on writing to learn is, I believe, important for all teachers.

WRITING PROCESSES

Our ideas about the way people write have changed dramatically in the past ten or fifteen years. Traditional wisdom held that composing was supposed to go like this: you get ideas and make an outline; you write your piece; you revise as necessary; and you write the final draft. This approach was commonly taught by composition texts and composition teachers, but it was based on little actual data about how people compose. When Janet Emig (1971) collected information from sixteen professional writers about their planning practices, she found that only four of them made detailed outlines as urged by composition texts — and they did so only for expository writing. The rest made only a very informal outline. One of the writers, Max Bluestone, explained his use of outlines thus:

> The rough scheme (his form of plan) is a map to the territory of my thoughts. The map is never precise, first because the territory has not been thoroughly explored and second because writing is in itself the discovery of new territory. I usually anticipate discovery in the act of composition. (Emig, 1971, p.24)

Beginning with Emig, considerable research into composing has been carried out in the past two decades. Research into writing processes examines what people do as they compose. Many different methods have been used. Some researchers have interviewed writers or asked them to complete questionnaires. Some have observed writers writing and then interviewed them, asking questions about what they were thinking at critical points in the writing, for example, at points when they paused for a noticeable length of time. Some researchers have asked writers to do a "think-aloud." In this procedure, writers are asked to say aloud *everything* they think as they compose, thus providing a record of their thinking processes. Of course, writers cannot say everything they think. But even the incomplete record of their thoughts, when taken together with notes and the final piece of writing, has shed much interesting light on composing processes.

Flower and Hayes (1981) produced an influential model of composing based on think-aloud data provided by expert writers. Their model has three major processes in writing: *planning* or getting ideas for writing, *translating* or putting ideas into words, and *reviewing* which consists of evaluating and revising. The term *planning* may sound like the traditional "write-an-outline" step. In actual fact, however, the planning done by the expert writers studied by Flower and Hayes was very different from the tidy process suggested by "write an outline." One major aspect of planning is finding out what you have to say or *generating*. Generating ideas means getting relevant information out of long-term memory, or, if necessary, consulting other sources to supplement the information in long-term memory. The writer calls up different kinds of information during generating information about the topic, to be sure, but also information about the audience the piece is to be written for, and information about how to go about writing the particular kind of writing (poem, book review, story, argument, and so on).

Planning is driven by the writer's goals. Transcripts of expert writers' think-alouds show that they are constantly setting goals for themselves. Goal setting is not usually a conscious act, yet the goals they set drive their writing process. When a writer says, during a think-aloud, "Let's doodle a little bit," he is setting himself the goal of doing some free-ranging exploration of the topic. When he says, "I need to open with something that will grab their interest," he is setting himself the goal of finding a particular kind of opening. When experts write, they spend considerable time exploring the task from every aspect. As they explore, their plan for writing gradually becomes clearer. Sometimes they make written notes about their tentative plan, and sometimes not.

Difficult writing tasks are not accomplished without a good deal of such exploration. Exploration may take place over days or weeks. The planning of expert writers may not look like planning to someone watching. It may happen as the writer drives in her car, or walks on the beach, or does chores around the house as well as when she sits at her desk or computer. Psychologist Jerome Bruner explores the topics he will write about by talking with friends (Emig, 1971). Novice writers have much less idea of how to go about such free-ranging exploration of the task. Elementary school children — and many older students as well — begin writing within a minute of being given a writing assignment. In one study, elementary students who were being encouraged to plan were told that adults often plan for 20 minutes or even longer before they start to write. Many of the students were astonished and wondered whatever adults could find to think about for so long. Indeed, they were inclined to view such a slow start as the mark of an incompetent writer (Burtis, Bereiter, Scardamalia, and Tetroe, 1983).

The free-ranging exploration that goes on before writing begins is part of planning. Sometimes the writer is not even aware that he is planning a piece of writing. However, planning is by no means confined to the time before writing begins. At any point in the process of composing, the writer may review the emerging piece and become aware of the need for another illustration, more information, or a different way of organizing what she has written. Reviewing, then, occurs throughout the process of composing and often leads to further rounds of planning; planning may occur at any point in the writing process. In other words, writing is not the neat, tidy, linear process of planning, writing and revision that it has often been represented as. Writing is a recursive process; bouts of generating, writing, reviewing, reorganizing and rewriting can occur in any order as dictated by the needs perceived by the writer.

As noted above, there are clear differences between expert and novice writers in the way they plan. A second aspect of composing that shows major differences between expert and novice writers is reviewing. Experienced writers constantly review what they have written and what they plan to write. When they review, they evaluate, and evaluation often leads to revision. Nancy Sommers (1980) found that novice writers' ideas of revision differ greatly from the ideas of expert writers. Her novice writers saw revision as being largely a matter of changing words: *Reviewing means just using better words and eliminating words that are not needed. I just review every word and make sure that everything is worded right* (p. 381). For her expert writers, however, revising and rewriting were an inherent part of writing: *I rewrite as I write. It is hard to tell what is a first draft ...* (p. 383). *I have learned from experience that I need to keep writing a first draft until I figure out what I want to say* (p. 384).

Composing processes differ for different writers. Some writers do much composing in their heads and produce a first draft that requires virtually no revision, while others write multiple drafts. Composing processes differ also with the task. Easy writing tasks or well-practised tasks require much less in the way of idea generation and organization and also less revision than difficult, unfamiliar writing tasks. A professor who is asked to write a letter of reference has done the task many times before. She needs to think of some relevant points to make, but the required structure and tone of such a letter are well known. The music or theatre critic who arrives home from a performance close to midnight and who must have his review in by 2 a.m. has little time and little need to belabour the task. He has written many reviews in the past and has the general format and the requirements of the task clearly in mind. It is a very different matter when we grapple with a topic not yet clearly defined in our minds, or when we struggle to write in a genre that we have not written in previously.

Traditional views of composing saw it as an orderly, linear process of planning followed by writing followed by revision. Writing could be done promptly in response to the teacher's assignment. But research reveals composing as a recursive, sometimes disorderly process in which planning, writing, reviewing and rewriting can occur at any time. The pace of writing, as Emig (1981) points out, may be very slow since writers must create not merely sentences and paragraphs but meaning. Moreover, writers sometimes engage in processes that they are scarcely aware of.

TEACHING WRITING

Just as traditional ideas about how people write were different from those currently held, so also were ideas about teaching composition different. When I started to teach English, years ago, I believed that I clearly understood my responsibilities as a teacher of composition. I was supposed to find a topic likely to interest my young students. On composition day, I announced what they were to write about. The next step was to motivate them. I prompted them to share their ideas on the topic and listed the best suggestions on the board. I elicited good words and phrases that might be useful to them as they wrote. When I felt they were well primed, I told them to begin their first draft and circulated around the room, encouraging slow students to get on with the job. Before the lesson ended, I told them when I expected them to hand in the finished version, neatly written, without errors, in their composition books. My task then was to mark out all their errors, to draw attention to weaknesses, to write a comment at the end, and to give them a mark or grade which I duly entered in my mark book. I found teaching composition a discouraging business. Only a few wrote interesting pieces, while the rest handed in the obligatory page or so filled with monotonous prose and dotted with the same errors week after week no matter how many times I marked them out.

I am sure that writing was discouraging for my students also as they received back their pages covered in the red ink that I so conscientiously applied. Indeed, there is good reason to believe that the constant criticism doled out to student writers produces large numbers of high school graduates, and even of university graduates, who believe they cannot write. Not many students in our classes will grow up to be noted authors. But most of them can learn to write competently if we adopt methods in keeping with what recent research has taught us.

Approaches to teaching composition that are informed by recent research are very different from the traditional approaches that I employed and that are still widely practised. Many of those who are informed by research believe that writing is learned rather than taught. In fact, some believe that children will learn to write as naturally as they learn to speak if they are encouraged to use writing for their own real purposes. The major task for the teacher, then, is to provide the kind of environment that will facilitate students' learning.

To view the teaching of writing in this light is not to deny that teachers have a good deal of knowledge that can help students to become more skilful writers. It does, however, have a lot to say about the ways in which teachers should pass on their knowledge. They should pass on their knowledge to those who can profit from it in circumstances when they can use it in their writing rather than to whole classes of students whether they need instruction or not.

What, then, are the major areas in which teachers can help students? In order to become proficient writers, students need to learn how to engage in the kinds of processes that expert writers use. They need to learn how to find topics to write about, and how to locate content on their chosen topics; they need feedback from responsive, sympathetic listeners — feedback that will help them to develop their emerging piece of writing and to revise as necessary. They need real purposes for writing. They need help learning mechanics. Each of these topics is addressed in turn in the following pages. The last two topics in the section focus on the role of the teacher of writing and evaluating writing.

FINDING TOPICS AND LOCATING CONTENT

When I began teaching, I considered it part of my job to devise topics that would be interesting for my students to write about. In the composition class, all students would write on the same topic. They would start the composition on the same day and were all expected to have it finished on the day I told them it was due. Classrooms following a process-oriented, workshop approach to writing are very different. Students will usually be writing on their own self-selected writing assignments. On a given day, some students may be beginning a new topic, some may be continuing a piece started the day before, some may be conferencing with the teacher or with a classmate about a piece of writing in progress, some may be doing the final editing of a piece ready to be published. Some may be working in a small group preparing a report on Sweden for social studies, or working on a group science project.

It takes time, of course, before the writing workshop can operate in this way. It takes some months for students to learn independent ways of working if they have not participated in writing workshops previously. Also, it requires that several hour-long periods in a week be devoted to the writing workshop — as many as three or four in an elementary classroom where students are working on writing for other subjects as well as for language arts.

A key ingredient in getting the program established is helping students to find topics that they are interested to write about. Eventually, each student will have a list of possible topics. However, those who have not previously engaged in workshop approaches may initially have difficulty identifying topics. A good way of beginning is to use a simple procedure based on listing and free writing. This procedure will help them find a topic and locate relevant information related to the topic. It also enables you to model several key aspects of a workshop approach to writing.

Start out by telling the class that they will be doing some writing on the following day and asking them to think of three things that they might write about. On the following day, ask them to write across the top of a page their three chosen topics. They then list under each topic as many words and phrases they can think of associated with that topic, taking two or three minutes for each topic. (You can model desired behaviours by joining in and writing your topics and word lists on the board.) At the end of this listing exercise, they may have selected one topic as the most interesting. If not, tell them to select the one with the longest list. They should now write for five to ten minutes without stopping on their chosen topic. Tell them not to worry about spelling, handwriting, or even about writing in complete sentences. They should not think of this as a piece of writing, but as a means of getting down some ideas that they can later use in a piece of writing if they choose to do so. This draft — along with all writing — should be kept in a writing folder. First drafts like this one are kept in the first pocket of the folder along with idea lists for possible pieces of writing in the future. (The other two pockets of the folder are kept for work in progress, and for finished pieces.) Note that first drafts do not necessarily become work in progress. First drafts that do not strike warm may be abandoned. They are always saved, however, since ideas that do not appeal today may appeal next week or in three months.

There are some topics that commonly strike a chord for everyone in the class. Ask them for example, to think of a place that has been important to them in some way. It might be as big as a town, or as small as a room or a corner of the garden. The same procedures of listing and free writing will give them the start of another piece. Other likely topics that can be treated in similar fashion are: a significant person — they may start by listing half a dozen people they know and then selecting one that seems interesting; a memorable incident — humorous, embarrassing, exciting.

Every student keeps a list of possible topics and adds to the list frequently. For example, the two topics not used on the first day go on the student's topic list. You might distribute, at the beginning of the year, a list of topics that have appealed to previous students. The list might include such things as favourite sports (soccer, swimming, skate boarding), hobbies (photography, chess, collecting hockey cards) general topics (parents, younger/older brothers or sisters, rock stars, the environment) controversial topics (keeping whales/animals in captivity; banning fire arms). The suggestions they find interesting are noted as possible topics for future writing.

You might occasionally take a few minutes at the beginning of a workshop to list topics that you yourself might write about: interesting or controversial topics discussed in the media; incidents you observed on an outing, while shopping, or while waiting for the bus; incidents that occurred at your house over the weekend. You might then ask students to pair up and tell their partners all the topics they can think of that they might write about. All their suggestions are, of course, listed and kept in the ideas section of their writing folders.

If, on a given day, a student is having trouble thinking of something to write about, the teacher may hold a brief **topic conference** (Atwell, 1987) with her. It may be enough simply to take her through the list of topics and interests in her writing folder. If no topic strikes warm, the conference may become a brief interview. The teacher asks open-ended questions to probe the writer's experiences and interests, for example: "What did you do on Saturday?" "Tell me about your neighbours." "Tell me what you like to do most/least." Careful attention to the answers, especially those that show emotional involvement, will often reveal a potential topic within a few minutes.

Similar procedures may be used to help students to locate possible research topics in a subject area. They may, for example, list what they know about the

Middle Ages, and what they would like to know. They may list questions related to science or a specific science topic that they would like to know the answers to. Items in newspapers and on radio and television are a rich source of possible topics for your students to research. On the day when I was writing this chapter, a minor item on a morning radio program mentioned that fear of insects, bugs, spiders, snakes, and other "loathsome" creatures seems to increase with age. A student might prepare a questionnaire to sample the attitudes of people of different ages, then write a report that gives the results of the questionnaire and a research report on one of the feared creatures. In fact, a group of students could prepare a booklet with reports by different group members on various feared creatures.

Potential topics for writing are limitless. The trick is to develop an eye for seeing them and to help your students learn how to recognize them as well. For some topics, students need to look within themselves for the content to write about. Listing and free writing are useful ways of getting out information from long term memory. For some topics, they will need to consult resources in the library and elsewhere. Strategies for note-taking and report writing are discussed in greater detail in the next chapter.

RESPONSE AND REVISION

When I began teaching, I responded to my students' finished writing by marking out their errors, making a summarizing comment, and assigning a grade. Some students were warmly commended for their writing, but most wrote perfunctory, error-ridden compositions and received responses that were not encouraging. What is more, for all my correcting, the same errors appeared over and over again.

A different approach to response is needed, one that is more useful and less discouraging. What students need is not information about their errors after the piece is finished, but response during the process of writing that will help them with the writing of the developing piece. Response should serve two purposes: (1) to encourage students to press on with the difficult, demanding, but potentially rewarding task of writing; and (2) to provide feedback that will help them to produce a better piece. Responding is an activity that both teacher and students should engage in.

Teacher Response

The teacher responds in two kinds of situations: (1) she responds publicly in front of the class in order to model responding so that students will learn how to do it; and (2) she responds in individual conferences she holds with students during the writing workshop.

Public Responding The teacher begins to model responding on the first day of the writing workshop. After students have engaged in free writing on their first chosen topic as described above, volunteers are asked to read their first rough drafts. The teacher responds to content only with encouraging comments like: "I liked it when you said the wind was 'bending the trees to the limit'. It helped me to imagine how strongly the wind was blowing." "I like the specific examples you gave of your cousin's mischievous behaviour." On subsequent days she continues to respond positively and, in addition, makes specific suggestions that will help the student in the development of his draft. She might say, "I'd like to know what it was about that old house that made you feel scared when you went in through the window."

Responses of this kind perform several different functions. First of all, they are encouraging — designed to make the student want to keep working at his writing. Secondly, they model responding so that students also will learn how to respond. The teacher's responses have three characteristics: (1) they start with positive comments; (2) they are personal statements, often beginning with *I*; (3) they are very specific. The third function performed by the teacher's responses is that they emphasize, from the very beginning, that writing is not something that is completed in one go. Writing is something that you work at — revising and rewriting, adding details and illustrations, and cutting out words and sentences in order to tighten. In other words, when teachers respond, they are helping to develop a concept of rewriting or revising.

Responding During Conferences In addition to responding publicly to the writing of volunteer readers, the teacher responds to students' writing in individual conferences. During the times allotted to the writing workshop, much of the teacher's time will be spent in conferences with individual students. Conferences will usually be short — from one to five minutes — though occasionally they may be longer. Conferences may be held for a variety of purposes. A **topic conference** has the purpose of helping the student to find something to write about. A **content conference** is held to help students clarify their intentions in writing a piece, or to deal with some problem that has arisen—how to find a more gripping introduction, for example. A student will usually have many content conferences in the course of writing a piece. Such a conference is brief, focusing on just one part of the writing or one problem, preferably a question or problem that the student has identified. Its purpose is to move the student forward, not deal with every problem in the piece. The purpose of an **editing conference** is to give students the benefit of the teacher's expert editing skills before the final draft is written.

The two most important behaviours of a teacher in conferencing are asking open-ended questions and listening. The purpose of the questions is to help students find out what they have to say or how they want to say it. It is not the teacher's role to tell students what to say and how to say it. The teacher listens in order to discover what it is that the student is trying to do in the piece. He listens and reflects back to the student what he hears, and thus helps the student to clarify her intentions. Useful things to focus on are: things you do not understand; things you want to know more about; things that may be worrying the writer; what the writer likes best about the piece; what she plans to do next.

Peer Response

The kinds of responses made by the teacher may also be made by students. They may respond in the large, whole-class group, in small groups, or in individual conferences with their peers.

After the teacher has modelled responses the first few days of the writing workshop, students should be asked to respond to a partner's writing. At first they should be told merely to respond positively to specific things that they liked. Later they should add to their positive comments by indicating parts they do not understand, or places where they would like more information.

Students can learn to make excellent responses to the writing of their peers. Note, for example, the discriminating comments made by fifth graders who worked in a small group and responded in writing to the composition of each member in their group. They were asked to mention at least one thing they liked and one thing that might be improved (Crowhurst, 1979):

- I like the part where it said, "he fumbled with the radio with a worried expression."

- You had realistic dialogue. What I mean is that sometimes when people write dialogue for teenagers, it doesn't sound real. Yours did.

- This is really good. I could never make a poem so long and expressive. I like the words *giddy, fragrant, solemn, creamy.* And the way you phrased it just perfection. Thus you must have spent hours working on it. No, absolutely no suggestions!!!

- That bear part was good. So was that barrel part. When you met Lorrie was another good part in your diary. Bad points: first, spelling mistakes. It was sort of mixed up. One day you were on the other side of the island, the next you were in Toronto. Who is J.J.? Where did you get the shells for the gun?

Students may sometimes meet in small groups to take turns reading their pieces and getting oral response from each of their peers. This procedure allows students to get a response to a whole piece of writing, whereas conferences will usually focus on one part of a composition, or on a particular problem. The following procedure is a useful one to follow for oral group response (Crowhurst, 1993):

Group members take turns at reading their pieces.

.. The reader reads her piece aloud.

3. After the first reading, group members take thirty seconds to note down their general responses. The page for their notes is divided into two columns headed "+", and "−".

4. The reader reads her piece a second time. As she reads, group members jot down words, phrases, and ideas in the positive column or the negative column. They are especially looking for words or phrases that catch their attention, for things they especially like, and for parts that affect them in some way.

5. After the second reading, group members take turns in responding while the reader makes notes of the things they say. The reader never argues with a group member's reaction. She listens, considers, and uses the feedback if it seems useful. If it does not seem useful, she ignores it. But she *never* argues.

Revising

Revising is difficult for students. One reason is that they have a very poorly developed idea of what it means to revise. Most students — and many teachers — think of revision as something that happens after the first draft is finished. For many students, revising means little more than writing out a good copy with the mistakes fixed up.

A second reason for students' difficulty with revising is that it is difficult for young students to change text once they have committed it to paper. Another reason is that even when they sense that something is wrong with a sentence or segment of text, they cannot always think of good ways to fix it.

Sometimes teachers have problems explaining revising to their students. One elementary teacher told me she found it hard to get her students to revise and hard to know how to help them. Sometimes she could find nothing more useful to say than, "Go away and change something." Her ideas about revision changed drastically when she engaged in a prolonged workshop experience in which she took a poem through many drafts until, at last, it satisfied the mental image that she had been struggling to get on paper.

Writers revise when they perceive a problem. Problems may be perceived at any point in the process of writing, even before pen is put to paper. If I think to myself, "I will start my article this way" and, later, decide that it would be better if I started in a different way, I have revised. I have revised a mental plan.

Writers who perceive a problem have various strategies for dealing with it. They may rewrite; they may add an illustration or anecdote to explain or clarify;

they may reorganize in a more logical way; they may omit unnecessary detail. If they perceive no problem, they do not revise. They certainly do not revise because revising is the third stage in the writing process. Revising is a response to a mismatch between what they want to say — their mental image of the piece — and what they see on paper. The clearer their mental image is, the easier it will be for them to detect a mismatch and the need to revise (Crowhurst, 1993).

In a workshop approach to writing, students are encouraged from the very beginning to view their writing as a draft. When volunteers read out their description of a favourite place or a significant person, it is assumed to be a draft. It is represented to them as the start of something that may *become* a piece of writing.

Students are constantly invited to examine their intentions as they confer — throughout writing — with teacher and peers. Open-ended questions help them to clarify their purpose; feedback from peers and teacher directs them to parts that may not be clear to a reader. These activities inevitably lead to changes. Students may not always realize that they are revising. But of course they are. Revising is part of writing. It is important for both teachers and students to understand that this is so.

WRITING FOR REAL PURPOSES

Purpose is central to language learning. Children learn to talk because language enables them to do things. By talking, they can greet, complain, request, inform, socialize. They do not talk merely to practise talking.

Purpose is of central importance in learning to write as well as in learning to speak. Research in both the United Kingdom (Britton, Burgess, Martin, McLeod, and Rosen, 1975) and the United States (Applebee, 1984) indicates that school writing is done almost exclusively for a teacher audience with the purpose of testing. Students write so that teachers can test their knowledge or their ability to write. But there are other purposes and audiences readily available for student writing. They can write to inform, to amuse, to entertain, to persuade, to request, to thank, to advertise — all of these in many forms. They can write for classmates, for students in other classes or other schools, and for journals that print student writing; they can write to the teacher for purposes other than testing, to the principal, to the editors of newspapers, to politicians, to businesses, to authors. The following list of genres developed by children that appear in Atwell (1987) implies both purposes and audiences for student writing:

Personal experience narratives   Poetry

Fictional narratives: Ballads

    Short stories and novellas   Limericks

(tall tales, sci-fi,
historical, romance,
fairly tales, contemporary
realism, etc.)

Autobiographies

Biographies

Essays

Research reports

Textbooks

Reviews of books, records,
movies, and TV shows

News stories

Reports of current events and
features

Children's books

Jokes and riddles

Games and puzzles

Captions and labels

Cartoons

Advertisements

Song lyrics

Diaries and Journals

Field journals and learning
logs

Petitions

Scripts:

Skits

Plays

Rhymed couplets

Acrostics

Counted-syllable formats

Free verse

Correspondence:

Friendly letters (to pen
pals, teachers, friends,
relatives)

Invitations

To the Editor

Marking special occasions

Requesting permission

Letters of thanks, love,
complaint, application,
sympathy, inquiry, fare-
well, protest, advice,
apology, congratulation

Editorials and opinions

Recipes

Memoranda and messages

Interviews

Instructions and advice

Rules and regulations

Lists and notes

Mottoes and slogans

Scrapbooks (and accompanying
texts)

Yearbook blurbs

Radio plays	Awards and inscriptions
Puppet shows	Resumes and cover letters
TV commercials	Public notices:
Speeches	Posters
Last will and testaments	Dittoed announcements
Eulogies	Intercom announcements

The purposes for which students may write are many. Providing them with real purposes for writing does much to provide the motivation that encourages them to persevere with their writing.

MECHANICS

The main aspects of writing covered by the term *mechanics* are spelling and punctuation.

Punctuation

Many students will pick up the conventions of punctuation in much the same way as they pick up the conventions of spelling. They can be encouraged and instructed, briefly, in individual conferences as the teacher responds to their writing and helps them with the final editing. Some instruction can also be given in mini-lessons delivered to a group of students who have a common need. Sometimes that group may be the whole class; sometimes the group will be smaller.

Marland's (1977, pp. 205) useful suggestion for teaching punctuation is that it be taught by *function* rather than by *sign*. The use of the period at the end of a sentence is quite different from its use to indicate an abbreviation. Thus there is little to be gained (and much to be lost) by taking a given sign and listing its various uses. Rather, students should be taught, for example:

1. seven ways of marking off a "sense group," namely: the comma; the semicolon; parentheses; the period followed by a space and an upper-case letter; the paragraph indentation; the space or signs for section divisions; the chapter-ending space;

2. the three ways of marking interruptions, namely: a pair of commas, a pair of dashes, a set of parentheses; or

3. ways of showing that a word or phrase has been borrowed or is being used in a special way, for example, underlining, or quotation marks (or italics or boldface if these can conveniently be used as when using a word processor).

A useful means of practising recently taught punctuation is to prepare passages that illustrate a particular kind of punctuation, to record the passages on an audio tape, and to provide students with photocopies of the passages so that they can listen to the tape and insert the required punctuation. This procedure has two advantages. Students can get practice without having to do tedious and time consuming writing. Secondly, it encourages them to note that punctuation is often used to mark features of spoken language.

Spelling

Spelling often assumes a significance out of all proportion to its importance. Spelling is neither as important nor as difficult as many other aspects of writing — such as finding something useful or interesting to write about, or expressing oneself with clarity and style. Yet many people, both members of the general public and teachers, talk as if spelling were the most important aspect of writing. *If he can't spell, he can't write* seems to be the attitude.

Several years ago I heard a well known talk-show host interviewing a famous Canadian author on a CBC program. In the conversation, it emerged that the host of the program had once been the author's editor. The host chuckled as he talked about the author's abysmal spelling. "You didn't know how to spell!" he said. "No, I didn't," said the author, "and I still don't. It's up to my editor to worry about my spelling!" We teachers cannot afford to let our students take such a cavalier attitude towards spelling. Careful spelling is something we must encourage. However, we should be clear — as the author was — that spelling is not the same thing as writing. The two often seem to be equated by people who think that if a student is a poor speller, he is a poor writer. If he makes a lot of spelling mistakes, he is a poor *speller*. Whether or not he can *write*, that is, compose, is a different question (Crowhurst, 1993).

Teaching spelling is part of the teacher's job. All teachers should encourage careful spelling. Subject area teachers will certainly want students to learn to spell the special vocabulary of the discipline. The purpose of this section, then, is to suggest some principles that should guide the teacher in encouraging careful spelling and in adopting teaching practices that will help students to learn to spell.

1. *During drafting, students should concentrate on content.* The major focus of students' attention during the early stages of writing should be to get down their ideas with clarity and effectiveness. All students should know that they should not risk losing a good idea by switching attention from what they want to say in order to worry about the spelling of a word. Especially in the early primary grades, students should be encouraged to spell words the best way they can.

2. *Before publication, it is the student's responsibility to try to ensure that every word is spelled correctly.* Encourage your students to take pride in correct

spelling. When composing is finished, it is time for careful editing to ensure that the finished product is free from irritating errors. The student should enlist the aid of others in the class to help with proof reading. (You should not worry students who are just learning to write in the early primary grades by insisting on correct spelling.)

3. ***In teaching spelling, concentrate on "demon" lists.*** A high proportion of spelling errors at every grade level involves a comparatively small number of very common words. The following list contains errors commonly misspelled by elementary children and should be learned by every child:

about	address	afraid	afternoon
again	all right	along	along
already	always	am	an
and	answer	anything	anyway
April	are	arithmetic	aunt
baby	balloon	because	been
before	birthday	bought	boy
brother	brought	can	cannot
can't	children	Christmas	close
clothes	come	coming	couldn't
cousin	daddy	day	December
didn't	different	doing	don't
down	Easter	enough	every
everybody	father	February	fine
first	for	fourth	Friday
friend	from	front	getting
goes	going	good	good-bye(-by)
grade	guess	guest	had
has	have	haven't	having
he	hear	hello	her
here	his	home	hope
hospital	house	how	hundred

I'll	I'm	in	isn't
its	it's	I've	January
just	knew	know	letter
like	little	lots	loving
made	make	maybe	me
morning	mother	much	my
name	nice	now	o'clock
October	off	on	once
one	our	out	outside
party	people	play	played
please	pretty	quite	receive
remember	right	said	Santa Claus
Saturday	saw	school	send
sent	sincerely	some	something
sometimes	soon	store	studying
summer	Sunday	suppose	sure
surely	swimming	teacher	Thanksgiving
that's	the	their	them
then	there	there's	they
they're	think	thought	through
time	to	today	together
tomorrow	tonight	too	toys
train	truly	two	until
vacation	very	want	was
weather	well	went	we're
were	when	whether	white
will	with	won't	would
write	writing	you	young
your	yours		

The following is a list of words most commonly misspelled by secondary students (Penner and McConnell, 1977):

absence	different	occasion
accommodate	disappoint	occurred
all right	discipline	opportunity
amateur	doesn't	parallel
appearance	embarrass	pleasant
argument	excellent	privilege
athletics	experience	receive
beginning	February	repetition
believe	foreign	restaurant
benefit	forty	schedule
busy	friend	secretary
business	government	seize
cemetery	grammar	separate
clothes	height	similar
column	hoping	surprise
committee	independent	tragedy
conscience	later	truly
deceive	leisure	until
definite	losing	Wednesday
describe	necessary	writing
develop	noticeable	written

4. *Establish a firm grasp of letter-sound correspondences in the early grades.* Despite many vexatious problems with English spelling, a high proportion of words are spelled phonetically. Grades 2 and 3 are an important time for students to become well grounded in letter-sound correspondences.

5. *Teach useful spelling rules.* There are a few spelling generalizations that have few exceptions. They are well worth teaching to students in appropriate ways and at appropriate times. Students in the high school who are poor spellers are very likely to be making errors involving these rules.

1. *ie and ei.* The old rhyme that gives guidance on the spelling of the /i/ sound as in *niece* should be known by every student:

    i before *e*
    Except after *c*
    Or when it says /e/
    As in *neighbour* and *weigh*.

    This rule will give students guidance on the spelling of words like: *believe, piece,* and *receive.* The only common exception to the rule is *seize. Leisure* is also an exception if your pronunciation rhymes with *seizure,* but not if your pronunciation rhymes with *pleasure.* Note that *height* and *weight* are not covered by the rule because the vowel sound is not /i/.

2. *Dropping/keeping a final silent -e before a suffix.* Words ending in a consonant and a silent *e* drop the *e* before a suffix beginning with a vowel (*come-coming; fame-famous*) but keep the *e* before a suffix beginning with a consonant (*love-lovely; excite-excitement*). Note that *true-truly* and *argue-argument* are not exceptions to this rule since *true* and *argue* do not end with a consonant and a silent *e.* This fact should be drawn to your students' attention. Note also that words ending with *c* or *g* and a silent *e* must keep the *e* before a suffix beginning with any vowel but i or *e* (*courage-courageous; notice-noticeable*). The reason for this is that "soft" *c* (sounding like *s*) and "soft" *g* (sounding like *j*) must be followed by *e* or *i*.

3. Doubling the final consonant. There are two related rules governing the doubling of final consonants.

    a. For words of one syllable that end in a single consonant preceded by a single vowel, double the final consonant when adding a suffix beginning with a vowel (*knit-knitting; stop-stopped-stopping*).

    b. For words *accented on the last syllable* that end in a single consonant preceded by a single vowel, double the final consonant when adding a suffix beginning with a vowel (*begin-beginning; occur-occurred-occurrence; equip-equipped;* compare *murmur-murmuring; gallop-galloped-galloping*). Note that American English is consistent in following this rule but that British English is not. Compare *traveled* (American English) and *travelled* (British English). The rule is so useful that you might consider teaching it to your students in upper grades no matter what your personal preference is between American and British spellings.

6. **Teach students to recognize common prefixes and suffixes.** Students are less likely to misspell *disappear, dissimilar,* and *unnoticed* if they note that these words are *dis+appear, dis+similar,* and *un+noticed.*

7. Pair cognate words to help students with silent letters and unstressed vowels.

1. Words with silent letters will be easier to remember if they are paired with cognate words in which the formerly silent letter is pronounced. Compare the following pairs:

sign	signature
bomb	bombard
crumb	crumble
muscle	muscular
condemn	condemnatory

2. Many unstressed vowels in English are pronounced with the schwa sound, represented as /ə/, no matter how they are spelled. Notice your pronunciation of the vowel sound in the last syllable in each of the following words: *current, currant, grammar, doctor, circus, porpoise, mountain, robin*. In each case, the vowel in the last syllable is pronounced /ə/. The pronunciation of the words gives little indication of the spelling of the unstressed vowels. If you pair words with cognate words in which stress has moved to the syllable that was formerly unstressed, you will help students spell the particular words, and teach them a useful strategy. Compare the words in the following pairs, and note how the pronunciation of the second word in the pair helps with the spelling of the unstressed vowel in the first word:

definite	define
grammar	grammatical
history	historical
president	preside
abolition	abolish
competition	compete

THE TEACHER'S ROLE

Students learn to write primarily by writing. They do not learn by listening to lectures about writing or reading texts on how to write. One of the most important things a teacher can do, then, is to provide students with opportunities to write for real purposes, and to support them as they write. However, it would be misleading to suggest that the teacher has no instructional role other than providing an enabling, supportive environment. The teacher who herself writes regularly has much expert knowledge about writing to share with students. The purpose of this section is to make explicit what is implied in earlier sections about the various roles the teacher plays in teaching writing.

The writing workshop is a time where most student time is spent on writing and related tasks like conferencing and responding. There are nonetheless many occasions during writing workshops when the teacher engages in instruction, though not usually the formal instruction of a lesson delivered to the whole class. When teachers confer with students, for example, they coach them, individually, in many aspects of writing: locating topics to write about; finding good leads; recognizing tedious passages that need to be deleted or tightened.

Another way for the teacher to instruct is by modelling. She models responding. She models finding topics. She models the writing process with her own writing. She sometimes discusses her writing with the class and describes problems she has had and how she solved them. Sometimes she may simply present a problem and listen with interest to suggestions her students may have for her. She may photocopy drafts of her work that show the kinds of revisions she has made, and explain why she made them. Perl and Wilson (1986) describe how astonished Audre Allison's 11th grade students were to learn that she had awakened, early in the morning, anxious because she had made little progress with a piece of writing she had planned to bring to class to share in a group. It was instructive to them to discover that she was plagued with the same kinds of problems that they themselves faced.

In addition to modelling and individualized coaching, the teacher should also give instruction to the whole class, when appropriate, in short "mini-lessons" at the beginning of the writing workshop. A mini-lesson lasts five or ten minutes and deals with some particular aspect of writing that many students need help with. Sometimes a mini-lesson will be given to a small group called together briefly during the writing workshop because they share the need for a particular kind of help.

Topics for mini-lessons are endless. Early in the year the focus is likely to be on procedural matters (e.g., the use of writing folders), on finding topics, on responding and conferencing. Sometimes a mini-lesson may focus on a particular genre, on the required form and tone of a business letter, for example, or a haiku poem. Sometimes it will be appropriate to give a mini-lesson on spelling or punctuation or on style. The determining criterion for scheduling a mini-lesson should always be that the students — some or all of them — need it and are ready to profit from it. A mini-lesson should be given only to those who are ready for it.

The teacher's knowledge and expertise are an important resource for his students. There are many appropriate occasions for him to share his knowledge with students who are ready to profit from it, and many ways for him to do it.

EVALUATING WRITING

The subject of evaluation is taken up in greater detail in Chapter 12. However, evaluating writing has been such a special and different form of evaluation that it deserves brief consideration here. Zemelman and Daniels (1988) claim that evaluating writing is dramatically different from the kind of evaluation done in other areas of school learning. Composition teachers spend enormous amounts of time grading, marking, correcting, and giving, detailed written feedback. English teachers are obsessed with evaluation, say Zemelman and Daniels. "What other teachers have as their unabashed goal to correct every error that every student ever makes on every piece of work they ever attempt?" (p. 206). What is more, all this grading, and correcting, and commenting avails little, according to Hillocks' (1986) important review of composition research. The excessive, error-detection kind of evaluation that writing teachers[2] have believed it their duty to engage in has produced multitudes of educated people who feel bad about their writing and themselves as writers.

While the subject of evaluation is taken up in more detail elsewhere in the book, I wish to enunciate here certain principles that may guide teachers in evaluating writing.

1. ***Distinguish between formative evaluation and summative evaluation.*** We evaluative formatively for diagnostic purposes. We note what students do well and what they need help with in order to help them learn. Summative evaluation has as its goal describing performance at the end of some time period — the end of the term or the end of the course. Its purpose is to inform administrators, parents, and the students themselves how they are doing — often in comparison with others in the class. We should collect a large amount of information in order to diagnose our students' abilities and to guide their learning. Not all of the information gathered for formative evaluation will necessarily be used in determining final grades.

2. ***Do not grade every piece of writing a student does.*** Students need to spend much time writing in order to learn how to write. If teachers think they have to read and grade everything students write, students will not be able to do as much writing as they need to do in order to develop skill. We do not mark them on every piece of reading they do, or on every math problem. Neither should we take that approach to writing.

3. ***Realize that the teacher plays many different roles in responding and evaluating.*** The kind of role we play varies with the purpose of the writing and the stage at which the writer is working. When the writer is looking for

---

[2] It should be said that some teachers in other subject areas also believe it their duty to mark out all errors in writing.

a topic or generating ideas, the teacher's appropriate role is to listen in order to encourage, and to probe the writer's knowledge and interests. During the time when the writer is going through rounds of drafting/revising/rewriting, the teacher plays varied roles: listening to help identify problems and to encourage; questioning and challenging to help the writer sharpen focus and clarify ideas; suggesting possible ways of proceeding. When drafting and revising are finished, the writer needs to edit for publication. Here the teacher makes use of his expertise as an editor to help the writer eliminate mechanical errors and awkwardness of expression. As explained above, the writer's peers may also play all these roles. When the piece is finally finished, it will be presented to whatever audience it was intended for. A letter will be sent to the addressee; a book for a lower grade will be delivered to that grade. If the teacher is part of the audience for whom the piece was written, then the teacher will respond as a reader — with interest and appreciation, it is hoped. Only occasionally, for some pieces, should the teacher's role be to grade.

4. *When determining a grade for the writing segment of a course, assign credit for various aspects of composing.* The writing grade has usually been assigned for overall performance on each of several pieces of writing. When I began to teach, for example, I would have in my mark book at the end of a term nine or ten marks for nine or ten pieces of writing. The writing mark, then, became the average of those marks. Certainly, overall performance in some pieces of writing will be part of the writing grade, but other things are to be taken into account as well. It is best that the writing grade be based on a portfolio of work. The following is a useful list of questions for teachers to consider when evaluating ability to write (Crowhurst, 1988):

- Is he/she writing more — longer pieces? more pieces?

- Is he/she doing more kinds of writing?

- Is he/she writing for more audiences?

- Is he/she suiting content, language, and tone to the intended audience?

- Can he/she find things to write about?

- Can he/she ask for help when needed?

- Can he/she use help given in conferences to revise and rewrite or to press on with the task of composing?

- Does he/she like to write?

5. *Separate the roles of responding and grading.* When you are responding, all your resources as a helpful listener and guide should be at your students'

disposal. How can you make your best resources available if you know that, ultimately, you are going to give this piece of writing a grade? When you are responding, you give guidance and help. When you are grading, however, do not spend time marking out errors or making comments. Adopt the procedure of reading swiftly and giving a holistic mark. This should be done for only one or two pieces per grading period. You might decide to use one piece selected from the writing folder by the student, and one piece written in class if you wish, depending on the age of your students. When grading pieces of writing, it is useful, if possible, to cooperate with another teacher who teaches the same grade so that you have two opinions for each piece of writing. Belanger (1985) suggests the following procedure:

1. To preserve student anonymity, have each student staple to the back of the paper an envelope containing his or her name.

2. To ensure independent assessments, the first rater places the assigned grade on an upper corner of the last page and folds the corner over. The second rater does not inspect the first grade until after assigning a grade. The final grade is the average of the two marks if there is perfect or near agreement. In the case of disagreements, a third rater is engaged or, if none is available, the two raters discuss the paper and their grades.

This procedure is possible if many pieces of writing are read and responded to, but only a few in a year are graded. When pieces are graded in this way, the sole purpose is to read rapidly and assign a grade; no comments or corrections are made.

CONCLUSION

Ideas about composing and about teaching composition have changed a great deal in recent decades. Research on composing has greatly influenced our understanding of composing processes.[3] Our different understanding of composing has led to a different view of the teacher's role in facilitating students' development of writing. As a teacher of writing, your major tasks are to help students discover what they have to say, and to help them to say it as clearly and effectively as they can. You have a duty also to help them master matters of form and mechanics, but these skills should be kept in appropriate balance and not equated with writing. Old-fashioned ideas about evaluating writing have often led to writing being negatively viewed by large numbers of students. While summative evaluation is part of the teacher's task, major emphasis should be placed on formative evaluation, on the teacher's role as coach and helper rather than as judge.

---

[3] It is interesting to note similarities between composing in writing and composing in other fields such as music, art, and architecture.

EXERCISES

1. Select a topic that you might write about: some influential person you have known, a place that has been important to you, a brush with death, a memorable incident from the past. Then do the following:

    a. Spend four or five minutes jotting down single words and phrases associated with your topic. Write down everything that comes to mind without pausing to weigh or evaluate.

    b. Now ask yourself: What was special about this person, this place, or this incident that makes it memorable for me? What is its central importance for me? Take a few minutes to record your thoughts.

    c. Now ask yourself: Is there anything else that is important about this topic? What have I forgotten to include? Take a minute or two to record your thoughts.

    d. Now read through your notes, and, when you have finished, begin a piece of free writing about your topic. Do not worry about spelling, or even, necessarily, about complete sentences. Do not stop to evaluate or organize. Think of this part of the exercise as getting down in continuous prose thoughts that you may later use in a piece of writing. Write for 15 or 20 minutes, or longer, if you wish.

    e. When you have finished, read over what you have written and consider what form this piece of writing is best suited to: an essay, a poem, a story, a play? When you have decided, begin writing in the form you have decided upon.

    f. At the end of this exercise, take a few minutes to record in your journal your response to the exercise. What did you find helpful? Where did you get stuck?

2. For this exercise, you need a partner to work with. Select a person you respect and feel comfortable with, but preferably not one of your best friends. The procedure is as follows:

    a. Each select a topic that you have strong feelings about.

    b. Now take turns in exploring your topic, orally, with your partner. It may take 20 to 30 minutes for each of you to explore your topic. In the role of the "explorer," your task is to talk about your topic and why it seems important to you. The role of the listener, is to respond by:
    *   reflecting back what the explorer said;
    *   noting points of strong feeling;

- asking questions of clarification.
- Your task is not to contribute your own thoughts and feelings on the topic.

c. At the end of your exploratory session, jot down notes of important points that became clear as you talked.

3. Test your knowledge of the spelling rule for final silent -e by joining the word and the suffix in the following examples:

grade + able	desire + able	like + ly
place + ment	adventure + ous	use + able
like + able	private + ly	enforce + able

4. Account for the spelling of the following words by explaining why the underlined letter has been doubled or why not:

develo<u>p</u>ing	refe<u>rr</u>al	defe<u>rr</u>ed
sta<u>bb</u>ed	refe<u>r</u>ence	defe<u>r</u>ence
regrou<u>p</u>ed	spiri<u>t</u>ed	regre<u>tt</u>ed
diffe<u>r</u>ed	infe<u>rr</u>ed	occu<u>rr</u>ence

5. The unstressed vowel has been omitted from each of the following words. Pair each word with a cognate word that would help with the spelling of the omitted vowel.

manag r	maj r	ind stry
ill strate	janit r	comp rable
neg tive	fert lize	narr tive

———————   ▬▬▬▬▬   ———————

REFERENCES

Applebee, A.N. (1984). *Contexts for Learning to Write: Studies of Secondary School Instruction.* Norwood, NJ: Ablex.

Atwell, N. (1987). *In the Middle: Writing, Reading and Learning with Adolescents.* Portsmouth, NH: Boynton/Cook.

Belanger, J.J. (1985). Conflict between mentor and judge: Being fair and being helpful in composition evaluation. *English Quarterly,* 18 (4), 79-92.

Britton, J.N., T. Burgess, N. Martin, A. McLeod and H. Rosen (1975). *The Development of Writing Abilities (11-18)*. London: Macmillan Education.

Burtis, P.J., C. Bereiter, M. Scardamalia and J. Tetroe (1983). The development of planning in writing. In B.M. Kroll and G. Wells (eds.), *Explorations in the Development of Writing: Theory, Research and Practice* (pp. 153-176). Chichester, England: John Wiley and Sons.

Crowhurst, M. (1979). The writing workshop: An experiment in peer response to writing. *Language Arts*, 56, pp. 757-762.

Crowhurst, M. (1988). Prerequisites for teaching writing: What the writing needs to know and be. *Canadian Journal of English Language Arts*, 11 (3), 5-12.

Crowhurst, M. (1993). *Writing in the Middle Years*. Markham, Ont. Pippin Publishing.

Emig, J. (1971). *The composing processes of twelfth graders*. Research Report No. 13. Urbana, IL: National Council of Teachers of English.

Emig, J. (1981). Non-magical thinking: Presenting writing developmentally in schools. In C.H. Frederiksen and J.F. Dominic (eds.), *Writing: The Nature, Development and Teaching of Written Communication. Vol.2. Writing: Process, Development and Communication* (pp. 21-30). Hillside, NJ: Lawrence Erlbaum.

Flower, L., and J.R. Hayes (1981). A cognitive process theory of writing. *College Composition and Communication*, 32, 365-387.

Hillocks, G. (1986). *Research on written composition: New directions for teaching*. Urbana, IL: National Council of Teachers of English.

Marland, M. (1977). *Language Across the Curriculum*. London: Heinemann Educational.

Penner, P.G., and R.E. McConnell (1977). *Language on Paper*. Macmillan.

Perl, S., and N. Wilson (1986). *Through Teachers' Eyes: Portraits of Writing Teachers at Work*. Portsmouth, NH: Heinemann.

Sommers, N. (1980). Revision strategies of students writers and experienced adult writers. *College Composition and Communication*. 31, 378-388.

Zemelman, S., and H. Daniels (1988). *A Community of Writers: Teaching Writing in the Junior and Senior High School*. Portsmouth, NH: Heinemann.

Chapter 10
WRITING TO LEARN[1]

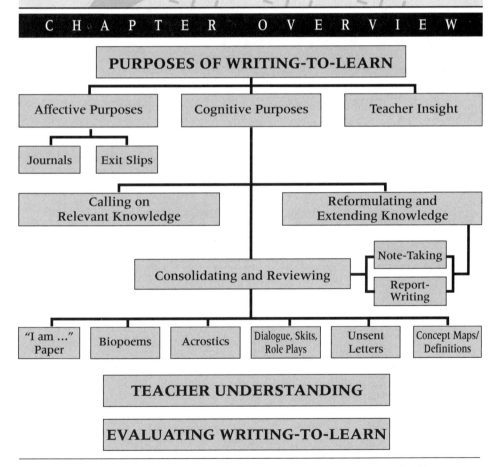

CHAPTER OVERVIEW

PURPOSES OF WRITING-TO-LEARN

- Affective Purposes
  - Journals
  - Exit Slips
- Cognitive Purposes
  - Calling on Relevant Knowledge
  - Reformulating and Extending Knowledge
    - Note-Taking
    - Report-Writing
  - Consolidating and Reviewing
    - "I am ..." Paper
    - Biopoems
    - Acrostics
    - Dialogue, Skits, Role Plays
    - Unsent Letters
    - Concept Maps/ Definitions
- Teacher Insight

TEACHER UNDERSTANDING

EVALUATING WRITING-TO-LEARN

---

[1] Some of the material in this chapter was published previously as "Writing to learn: Promise and problems," in S. Straw and S. Baardman (eds.) *Social Reflections on Writing: To Reach and to Realize*. (Winnipeg, Manitoba: Literacy Publications, 1993), and in M. Crowhurst, *Writing in the Middle Years* (Markham, Ont. Pippin Publishing 1993.)

Putting thoughts into words is of critical importance for learning. Expressing our thoughts raises to consciousness what we are only dimly aware of. Once expressed, thoughts can be developed or modified. We have all heard people say — and have probably said, or thought, ourselves — "Well, I know what I mean, but I just can't put it into words." What we usually mean is that the ideas are not clear enough in our minds to give expression to them. The act of expressing our thoughts helps us to clarify them and to discover what it is that we actually know, and feel, and believe.

The two ways of putting thoughts into words are speaking and writing. Each is important for learning. They are complementary activities. They share some similarities and some differences. The great similarity is that both speaking and writing force us to clarify our thoughts. But each of the two modes has different values. When we speak, we may have immediate input by others who corroborate, qualify, challenge and develop what we say and thus contribute to the development of our thoughts. The unique value of writing is that it allows us to capture fleeting thought and to hold it for further contemplation and development.

The three great values of writing as a means of learning are its *explicitness*, its relative *permanence*, and the fact that writing requires *active participation*. The act of committing ideas to paper forces us to be explicit, to find words, to express them in complete thoughts, and to arrange those thoughts more or less coherently. The permanence of writing allows us to work on our thoughts. As Gage (1986, p. 24) has said:

> Writing is thinking made tangible … Writing is thinking that can be stopped and tinkered with. It is a way of holding thought still enough to examine its structure, its flaws. The road to clearer understanding of one's thoughts is travelled on paper.

Writing requires action. Emig (1977) attributes the value of writing to the fact that it is a multisensory, multimodal activity involving hand, eye, and brain. The hand is active producing an image (the written product) that the writer can see; and the writer also learns by representing meanings symbolically in words.

A series of important research studies on the relationship between writing and learning were conducted by Langer and Applebee (1987). The final, culminating study of the series involved 112 ninth-grade and eleventh-grade students. The purpose was to determine the kinds of thinking and learning that resulted when students engaged in various kinds of writing activities in conjunction with reading a text. Students read two different passages from social studies texts and then, for each reading, engaged in one of the following kinds of writing: **comprehension questions** requiring students to write short answers to twenty questions; **a summary** requiring students to write a cohesive summary of the reading in 200-250 words; and **analytic writing** requiring students to write an essay supporting a particular interpretation or point of view related to the text. A fourth group of students spent the entire time reading and studying the texts but did no writing of any kind. The two most important findings of the study were as follows:

1. Writing proved to be a powerful means of fostering students' learning. No matter what kind of writing students did, they remembered more and remembered longer than the students who read and studied but did no writing.

2. Different kinds of writing led to different kinds of thinking. Comprehension questions led to a wide but superficial review of the material. In summary writing, students focused on less of the content, but looked for more relationships among ideas than for comprehension questions. In their analytic writing, students focused on an even smaller proportion of the content of the original text, but processed it more extensively and remembered it longer.

The focus of the previous chapter was on writing processes and strategies you might use to engage students in the kinds of processes that will help them learn to write. The focus in this chapter is not on learning to write but on writing as a means of learning. The last chapter focused on learning how to write so as to produce a finished written product that could communicate successfully with others. The goal of the kind of writing discussed in this chapter is to promote understanding and insight through writing.

The distinction between writing to communicate and writing to learn is not absolute. Some kinds of writing-to-learn result in a finished, polished product — report-writing, for example. However, writing to learn does not necessarily involve the production of a finished, polished piece of writing. The writing may be informal, scrappy, and incomplete. It may not even be written in complete sentences. Our primary interest when we ask students to write in order to learn is not a product on a page but a product that is in the student's head— knowledge, insight, understanding.

PURPOSES OF WRITING TO LEARN

Writing can foster learning in various ways. It can serve both *affective* and *cognitive* purposes. It can also aid the learning process by providing a window through which teachers can view the thinking and understanding of their students thus making them better able to plan future activities. Each of these — affective purposes, cognitive purposes, and ways in which writing can give the teacher insight into students' thinking processes — is discussed in the sections that follow with illustrations of kinds of writing that may serve these purposes. In the final section of the chapter some suggestions are made about evaluating writing to learn.

AFFECTIVE PURPOSES

Affect refers to the emotions. Emotions affect learning for good and for ill. Negative emotions like anxiety, fear, and anger often inhibit learning. If we fear we will not hit that high note, or clear that high hurdle, we probably will not. Writing anxiety and math anxiety are well known phenomena that inhibit performance in each of those two subject areas. When we are angry, the energy we expend on our anger leaves us less energy to expend in more profitable ways. Writing can be a useful tool for defusing negative emotions in the classroom.

Positive emotions, on the other hand, are a great asset. Liking and trust for the teacher are positive forces that can facilitate the learning process. Certain kinds of writing are useful in establishing understanding and trust between students and teacher. If students feel that their ideas are accepted and valued, and that their questions and problems are addressed, they are likely to enter a class with positive feelings that make for a healthy learning environment. Writing can help to establish a positive, cooperative, trusting classroom climate.

Two kinds of writing that offer good opportunities for student/teacher interactions of the kind that are likely to establish trust are journal writing and exit slips.

Journals

Journals — or learning logs, as they are sometimes called — are used by teachers in many different ways. They are described by Gere (1985) as being central to writing to learn. The journal is a convenient place for keeping many of the kinds of writing described throughout this chapter. In their journals, students are encouraged to observe, to react, to analyze, to evaluate — to catch thought in progress. They are not intended exclusively for writing for affective purposes. But the journal is ideally suited for this kind of writing.

Free writing exercises at the beginning of a class or unit may serve affective purposes as well as cognitive. A preliminary brief writing exercise makes it easier for many students to participate in a class discussion in contrast to oral questions that tend to result in contributions by the same few articulate students who can gather their thoughts quickly. In a home economics class, the teacher showed students a picture of a room and asked them to do five minutes' spontaneous free writing on whether or not they would be comfortable living there. At the end of five minutes, students were invited to read their answers. Many students volunteered. Opinions read out were discussed and elaborated on by others. The discussion served as an introduction to a unit on elements of housing design. The activity served affective purposes in more than one way. Students found it encouraging to know that they already possessed useful knowledge about the unit they were about to begin. Since all opinions were accepted as valid, the activity helped to build confidence and to encourage cooperation and questioning. Such activities help to build a comfortable, non-threatening, interactive classroom — an ideal climate for learning. The contribution of the writing exercise is that it encourages all students to gather their thoughts and have something ready to contribute.

Exit Slips

Exit slips are even more informal than journal entries. Simply have your students take half a sheet of paper at the end of the class, and write you a message as the "price" of getting out of the class. I do it frequently in the early weeks of every class I teach. For my students who are university graduates it is usually enough for me to say, "Tell me anything you want me to know about the class." It is sometimes useful to ask more specific questions, especially with younger students: *What did you like most/least about today's class? What was the hardest thing you did in today's class? Was there anything in today's class that you would like more help with? What would you like to know more about? How is this course going for you?*

Exit slips are responded to by the teacher overnight and returned promptly. It takes a little time to respond, but the pay-off is high. You find out what your students think and how they feel, what they understand and what needs further explanation. The fact that they can express their feelings helps to dissipate anxiety and to establish a trusting teacher-student relationship. It can be difficult to establish these kinds of relationships with students if you are teaching many students in four or five different classes a day, as will often be the case for secondary school teachers.

This kind of writing can, of course, be done in the journal. However, it is a lot easier to carry home thirty pieces of paper than thirty journals. In any event, exit slips can subsequently be kept in a pocket in the journal to provide part of the ongoing record of the student's response to the course.

You may not be able to maintain the practice of responding to frequent exit slips throughout the term. However, once you have established the idea of teacher-student communication through several exit slips completed by all in the class, a **comment box** may be left in the room so that students can comment any time they wish on issues of concern.

COGNITIVE PURPOSES

Langer and Applebee (1987) suggest that writing can serve three kinds of cognitive purposes: (1) to draw on relevant knowledge and experience in preparation for a new unit or activity; (2) to consolidate and review recently acquired information; and (3) to reformulate and extend knowledge. Each of these is discussed in turn with illustrations of appropriate writing activities. Note-taking and report-writing are common activities in many subject areas. At their best, note-taking and report-writing can serve a variety of cognitive purposes. At their worst, they involve wholesale plagiarism and great teacher frustration. Note-taking and report-writing are discussed in separate sections.

Calling on Relevant Knowledge

The importance of preexisting knowledge for comprehension was discussed in Chapter 7. Prior knowledge is critical not only for understanding what we read but also what we hear. Whatever we learn is learned on the basis of what we know when we come to new material. Setting students tasks that activate their prior knowledge serves two important purposes. It calls up relevant knowledge as a basis for the material about to be studied; and it informs you about your students' knowledge and, sometimes, about misconceptions that you will need to address. The way you go about teaching a unit is determined by what your students already know.

Two kinds of simple writing activities that are very useful for calling up prior knowledge are free writing and listing.

Free Writing   A fourth-grade teacher who was about to teach a unit on states of matter, asked her students to do a free-writing exercise telling all they knew about matter. Some knew a lot. One boy wrote (Crowhurst, 1993):

> Matter is solids, liquids and gases. Gas material is oxygen, helium fumes and so on. Liquid material is water, acid, milk, pop and so on. And solid's material is metal, plastic, gels, wood, and so on. Liquid is sort of like water. And solids are like metal. And gases are like oxygen.

Others were not as well informed:

> Gases are mostly used in veaclals and is bad for the ozone. Saturn is made out of gas. Gases are found in the seabeds and in Texas. Gases can kill lots of water creatures and birds. Liquids are a drink that living things could drink like water. Flowers have liquids and it's called nectore. Solids. Trees can be solids. What else is solid?

Listing   Some uses of listing have already been described in Chapter 8. Ogle's (1986) K-W-L procedure, for example, is as useful to introduce a new unit as it is to introduce a reading. It may be simplified for very young students. A teacher of primary students aged 6 and 7 was about to begin a unit on dinosaurs. In the weeks prior to beginning the unit, a display on dinosaurs was set up in the room. A large, informative poster decorated the wall, and the display included many books that students were free to read if they wished to. When it came time to start the unit the teacher introduced it by distributing a sheet that asked them to list three things they knew about dinosaurs and three things they wondered about. A selection of their sentence completers for "I know...." were:

- that dinosaurs lived long ago. Because scientists dug up them.

- that they had tails.

- that tyrannosauris rex is a meat eater.

- a long long time ago there were dinosaurs it was 225,000,000 year's ago.

- dinosaurs lived in hot ereaus (areas).

- long long ago the land was together.

- dinosaurs had cold blod.

- the world was atched (attached) together.

- brontosauris is as tall as a house he is as long as two buses and he is as heavy as five elephants.

- dinosaurs had a small brain.

- there were 500 kinds of dinosaurs.

Some of the things they wondered were:

- how the dinosaur's died.

- why they died.

- why the land was warm long long ago.

- if the land will every go back to how it was befor.

- How did the croc(odile) survive.

- if they live in space.

- if they are ikskikt (extinct).

The writing exercise undoubtedly whetted their appetites for the unit to come and gave the teacher useful information on which to base her planning.

Note that listing is a useful procedure not only for calling on background knowledge, but also for extracting information available by observation. A geology teacher provided groups of students with rock samples representing the major types of rock and asked them to list similarities and differences among rocks. An art teacher (Zimmerman, 1985) brought in a still life painting and asked her students to list all the objects they could see. That done, she asked them to write a description of the person who might own these objects. In both cases, the simple writing task of listing was a first step that eased students into a much more demanding task: in one case, categorizing rock types; in the other, interpreting a painting.

Consolidating and Reviewing

Many interesting writing tasks may be used to encourage students to consolidate or to review recently studied material. If students are asked merely to repeat back material you have given them, you cannot tell how well they understand the memorized words and phrases they write. The kinds of writing tasks described below require them to engage in cognitive processing beyond memorization. The activities are helpful for review and also for showing what they understand and what has been misunderstood.

1. *"I am ..." Papers*   (Watson, 1985). Students are required to write about a person, a process, an animal, or an object in the first person. For example, the primary students who studied dinosaurs might have written "I am ..." papers on "I am tyrannosaurus rex" or "I am a brontosaurus" or "I am a paleontologist." (They did indeed know this word!!) Figure 10.1 shows a biology student's effort on "I am an ulva algae." A music teacher suggested that students could write "I am" definitions beginning "I am rhythm ..." or "I am a 3/4 time signature ..." Another music teacher's "I am ..." poem on key signatures is shown in Figure 10.2. Note how thoroughly this elegant poem covers key signatures. Note also, however, that writing does not need to be polished or elegant in order to serve the purpose of having students review a topic.

2. *Biopoems*   Biopoems may be written about people, objects, animals, materials. The form of the biopoem (Gere, 1985, p.222) is as follows:

    Line 1. First name

    Line 2. Four traits that describe the character.

    Line 3. Relative ("brother," "sister," "daughter," etc.) of   .

Figure 10.1
I Am an Ulva Algae

I am Ellie the ulva algae. One day when I was just a little algae I asked my mommy where I came from and this is what she told me.

Mommy used to be a sporophyte. That meant she was diploid and had 2n chromosomes. One day after she underwent meiosis, she produced four spores that were haploid. That means they only had n chromosomes. These four spores in turn grew to be gametophytes and they produced gametes which were also haploid. Then it happened. Two of the haploid gametes joined together to form a zygote. This zygote was diploid 2n and grew to be a sporophyte. That's me. Now I still didn't understand Mommy very well so she drew a diagram for me to see.

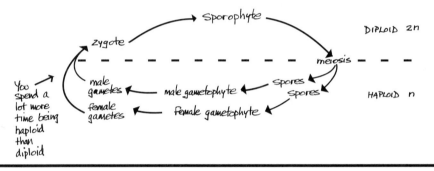

Source: Written by a Grade 11 student (with minor revisions).

Line 4. Lover of   (list three things or people)

Line 5. Who feels   (three items)

Line 6. Who needs   (three items

Line 7. Who fears   (three items)

Line 8. Who gives   (three items)

Line 9. Who would like to see   (three items)

Line 10. Resident of   .

Line 11. Last name (or alternative name)

The biopoem in Figure 10.3, which was composed by a group of second-graders, does not conform perfectly to the prescribed form. Note, however, how attempting to complete the various lines encouraged the students to review their material on dinosaurs from different perspectives. Teachers of young students who use forms like the biopoem may allow their students a lot of latitude; older students often find it an enjoyable challenge to try to complete all lines as prescribed.

Figure 10.2
"I am ..." Poem

I am a Key Signature

I am a key signature,

Standing mostly to the left of the page,

In a pile of sharps or flats.

I am the first thing you should notice.

Look closely,

For I predict the piece.

I could be a happy major,

Or sadly minor.

What I say goes.

A sharped "F" remains sharp,

Unless I say it changes,

And my only enemy is an accidental.

I am

A key signature

I am.

Barbara Elwood

Figure 10.3
Biopoem Written by Second-Graders

Brontosaurus
Big, slow, small brain, heavy
Relative of the crocodile
Lover of jungles, swamps, heat
Who needs water, lots of plants, other brontosauruses
Who fears flesh-eaters
Resident of millions of years ago
Dinosaur

3. *Acrostics*   To write an acrostic, students select a topic and write successive lines beginning with successive letters of the name. Each line must convey a significant fact about the chosen topic. An acrostic on lobsters written by a third grader is shown in Figure 10.4 (Maxim, 1990). The acrostic on sand in Figure 10.5 was written by a geology major with a flair for poetry. A slightly different use for an acrostic was used by a biology teacher who asked her students to make up a mnemonic to help them remember the levels of classification used in biology: namely, kingdom, phylum, class, order, family, genus, and species. Two suggestions were:

Kissing	King
People	Philip
Can	Came
Only	Over
Form	For
Good	Good
Skills	Sandwiches

4. *Dialogues, Skits, Role Plays*   The characters in dramatic forms of writing may be people — historical characters, for example, or characters from a novel. They may also be inanimate objects that are personified.

Figure 10.4
Acrostic

LOBSTERS
Lays up to 5,000 eggs
One claw is to crush their prey
Bait is what they use to catch lobster with
Sometimes if you hold one it might pinch
Turns red when it is cooked
Eats pogies, mackerel, bluefish, and redfish
Return females with eggs to the ocean
Scavengers!

Source: Reprinted with permission from Betsy Beck and Robin L. Beck. In "Beginning Researchers" by D. Maxim, In N. Atwell (Ed.), *Coming to Know: Writing to Learn in the Intermediate Grades*. (Heinemann, a division of Reed Publishing (USA) Inc., Portsmouth, NH, 1990) p. 8.

Figure 10.5
Acrostic Poem

SAND
Some are white and pretty nifty.
Always small and kind of sifty.
No two grains are quite the same.
Dancing waves are all to blame.

Dwayne McBeth

Zimmerman (1985) asked the students in her art appreciation class to review concepts recently covered in class by writing a dialogue between a gallery owner and a visitor whose opening utterance was, "How on earth can that painting be worth $100,000?" A business education teacher asked marketing students to write a dialogue for a sales presentation. A chemistry teacher had his students write a dialogue between carbon as diamond and carbon as graphite. Another chemistry teacher suggested that a dialogue between elements in the periodic table might help students remember properties of different families. An example of a dialogue is shown in Figure 10.6. Note that turns should be fairly short and four to seven exchanges for each participant is usually enough.

Students in a biology class who were studying pathogens were asked to work in groups to produce a skit entitled "How I caught malaria." Group members played various roles — the patient, the mosquito, body parts, props — and found the activity both enjoyable and instructive.

5. *Unsent Letters* Unsent letters — "unsent" because they are not sent to the addressee — may be written to living persons, characters from history or literature, or to inanimate objects that are personified. Figure 10.7 shows a personal ad written by the element, chlorine, and a letter of reply by the element, sodium. Note how students must review what they know in order to write such pieces.

6. *Concept Maps and Concept Definitions* Concept maps and concept definitions are excellent ways of reviewing concepts and vocabulary. To assign a concept map, use the following procedure. Arrange a set of terms on a page. Terms may be concepts, events, objects, laws, themes, characters, or processes. Tell students to consider each term together with every other term on the page and to link terms that are related in any way. The nature of the link is written on the line joining the terms. Most terms are linked to several others. Students may work individually, in pairs, or in groups. Figure 10.8 shows a concept map made by two biology students with the assistance of their text as a means of reviewing for a test. Note that completing such a

---

Figure 10.6
Dialogue Between a Period and a Comma

PERIOD:	Well, the first thing is that I am a better shape than you. A circle is a perfect shape.
COMMA:	I think I have a more interesting shape. Perfectly even shapes are so-o-o-o boring!
PERIOD:	Well you can't deny that I'm more powerful than you. When the reader sees me, he comes to a full stop. That's what they call me in Australia—a "full stop".
COMMA:	I also make the reader pause.
PERIOD:	Yes, but it's such a little pause you can hardly notice it.
COMMA:	You might think you are more powerful, but I am more useful. You are just used to end a sentence, but I am used for all kinds of reasons.
PERIOD:	I am not used just at the end of a sentence. I am also used after an abbreviation and in a decimal number.
COMMA:	In French, they use a comma in a decimal number.
PERIOD:	Well, anyway, what are all these different things you are used for?
COMMA:	Well, I separate the nouns in a list; and I separate adjectives like in "a scrawny, freckled girl"; and I separate introductory phrases like in "After cleaning the car, I had to dig the garden." And I could think of other things too.
PERIOD:	It's true you are used for a lot of different things.
COMMA:	Yes. You count the periods and the commas on a page. There'll nearly always be more of me.
PERIOD:	I guess, really, you'd have to say that you have your work to do and I have mine. We are both important in different ways.

Source: Crowhurst, 1993

task encourages them also to look for new relationships among terms since not all terms are directly related in ways mentioned in their text.

Completing concept definitions like that illustrated in Figure 10.9 is another useful means of revising concepts. The term being defined, *wedge*, is written in the centre of the page. Above the term is written the more general category to which the term belongs, in this case, *simple machine*. To the left of the term is written an example of a concept that is related to the concept being defined; it should also be a member of the more general category. In this case, the example chosen is *inclined plane*. To the right of the concept are listed some of its properties. Below the concept are written examples of the concept that is being defined: *knife*, *axe*, and *front teeth*. Writing definitions in this way is a useful

Figure 10.7
Personal Ad and Letter of Reply

Reactive, attractive non-metal, interested in stable, long-term relationship, seeks alkali metal to bond with. Must have high electronegativity to ensure secure, long-lasting attachment; must be able to donate extra electron. Reply: "Chlorine," this paper.

Dear Chlorine:
I am replying to your recent ad in the personal column. I am one of the most eligible of the alkali metals. It is true I am small with an atomic mass of only 23.0 a.m.u. but don't let my size fool you! With an electronegativity of 0.9 I could easily displace other competitors from your side to win your respect and love. I have two orbitals. I could offer you an extra electron for your vacant space. When joined together, we would make beautiful crystals. The bond between us would be near impossible to break—not even fire could take me away from you. We would have a secure future as a stable octet unless water parts us.

Sodium

review. It may also be done as a way of trying to call up relevant knowledge — preferably by students working in pairs or small groups.

The kinds of writing activities suggested are both enjoyable and useful. They require students to review what they know about a topic and, often, to use newly acquired vocabulary, helping them to make it their own. Students do not always enjoy doing activities like these. It is hard work. Those who have perfected the skill of getting good grades by regurgitating facts committed to memory may want to be left in peace doing what they know how to do very well. Activities such as these, however, make them think about material in different ways.

Reformulating and Extending Knowledge

Nothing is more important for our students than to learn how to use the information they acquire. It is not enough to supply them with facts for them to memorize and parrot back. The world is changing rapidly. New applications for information are constantly demanded. Workers are needed who can adapt, create, hypothesize, and find new ways of working with materials and data. To prepare our students, we must invite them not merely to master information, but to reformulate and extend the knowledge they have acquired.

Teachers' questions are an important medium for promoting students' thinking. As discussed elsewhere in the book, teachers' questions are predominantly factual questions that ask students to answer by reproducing

Figure 10.8
Concept Map: The Cell

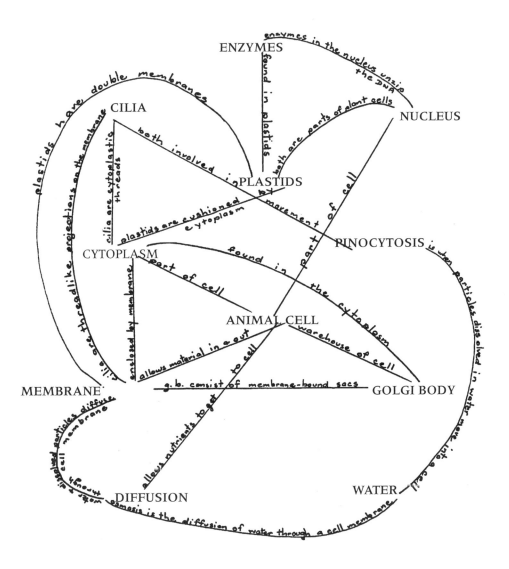

Figure 10.9
An Illustration of Concept Definition

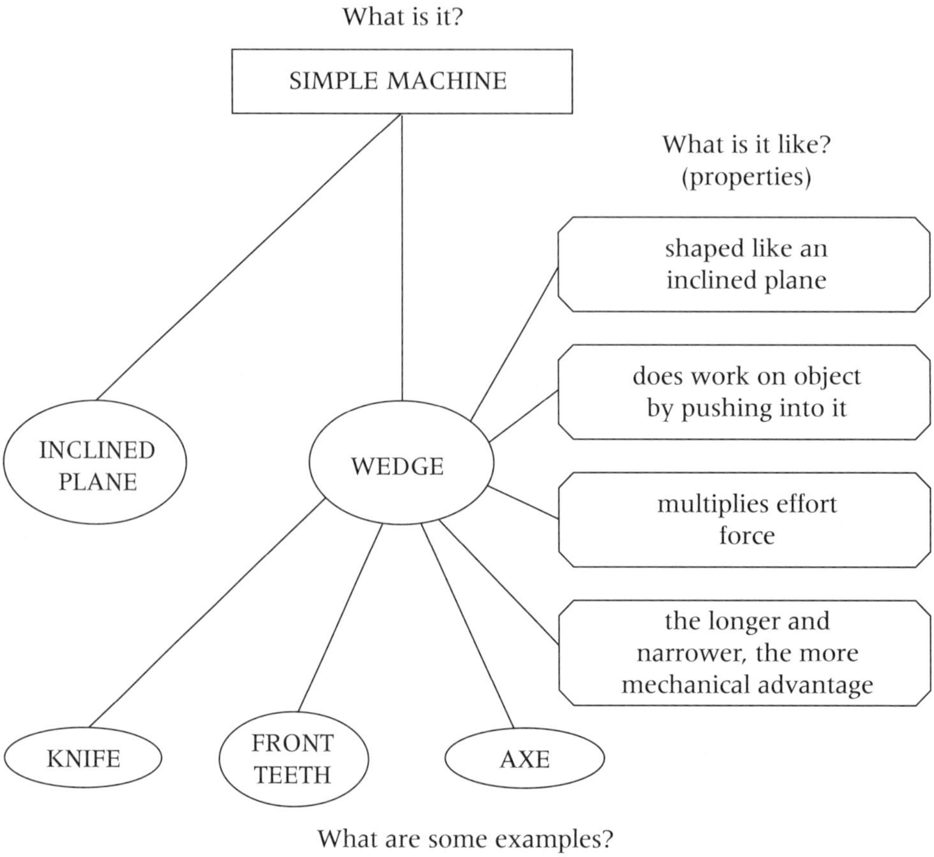

What is it?

SIMPLE MACHINE

What is it like?
(properties)

shaped like an
inclined plane

does work on object
by pushing into it

INCLINED
PLANE

WEDGE

multiplies effort
force

the longer and
narrower, the more
mechanical advantage

KNIFE

FRONT
TEETH

AXE

What are some examples?

Source: Student assignment.

memorized material. Other kinds of questions should be asked frequently. Students may need to be told that some questions are "thinking" questions rather than factual questions. A biology student was asked the question *Why do monerans not simply take over the earth if they produce asexually?* He complained in his learning log that he could not find the answer in his text. His teacher explained that this was a thinking question, not a factual one. Students who have spent many years in the education system may not expect to be asked thinking questions!

Questions that call for divergent thinking may be the stimulus for five or six minutes of free writing. The results of such exercises are good for students and refreshing for teachers when they discover what interesting things students can think of if we invite them to and are interested in their responses. "What if ..." questions can stimulate useful thinking in many content areas. Questions like: "What if there were no friction?" will cause physics students to think back to the fundamental principle behind friction and to extend their thinking to a new situation. Newton (1990) lists dozens of useful questions for English teachers to ask; teachers in other subject areas may also find them useful:

- What are the not-very-obvious reasons why...?
- What are some reasons that people with conflicting views could give why...?
- What alternatives to ... are possible/would have been possible?
- Which is the best (most efficient, most productive, etc.) alternative? Why?
- Is this person (this animal, this idea) more like a rock or a rose?

Jack Graves (Langer and Applebee, 1987), teaching *Romeo and Juliet,* asked students to work in groups to generate alternative courses of action that Juliet might have taken when her parents insisted that she marry Paris after she had secretly married Romeo. They were also to list pros and cons for each alternative. The following day they explored in class some of the alternatives the groups had generated: what problems would have developed, for example, if Juliet had decided to run away with Romeo? These activities helped to extend students' understanding of why Juliet took the drug.

The create-an-animal assignment used by a biology teacher working with Langer and Applebee (1987) is another example of a useful writing assignment that encouraged students to reformulate and extend their knowledge. Students in the class had been given the task: *Design a animal to live on land. Start with a chordate that lives in the water and decide what you have to do to get it to live on land* (p. 53). The task required them to consider the work they had done over the previous month and to use it to create something new. Another biology teacher, reading about the create-an-animal assignment, suggested a follow-up assignment: students could be asked to classify all the created animals. They would thus both revise the classification system and experience, first-hand, some of the problems of classification methodology.

Students will be prompted to think if they are encouraged to ask questions as well as to answer them. Journal-writing provides an excellent opportunity for asking questions. Some examples of questions asked by eleventh-grade biology students were:

- If viruses are non-living, then why are they in a biology textbook? Isn't biology the branch of science that deals with living things and their surroundings?

- In the text it says that when a paramecium has a lack of food, or in conditions of dryness, it goes into a cyst. I regard a cyst as a form of hibernation. Am I right? If so, how is it possible for a paramecium to die?

- According to the text, there's a theory that if you don't use a part of your body, it will go away. I find that my 5th toe is hardly in use while walking. Do you think humans will progressively get smaller 5th toes and fingers?

- How is it possible that living matter be made up of non-living particles (i.e., molecules)? … This entire concept of living matter from non-living particles is odd since it makes me wonder just what it means to be alive if you're made from dead stuff anyways.

Crowhurst and Kooy (1985) describe the kind of thinking ninth-grade students engaged in when they were asked to read and respond to a novel without any input by the teacher. The teacher distributed the novel — Robert Cormier's *I Am the Cheese* — with no introduction. The students were to read the novel and make journal entries, after every 10 or 15 pages, by responding to the following sentence starters:

- What impressed me in this section was …

- I noticed …

- I wonder about …

- I predict …

- I don't understand/I now understand …

The teacher responded to their entries by questioning (*What makes you think so?*), by sympathizing (*Confusing, isn't it!*), by encouraging (*Right on! What an interesting thought! That never occurred to me before.*) The students raised in their journals every conceivable question the teacher might have wished to discuss. They questioned, hypothesized and interpreted. They described their feelings about characters, events, and the book as a whole. They commented on the author's style, on the book's structure, and on its title. Teachers have to do much less telling when students are encouraged to think.

Note Taking

Note-taking is an activity that occurs in many different situations. Students may take notes of a lecture or speech, or of a film or other visual presentation. They will often make notes on something they read. Some situations require them to take quick notes — on the run, as it were. Other situations — like making notes from a printed text — allow them to take as much time as they want to. Virtually all students will benefit from some instruction in making notes. Even university students are often ineffective note takers. When instructing students in making notes, it is easiest to begin with note-taking from a written text. If you start with this kind of note-making, you can later have them make notes of oral presentations — of the lecture of a distinguished visitor to the class or school, or of the principal's remarks at a school assembly.

Students make notes from textual material for various purposes. Sometimes they want full, detailed notes of a chapter or reading as an aid to learning the material. Their notes, in this case, need to be a summary of the chapter. A second way of making notes for the purpose of learning from text is to make two-column notes. A third purpose for note-taking is to prepare some kind of report or research paper; in this case, notes must be taken from a variety of sources and should be selective rather than exhaustive. Students do not always recognize the different purposes of note taking and will often summarize huge amounts of irrelevant material when making notes for a report.

Summary Writing   Writing summaries helps students remember textual material (Langer and Applebee, 1987; Taylor, 1982). Learning to write summaries also draws students' attention to the organization of material in a text. Taylor (1982) devised a procedure for making hierarchical summaries that is easy to teach to students in the middle grades and beyond. The procedure consists of three steps: (1) previewing; (2) reading and outlining; and (3) studying and retelling.

1. ***Previewing***   Students are given a three to five page segment of text that has headings and subheadings. They quickly skim the text and, with the help of the teacher, make a skeleton outline consisting of Roman numerals, one numeral for each major section as indicated by a main heading. They then write a capital letter for each subheading in each major section, and leave five or six lines between capital letters. Students now have a skeleton outline consisting of Roman numerals and capital letters but otherwise empty. The outline serves them as a study guide for the next step, reading and outlining.

2. ***Reading and Outlining***   Using the outline to guide them, the students now read the first major section and do the following:

   • Leaving the space after the first Roman numeral blank, read the first subsection and write a topic sentence, in their own words, that expresses the main idea.

   • List two to four important supporting details for the main idea.

   • Follow these two steps for each subsection in the first major section of the text.

Figure 10.10
Example of a Hierarchical Summary for a Seventh-Grade Social Studies Text Selection Containing One Heading and Four Subheadings

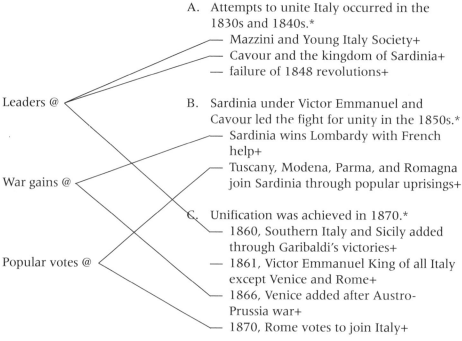

I.   The states of Italy united into a single kingdom in the second half of the 19th century.#

  A.   Attempts to unite Italy occurred in the 1830s and 1840s.*
   — Mazzini and Young Italy Society+
   — Cavour and the kingdom of Sardinia+
   — failure of 1848 revolutions+

Leaders @

  B.   Sardinia under Victor Emmanuel and Cavour led the fight for unity in the 1850s.*
   — Sardinia wins Lombardy with French help+
   — Tuscany, Modena, Parma, and Romagna join Sardinia through popular uprisings+

War gains @

  C.   Unification was achieved in 1870.*
   — 1860, Southern Italy and Sicily added through Garibaldi's victories+
   — 1861, Victor Emmanuel King of all Italy except Venice and Rome+
Popular votes @
   — 1866, Venice added after Austro-Prussia war+
   — 1870, Rome votes to join Italy+

  D.   United Italy had problems to overcome*
   — hostility of Pope Pius IX+
   — hostility between north and south+
   — republicans versus monarchists+
   — failure to include Italian areas in France and Austria+

\# Topic sentence for entire selection as designated by a heading
* Main ideas for subsections as designated by subheadings
\+ Supporting details for main ideas
@ Key phrases connecting subsections

- Having completed all subsections of the first major section, students now write a topic sentence, in their own words, for the section just completed and insert it beside the first Roman numeral (i.e., I).

- Write in the left margin of the outline any key words or phrases for subsections that seem to go together. Draw lines between key phrases and corresponding subsections. Figure 10.10 shows a summary outline for one section of a social studies text showing the major heading and four subheadings.

- Complete the remaining sections of the text in the same way.

The first few times a hierarchical summary is done, students will need substantial teacher guidance. Students should share and discuss their topic sentences for the first subsection, and then the supporting details they selected. Draw attention to sentences that are accurately and economically expressed, and gradually reduce the amount of help and guidance you give so that after five or six summaries, students can complete them independently. Note that writing a summary of this kind may be done as a group task.

3. ***Studying and Retelling Orally*** Taylor suggests that students should then study their summaries and work with a partner, telling everything they can remember of their summary.

A summarizing procedure is used when students need to read, understand, and remember the content of a text. Summarizing requires active processing of the text and leads to improved comprehension and retention. Summaries are also a valuable resource for reviewing for a test. Remember that Chapter 8 suggests other ways of summarizing texts graphically.

Two-Column Notes Two column notes may be used in various ways. One useful procedure is to have students list key words or concepts in the left hand column and use the right hand column to elaborate on the main ideas listed on the left. Students now have an excellent study aid. By covering the information on the right, students can easily test themselves on the concepts listed on the left.

A second use of two-column notes has been described by Berthoff (1981). The left-hand column is used to enter data or record information from text. The right-hand column is used to record reactions to the factual information recorded on the left. Students may record hypotheses, extend concepts by referring to their own experience, apply or evaluate new information, or record questions or problems that occur to them.

Taking Notes for a Research Paper Taking notes in preparation for writing a report or research paper is a related but different kind of activity from making notes in summary form. The major difference is that students need to learn how to take notes selectively on points of interest. Your goal is to have them take notes that are concise, informative, accurate, organized, and expressed in the student's own words rather than lifted, wholesale, from the source.

Maxim (1990) describes an effective procedure she used with her third-graders that enabled them to learn how to take concise notes without copying in a science unit on the ocean. After reading aloud to them from fiction and non-fiction books on the sea, she asked them to list facts they had heard, and to write questions the reading had made them wonder about. They did the same after a field trip and after film strips. Before they went to the library to research their individually chosen sea creatures, they wrote questions about their creature in their research notebooks. They read in the library without taking notes and were allowed ten minutes after returning to the class to record in their notebooks information they had found. The key features of Maxim's procedure were as follows: (a) Self selection of the specific animal to be researched increased the likelihood that they would be interested in the topic. (b) The questions they prepared before reading led to focused, purposeful reading. (c) Making notes from memory resulted in economy and eliminated plagiarism.

Two features of Maxim's procedure should always be used when students are researching individual topics, no matter what the grade level. The first is that students should be helped to identify a topic that is interesting to them. The second is that students should be encouraged to develop questions and categories of interest before they begin reading and note taking. The first will increase motivation. The second will help to focus their note taking and lessen the likelihood of their taking copious notes on everything they read whether relevant or not.

Suppose, for example, that each student in a fourth-grade class is to research a particular mammal. The teacher has the class brainstorm the categories of information that they want to make notes about (for example, description, habitat, food, family, relatives, enemies, other facts). A page (or more) may be devoted to notes on each category. The categories focus attention during reading and note taking, limiting the kind of information that will be collected, and providing a means of organizing notes.

In higher grades, the need for accuracy and greater detail may deter you from using Maxim's procedure of having students record information from memory. Students will need some instruction in how to take brief notes using key words and omitting all words and phrases not essential to the meaning. In higher grades, as in lower, students begin by brainstorming likely categories for their topic, and add categories (and subcategories) as they skim the various sources they have located, and as they read the first few source materials carefully. Categories and subcategories become headings for notes and, later, after some revision in the light of their completed research, will be headings and subheadings in the final report.

Senior students should be encouraged to take notes on index cards or, to save bulk, on slips of paper cut to the size of an index card. Making *bibliographical cards* and *note cards* as described below saves work and facilitates organization in writing a formal report.

1. ***Bibliographical cards***   For each book or article used as a source, a card should be made giving the complete bibliographical reference. The card is given an index number — 1, 2, etc.— to be written in the top right hand corner of the card.

2. *Note Cards*   Notes are made on index cards (or note slips), one note per card. The index number of the source is written on the top right-hand corner. The topic or subtopic of the note is written as a heading on the top left hand corner of the card. The page from which the note is taken is recorded. Summary notes are made in the student's own words.

Writing Reports

The writing of a formal report is greatly facilitated by notes taken on cards as described above. The cards should be read through carefully, and then arranged in piles according to topics and subtopics. Students should find a theme or thesis that will be the focus of their report. The introduction and conclusion need special attention. If students have a theme, they should be able to write a rough form of their introduction at the beginning. However, it may be useful for them to know that many writers find it easier to write the polished version of their introduction after they have written the body of the report.

Reports may take many forms other than formal written reports. This is especially true for students in the middle grades. Oral presentations may be made: speeches, plays, skits, interviews, or a debate between two students who take opposing views on a topic. Visual displays might consist of a bulletin board display with drawings, photographs, maps, and posters along with accompanying text; or a mural — a sequence of scenes, say, with accompanying text. Written materials might be the diary of a historical character; an illustrated book for younger students; or correspondence between two real or imagined historical characters.

Science students need to learn to write formal lab reports. Johnston (1985) suggests a different form of lab report. She asks students to "explain" their findings, and comments that this often leads to greater understanding than standard lab reports. Standard lab reports, she suggests, allow students little opportunity to show conceptual understanding or abstract reasoning. Instead, she asks her students to write one-page interpretations on the lab exercise they have completed. They are encouraged to draw conclusions, raise questions, and propose new theories. She believes that interpretive lab reports encourage students to think more deeply about what they do. They also find out what they understand and what they do not when they are asked to put their thoughts in writing.

TEACHER UNDERSTANDING

Writing-to-learn has been discussed thus far in terms of what it can do for students — helping them to call up relevant prior knowledge, to reformulate or to review what they have learned. The other great benefit of students' writing is that it informs teachers and puts them in a better position to plan future learning activities. Writing before, during, and at the end of a unit of work will give you a great deal of information about how well your students understand the material studied. Writing tasks such as those described above require students to draw on their knowledge and to express it in their own words without teachers' questions to prompt them. The results are more informative — and usually more interesting — than the repetition of material memorized from the teacher's notes. Examples given already have suggested how useful writing can be in informing teachers about the level of student understanding.

Exit slips and journal entries often contain direct student comments about their learning. Note how informative comments such as the following are for a teacher:

> **Grade 11 student:** The concept maps we did in class today were incredibly tedious. But I do know my vocabulary now and I didn't really study it. The words will stick in my memory because I actually had a chance to use them.

> **Grade 9 student on *I Am the Cheese*:** (A series of comments made at various points in her reading.) What is tapes ... Where is he talking to the doctor and why is what I don't understand ... and why do the tenses always change at the tapes ... His (bike) trip doesn't seem to be going on any more. I don't know why he stopped ... During the tapes, when it talks about Adam, it is written in a different person. In the chapters, it says "I leave Carver," when in the tapes it says "He shot out of blah blah" as if someone else is writing it ...

> **Grade 7 student:** Now I'm confused about multiplying and dividing (fractions) because one does the job of the other and reverse. So I don't know which one to do. I have got adding and subtracting down pat though.

> **Journal exchange between primary student and teacher:**

> **Student:** in math today we did subtrakion. I had to think when we got to the part when seventeen subtrakt four = fourteen because I didn't have anuff finggers. the part thet I thout was esey was when it went four take-away two = two

Teacher: When you ran out of fingers, what did you do?

Student: Got pencles, crayons, and stuff.

Comments such as these can be very informative.

EVALUATING WRITING TO LEARN

Evaluation is a vexed problem for teachers. The topic is taken up in greater detail in Chapter 12. Here, however, I want to emphasize that the primary evaluative use of writing to learn is for formative evaluation rather than summative evaluation. The writing that students do can give you a great deal of diagnostic information that will help you to plan further activities to promote learning. For many of the kinds of writing suggested in this chapter, it is not appropriate that you give numerical or letter grades. Moreover, students need to do much more writing than you can read and grade if writing is to become an important tool for learning.

Teachers sometimes feel, however, that students are unwilling to do work unless they get credit for what they do, that is to say, unless it earns them marks. This is especially true of students in higher grades who have had six or more years of education with a major focus on tests and grades. If you believe this to be true of the class or classes that you teach, there are many choices available to you for encouraging participation and giving credit for activities without letting grades dictate. You may find some of the following suggestions useful. The decisions you make about evaluation, marking and grading will be somewhat dependent on the grade level at which you teach.

1. You may wish to give a grade to some pieces of writing — for example, a major report.

2. Many pieces of informal writing have served their purpose once the students have written and shared their writing with a group or with the class. You may want them to keep such writing in a learning log or journal, or you may decide not to do so.

3. Some writing that you request them all to do — for example, exit slips — may simply be given a check mark to indicate that it was done. Keep a special sheet on which you record such check marks.

4. For some writing, you may give a check mark to indicate that it was done satisfactorily, a check with a plus sign to indicate that it was unusually thoughtful, and a check with a minus sign to show that it was done but not adequately. Keep a record.

5. If you have your students keep a learning log or journal, you will want to respond to some of the writing they do. Response is important in building student-teacher rapport, an important potential outcome of student writing.

Responding is not to be confused with marking or grading. Responding means writing a comment as one person to another.

6. There are various options available for giving credit for journals or learning logs.

a. Some teachers like to give full credit if it is done satisfactorily.

b. You may consider it as part of a general participation mark, and give it a mark or a grade, or use the check, check plus, or check minus system.

c. Rather than reading the entire journal, you may take the journal in periodically. Sometimes you will take it in to respond to a specific piece of writing you have asked them to do. You may also take it in regularly for a general check, asking students to indicate some specified number of entries that they consider to be thoughtfully done.

The main task is to consider your options and select a procedure that allows you to assign a grade — if you are required to — without letting grading dominate your teaching agenda.

Conclusion

Writing in content areas includes some common kinds of writing like note-making, lab reports, and report-writing. Writing to learn also includes many different kinds of writing. Some of it is informal, spontaneous, unpolished writing that may not even be in complete sentences. It is intended to promote learning. It is certainly not intended to be graded.

Writing can serve many purposes in content area classes. It can help to build student-teacher rapport. It can call up existing knowledge as a basis for new learning. It can serve to review and consolidate what has been learned. It can promote reflection and self awareness.

There is not always a clear line between activities described in this chapter and those in the chapters on reading (Chapter 8) and talking (Chapter 6). Many writing activities were suggested in the chapter on reading. Some of the activities in this chapter might be done cooperatively, in small groups. The kind of learning described throughout the book emphasizes engaging students in active meaning-making. Constructing their own meanings necessitates involving them in talking, reading, and writing. In many cases, an activity will involve all three. Putting what they hear, what they observe, and what they read into words is critical to meaning construction.

EXERCISES

1. Work with two or three people interested in the same content area and produce a portfolio of writing of various kinds on topics or concepts in that content area, e.g., an "I am ..." piece, a biopoem, an acrostic, a dialogue, a personal ad and reply.

2. Work with another person in your content area to prepare a concept map and *three* definitions for your subject.

3. Select a text for your chosen grade level and choose a section of 4-5 pages that has headings and subheadings.

    a. Make a hierarchical summary of the selection.

    b. Now do a graphic representation as described in Chapter 8.

    c. Compare the two forms of summary. What are the advantages of each? Show your two pieces to one or two peers and note their reactions to each.

REFERENCES

Crowhurst, M., and M. Kooy (1985). The use of response journals in teaching the novel. *Reading-Canada-Lecture*, 3, 256-266.

Emig, J. (1977). Writing as a mode of learning. *College Composition and Communication*, 28, 122-127.

Gage, J. (1986). Why write? In D. Bartholomae and A. Petrosky (eds.), *The Teaching of Writing* (pp. 8-29). Chicago: National Society for the Study of Education.

Gere, A. R. (ed.) (1985). *Roots in the Sawdust: Writing to Learn Across the Disciplines*. Urbana, IL: National Council of Teachers of English.

Johnston, P. (1985). Writing to learn science. In A. Gere (ed.), *Roots in the sawdust* (pp. 92-103). Urbana, IL.: National Council of Teachers of English.

Langer, J., and A.N. Applebee (1987). *How writing shapes thinking: A study of teaching and learning. Urbana*, IL: National Council of Teachers of English.

Maxim, D. (1990). Beginning researchers. In N. Atwell (ed.), *Coming to Know: Writing to Learn in the Intermediate Grades* (pp. 3-16). Portsmouth, NH: Heinemann.

Newton, J. (1990). *Ideas for Teaching English*, Grades 7-12. Winnipeg: Manitoba Association of Teachers of English.

Ogle, D. (1986). K-W-L: A teaching model that develops active reading of expository text. *The Reading Teacher*, 39, 564-570.

Taylor, B.M. (1982). A summarizing strategy to improve middle grade students' reading and writing skills. *The Reading Teacher*, 36, 202-205.

Watson, T. (1985). Writing to learn history. In A. Gere (ed.). *Roots in the sawdust* (pp. 137-147). Urbana, IL.: National Council of Teachers of English.

Zimmerman, P. (1985). Writing for art appreciation. In A. Gere (ed.). *Roots in the sawdust* (pp. 31-46). Urbana, IL.: National Council of Teachers of English.

Chapter 11
TEACHING STUDENTS FROM OTHER CULTURES AND LANGUAGE GROUPS

CHAPTER OVERVIEW

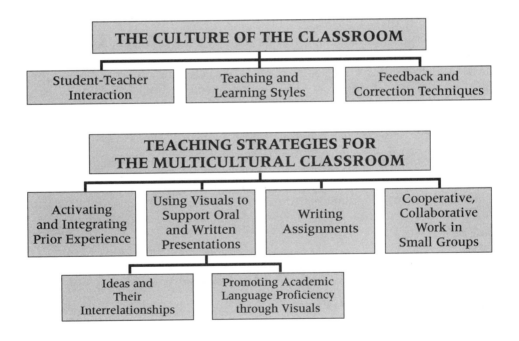

THE CULTURE OF THE CLASSROOM

- Student-Teacher Interaction
- Teaching and Learning Styles
- Feedback and Correction Techniques

TEACHING STRATEGIES FOR THE MULTICULTURAL CLASSROOM

- Activating and Integrating Prior Experience
- Using Visuals to Support Oral and Written Presentations
- Writing Assignments
- Cooperative, Collaborative Work in Small Groups

- Ideas and Their Interrelationships
- Promoting Academic Language Proficiency through Visuals

Canada is a multicultural country. A walk along the streets of any large city tells us this. The multicultural nature of the country is particularly evident in many of the country's classrooms. In large cities, it is common to find classes with a majority of students whose mother tongue is other than English. For example, approximately 50 percent of students enroled in schools administered by the Vancouver School Board and by the Peel Board of Education near Toronto are non-native speakers of English.

The multicultural nature of our country and many of its classrooms has a number of implications for teachers. It is of major importance that, since many children are being educated in a language that is not their mother tongue, teachers adapt their teaching to the multicultural classroom.

Language is only one of many variables in the school environment that requires adaptation in view of the multicultural nature of Canadian society and schools. Other facets of the school environment that may require attention are: variable learning styles; teaching styles and strategies; attitudes, beliefs, and actions of the school staff; the culture of the school and classroom; instructional materials; assessment and testing procedures; the formalized curriculum and course of study (Banks, 1988).

With regard to curriculum, comprehensive reform is needed in order to create curricula that reflect and respond to the cultural variety of our diverse society. What is needed is widespread integration of multiculturalism into the curriculum rather than an add-on approach characterized by single courses or individual units about multiculturalism (Banks, 1988). A number of useful studies across Canada (e.g., Bevan, 1984; Nova Scotia Human Rights, 1981) have evaluated textbooks for bias with regard to race, ethnicity, and minorities. But much work on comprehensive reform of the curriculum remains to be done.

There are, then, many aspects of schooling needing attention if the schools of our country are to reflect the nation's official commitment to multiculturalism. In this chapter, only two of these are considered in detail: the culture of the classroom; and strategies for teaching those whose mother tongue is other than English.

THE CULTURE OF THE CLASSROOM

The ways people interact verbally are determined by their cultural background. To some extent, classrooms are new cultures for all children. When they begin school, children must conform to the rules that govern school discourse. In classrooms with twenty or thirty students, they must learn new rules for getting a turn to talk. They must also learn what topics are appropriate for classroom talk, and that topics are often determined by the teacher (Cazden, 1988).

The problem of adjusting to the culture of the school is greater for some children than for others. The closer their home culture is to the culture of the classroom, the easier it will be for students to adjust to school. In the past twenty years, a number of studies have examined ways in which cultural differences have influenced children's participation in school.

In an important early study, Philips (1972) made observations, both in the school and in the community, of Warm Springs Indian children living on a reservation in Oregon. Her comments about the "silent" or "shy" Indian child are instructive. She found that children were especially reluctant to participate verbally in two kinds of situations: (1) when they were required to speak publicly in front of other children — to ask or answer a question, or to make oral reports or presentations to the class; and (2) when their speech was controlled or dictated by the teacher, especially in situations where she might correct them if they made an error in their responses, as, for example, in a small reading group. In games like Simon Says, or Follow the Leader they were very reluctant to act as leader when called on by the teacher to do so. The Warm Springs children's participation was very different in group situations in which the students controlled and directed the interaction. In group situations, Philips found

> ... a marked contrast between the behavior of Indian and non-Indian students. It is in such contexts that Indian students become most fully involved in what they are doing, concentrating completely on their work until it is completed, talking a great deal to one another within the group, and competing, with explicit remarks to that effect, with the other groups. Non-Indian students take more time in "getting organized," disagree and argue more regarding how to go about a task, (and) rely more heavily on appointed chairmen for arbitration and decision-making ....(p. 379)

In unsupervised playground activity, Indian children engaged in team games more often than non-Indian children, and sustained such activities longer and at younger ages than non-Indian children.

The Warm Springs children's behaviour in school reflected the kinds of participation that they experienced in everyday life in their community. Learning commonly involved three steps: (1) silent observation; (2) supervised participation with little verbal instruction, direction, or correction; and (3) private, self-initiated practice and self-testing. Skills once learned were demonstrated not by verbal performance, but by means of some material evidence or non-verbal physical expression. For social events in their community both attendance and participation were open to all. There were no designated leaders in control of the program, and no designated speakers, or soloists in dancing, singing, or drumming. It was left to individuals to decide whether or not to participate.

Philips summarizes her observations of Warm Springs children thus:

> Indian children fail to participate verbally in classroom interaction because the social conditions for participation to which they have become accustomed in the Indian community are lacking ... Educators cannot assume that because Indian children (or any children from cultural backgrounds other than those that are implicit in American classrooms) speak English ... that they have also assimilated all of the sociolinguistic rules underlying interaction in classrooms ... (p. 392)

Philips' study describes ways in which discontinuities between home and school cultures resulted in children's failure to participate in expected ways in school. Other studies have described changes in participation that were brought about when interaction patterns familiar to the children were introduced into the classroom (e.g., Au, 1980; Heath, 1983). Ethnographer Shirley Brice Heath spent several years studying interaction patterns in the homes of rural black and white working-class families in the Appalachian region of the United States. One of her observations was that black children from "Trackton" did not understand and did not respond to teachers "known answer" questions — a dominant form of talk in classrooms, as described in Chapter 4. Heath encouraged teachers to use forms of questions that were more familiar to the children. For example, in showing pictures to children, teachers learned to avoid the typical kind of teacher question asking for the identification of objects in the picture and attributes of the objects. Instead they asked the kinds of questions that children were more familiar with such as:

What's happening here?

Have you ever been here?

Tell me what you did when you were there?

What's this like? (pointing to a scene, or item in a scene)

Familiar kinds of questions such as these produced enthusiastic participation by the children. Over time, teachers gave students specific instruction and practice in answering the kinds of questions they were likely to meet in school situations — instruction, that is, that would help them learn to adapt to the culture of the school.

Dell Hymes (1981, p.59) points out that it is easy to recognize and respect certain kinds of cultural differences like religious beliefs and national customs. It is not always easy to recognize, however, differences that arise from "the culture of everyday etiquette and interaction" and how these differences may affect children in the classroom causing them to feel out of place and less able to participate than children whose home culture is more similar to the culture of the school.

The culture of the school in Canada reflects mainstream middle-class values. Often these values are implicitly held rather than explicitly recognized. We need, therefore, to look at the values that are intrinsic to Canadian middle-class society and how other value systems may differ. Damen's (1987) description of the general value orientations of North Americans is applicable to Canada as well as to the United States. In Table 11.1, mainstream, middle-class American values are contrasted with values from a different orientation. The values listed in the *Contrast Middle-American* column are not associated with a particular culture. Rather, they represent opposite orientations, one or more of which may be held by a variety of other cultural groups.

Beliefs and values influence behaviour. Different cultural experiences and values that students bring with them to the classroom are likely to result in behaviours different from those expected. Some likely areas of difference are: student-teacher interaction; teaching and learning styles; and feedback and correction techniques.

Table 11.1
Some Implicit Cultural Assumptions

North American (USA)	Contrast Middle-American
Personal control of environment	Nature dominating man
Change inevitable and desirable	Unchanging; traditional
Equality of opportunity	Class structure dominant; social hierarchy determines opportunities
Individualism valued	Interdependence but individuality
Future orientation	Present or past orientation
Action orientation	Being orientation
Directness and openness	Suggestive, consensus-seeking; group orientation
Practical, pragmatic, rational	Feeling orientation; philosophical
Problem-solving orientation	Inactive; enduring; seeking help from others
Cause-and-effect logic	Certain knowledge
Informality	Formality
Competition	Group process
Do-it-yourself approach to life	Dependence upon intermediaries for success

(Adapted from Damen, 1987, p. 195)

STUDENT-TEACHER INTERACTION

Canadian classrooms are characterized by a good deal of interaction between teacher and students. Students are permitted and expected to ask questions if they do not understand information or instructions. They are permitted — and, at times, encouraged — to express opinions, to hypothesize, and even, occasionally, to challenge the teacher. The argument has been made elsewhere in this book that teachers ought to encourage questioning and independent thinking more than is usually done. Nonetheless, these behaviours do occur with some frequency in classrooms in Canada and the United States.

In many other cultures, children have fewer rights to speak in the presence of adults, both at home and in school. Korean, Japanese, Chinese, and Punjabi children are apt to be considered rude and disobedient if they question or disagree with opinions expressed by their parents. Some cultural groups such as the American Indian emphasize nonverbal rather than verbal communication in rearing their children, and place little value on speaking in public situations.

In cultures which emphasize respect for elders (for example, Chinese, Japanese, and Korean), students are expected to accept the teacher's viewpoint and not challenge it. The expression of independent opinions is discouraged. The students' duty is to listen and learn from the greater wisdom of the teacher. Children who are discouraged from engaging in verbal interaction at home, and whose school experience has stressed unquestioning obedience will require time, support, encouragement, and specific instruction in order to feel comfortable interacting with teachers in ways that are common and expected in Canadian classrooms. Even asking questions for the purpose of clarifying instructions is not usual for children from a range of cultural backgrounds — Asian, Saudi, East Indian, and some European countries (Scarcella, 1990).

To require students to answer questions in the highly public forum of the large, whole-class group is especially difficult for many students from other cultural groups. An obvious problem is that inadequate proficiency in English may prevent them from formulating an answer as quickly as expected. There are, in addition, a number of cultural values that come into play in the large group question-and-answer situation that is so predominant in classrooms. Asian students, reared with an emphasis on humility, are often reluctant to display their knowledge by volunteering to answer questions. They may be deterred from answering also because giving a wrong answer brings shame not only on the individual, but on the family as well. Male children from Iran and Saudi Arabia, on the other hand, may display great eagerness to answer because, in their cultures, to be outgoing is valued. They expect that aggressiveness in volunteering to answer will be approved. A further problem likely to arise in question-and-answer sessions is that attitudes towards silence vary considerably from culture to culture. Teachers in our culture experience discomfort if a silence lasts much longer than a second. For many Asians and Native American Indians, however, reflection before answering is a mark of courtesy and respect.

Gender may be an additional complicating factor for some cultural groups. Gibson (1987) found that Punjabis, when first in America, were reluctant to speak in class except to give a factual answer to a teacher's direct question. The problem was compounded for Punjabi girls who were not accustomed, in Punjab village life, either to conversing with boys or to speaking in their presence. Coeducational classes were an experience for which their cultural background had not prepared them.

Eye contact is another area of cultural difference. Our cultural expectation is that those to whom we speak will make eye contact with us. If our students' gaze is fixed upon us, we assume they are attending. If they smile and nod, we assume they understand and agree. These non-verbal signals do not have the same meaning across cultures. Latin Americans and Native Canadians may look down when addressed as a mark of respect. Nods and smiles from Asian students may signal merely that they are listening, not that they understand or agree (Scarcella, 1990).

TEACHING AND LEARNING STYLES

Instructional strategies in Canadian schools are heavily dependent on language, especially spoken language. Most talk is done by the teacher who speaks about two thirds of the time in the average classroom. When students speak, they are most likely to do so, on command, in response to a question by the teacher.

The emphasis on verbal activities presents problems of various kinds for students from different cultures. If students are not fully proficient in English, they are likely to have difficulty processing academic language in teachers' lectures, and also in producing appropriate answers in the brief second or less that teachers typically allow for a student to begin to reply (Rowe, 1986).

Another kind of problem arises from the fact that not all cultures emphasize the verbal mode as we do in instructional situations. As noted above, Warm Springs Indian children learn in their everyday life with very little verbal instruction. For the Navaho, and others who live close to nature, careful observation is the dominant mode of learning. They "approach their world visually and by quiet, persistent exploration" (John, 1972, p. 338). Many Asian students also learn through observation (Cheng, 1987). Those whose learning style is strongly visual are not well served by the highly verbal instruction that dominates schools.[1]

A second characteristic of schools in Canada and the United States is their emphasis on individual learning and competition. Evidence of learning is given in competitive display before the group, or in written tests for which marks are given that categorize individuals as good, average, or poor. Many Asian, Latin-American, Afro-American, and Native Canadian students fare better in cooperative rather than competitive, individualistic learning situations.

---

[1] It is to be noted that there are many mainstream Canadian-born children who would also profit if the predominantly verbal mode of school instruction were complemented by visual aids.

FEEDBACK AND CORRECTION TECHNIQUES

The traditional style of teaching that predominates in schools is heavily oriented towards testing. Teachers present information either orally, or through reading assignments, or by a combination of the two. They then test students' acquisition of the information by asking questions. Students are thus required to demonstrate their knowledge in public. Making mistakes and being corrected in front of others is a common event in the school day. Public testing of this kind presents problems for students from other cultural groups. For some, like the Warm Springs Indians, the customary procedure is to perfect learning in private before demonstrating acquisition in public. For many Asians there is considerable loss of face, even humiliation, in making errors in public; this is especially so if older students are corrected in front of younger students.

Public criticism is not an enjoyable experience for any student. For Asian, Middle Eastern, and Mexican students, public criticism is likely to be viewed not only as unpleasant, but as rude, or gravely offensive, especially if a student is named and corrected by a teacher who is standing at a distance, across the room. Many Asians respond very negatively to direct confrontation of any kind, and will go to great lengths to avoid being confrontational themselves, even saying *yes* when they mean *no*, on occasion (Scarcella, 1990).

SUMMARY

The brief treatment of cultural differences in the preceding pages is suggestive rather than exhaustive. It does not give a blueprint for you to follow. In fact, you may well have, in your class, students from several different cultural groups who react differently in the same situation. Some students may vie aggressively to answer questions, while others answer reluctantly, or even refuse to answer at all. Some students may want you to come close and deal with them in personal, one-to-one encounters, while others expect you to maintain greater distance. Some expect the teacher to maintain close control of the classroom and all that happens in it, while others fare better if they have greater autonomy.

Given the heavy demands that will be placed upon you, especially if you are a beginning teacher, it may be some years before you can become well informed about the cultural values held by the various cultural groups that may be represented in your class. It is important to keep in mind, however, that we are all creatures of our own particular culture. Our values, expectations, and behaviours are conditioned by the culture in which we have been raised. Many of these values and expectations are implicitly held rather than explicitly recognized. We do not always realize the assumptions upon which our behaviour and reactions are based. It is easy to misinterpret the behaviours of those who do not share our cultural background. As teachers, we must remain sensitive to cultural differences and be aware of the potential for miscommunication both verbally and non-verbally.

TEACHING STRATEGIES FOR THE MULTICULTURAL CLASSROOM

Student teachers sometimes react with something close to panic when they find, during their practicum experience, that many classes have high proportions of ESL[2] students. This is especially true of secondary teachers who feel themselves under strong pressure to complete a demanding prescribed curriculum. It is hard enough, they feel, to teach high school physics, math, or literature to students who are proficient in English. Many feel themselves totally unequipped for the demands of teaching those with less than full proficiency in English. To the many who will teach classes with significant numbers of ESL students in them, I introduce this section on teaching strategies with a word of *warning*, and a word of *comfort*.

The warning is that you cannot proceed with your teaching assuming full English proficiency. Even though ESL students may sound as if they have mastered English, and speak with scarcely a trace of foreign accent, you must not assume that their English is adequate for academic purposes. They are quite likely to find academic language, both spoken and written, very difficult. Fluency in social conversation is achieved relatively quickly, but research shows that it takes many years for students to develop language proficiency sufficient to cope with academic subjects (Collier, 1987; Cummins, 1984).

Cummins examined data collected from grades 5, 7, and 9 students by the Toronto Board of Education and found that "it took immigrant students who had arrived in Canada aged six to seven or later between five and seven years on average to approach grade norms in English verbal academic skills" (p. 133). Similar results are reported by Collier on the basis of data collected in the United States. Given the obvious fact that students cannot wait until they perfect their English skills before getting on with the academic subjects that they must study, it is necessary for subject area teachers to adopt teaching strategies that will allow them to develop their English proficiency while they learn the content of the various subjects of the curriculum.

---

[2] For economy's sake, this term, standing for *English as a second language*, will be used to refer to those whose mother tongue is not English and who have less than full proficiency in English. It is acknowledged that ESL students may have two or more languages in addition to English. When my Hungarian husband learned, in his forties, that he was an ESL speaker, he asked me what the term meant. When I told him, he replied that he was indeed an ESL speaker, but that S stood for *sixth* not *second*.

My second introductory point — the word of comfort referred to above — is that you need not have special courses in ESL methodology in order to provide students with opportunities to develop their English while they study content area subjects. It is useful, of course, to have specialized training in ESL teaching, but the majority of beginning teachers do not have this kind of background. The purpose of this section of the chapter is to describe teaching strategies that are particularly useful for helping ESL students learn in content areas while at the same time developing English proficiency.

Four important strategies for you to emphasize in your teaching are: (1) the activation and integration of prior knowledge and experience; (2) the use of visuals to supplement and support lectures and reading assignments; (3) the use of varied writing assignments to help students master both content and the language of academic discourse; (4) the use of cooperative, collaborative group work to help them learn content and practise oral academic language. You will doubtless notice that the strategies suggested as beneficial for ESL students have been recommended throughout the book as being generally beneficial for all students. Indeed, all the strategies recommended in preceding chapters are relevant for ESL students. In other words, if you adopt teaching strategies that are good for students in general, you will be using strategies that will allow opportunities for ESL students to develop both in content area knowledge and in their English proficiency. It is good to have specialized ESL training; but you need not despair if you lack this background provided that you are sensitive to the special needs of your ESL students. In the discussion that follows, general strategies suggested throughout the book are made specific to teaching classes with ESL students.

ACTIVATING AND INTEGRATING PREVIOUS EXPERIENCES

Activating prior knowledge and experience is important for all students. Learning involves making connections between what we already know and new information. As discussed elsewhere in the book, it is always desirable to use strategies that encourage students to call up what they already know about a topic prior to beginning formal study or prior to reading a text. It is especially important that this be done for ESL students. They are involved in a situation where many things are somewhat strange to them — language and cultural norms, to mention only two. Exercises that activate prior knowledge serve to call to mind relevant concepts. What is known is the basis on which new knowledge can be added. Moreover, new vocabulary will be more easily learned if it can be connected to concepts already known.

Encouraging students to bring to the class their prior knowledge and experience has other values. Talking and writing about what they know about is valuable for promoting literacy in their new language. Moreover, encouraging ESL children to integrate their experiences from outside the class can help to build a pluralistic classroom community that will be beneficial to native-born and immigrant children alike. A primary teacher's journal contains the following heart-warming entry about the celebration of the Chinese New Year in her class.

> Our entire morning was planned with activities to reflect the Chinese culture. All the Chinese children in the class seemed elated when I discussed the plans for our day. James[3], in particular, contributed a lot to class discussions. He told us about the Chinese calendar and explained his own sign (the rat). He helped his classmates complete their Chinese brush painting projects and was proud to show the proper technique to everyone. He showed me how to write numbers beyond five. I asked him to correct his classmates' Chinese math papers, and he took pleasure, in a kind way, in showing them where they had made mistakes. We learned Chinese phrases and James printed the Chinese characters to go with the phrases. At the end of the day, he said, "Wow,! These weeks in Canada sure go fast. It's already Wednesday."

In allowing James to share his knowledge and experience, the teacher enriched the whole class. James was an expert for the day, his skill and knowledge recognized and appreciated by the class. The eight other Chinese children in the class saw aspects of their culture shared and valued. Those who were not Chinese responded with interest to what they learned about the culture of their classmates. One of them commented, "English is hard for them, but Chinese is doubly hard for us!"

Early (1990) describes how the teacher of a class of grade 4/5 ESL students used students' pre-existing knowledge and experience to build a classification tree to show where fish fitted in the hierarchy of animals. First she had them work in small groups organizing Leggo blocks and toy cars in as many different ways as they could, and then showed them how to display their categories in a tree diagram. Next she had them bring their own collections to school (stickers, stamps, coins, etc.) and work in pairs categorizing these in various ways, and making a tree diagram to illustrate their preferred system of categorization. Next, the teacher led the whole class in a discussion of how animals might be classified. She accepted and discussed many different classifications (e.g., lucky/unlucky, dirty/clean, good/evil). Gradually, after much discussion, the class produced, by means of skilful questioning by the teacher, a "scientific" classification tree as illustrated in Figure 8.1 on p. 181.

---

[3] James was a seven-year-old in his third year at school (grade 2) who had been in Canada for two years and who was receiving special ESL instruction from the ESL specialist on a daily basis.

There are many ways of incorporating what students already know into the classroom. Doing so allows them to talk about familiar things and is thus useful for the development of literacy skills. Prior knowledge also serves to enable connections to be made between what is known and what is new. Activating prior knowledge is important for all students; it is critically important for those whose language skills are less than fully proficient.

USING VISUALS TO SUPPORT ORAL AND WRITTEN PRESENTATIONS

Visuals have been described in some detail in Chapter 8 where it was suggested that students be encouraged to summarize texts in a variety of graphic forms to help them process and remember what they read, and to provide a useful summary for study purposes. Visuals come in many forms. Various kinds of charts, graphs, time lines, sketches, pictures, and models are the most common.

Visuals are important for ESL students for at least two different kinds of reasons. One is that students from some cultural groups, in particular, are more oriented to visual modes of learning than auditory modes. The second reason is that students whose verbal language skills are limited will profit greatly if visual representations are used to summarize material that is being presented verbally in a lecture or a text. The visual representation is much less demanding on their verbal skills than verbal explanations that are inevitably couched in academic language that is difficult for them. Visuals can both organize and simplify content. Note, for example, how clearly and economically Figure 11.1 represents changes of states of matter. The figure contains only eight words but they are critical words for students to learn. Note that, in addition to labelled illustrations, colour is used to convey meaning: *fusion* and *vaporization* are written in red to show that heat is added to produce the change; *solidification* and *condensation* are written in blue to show that heat is removed; *sublimation,* written in green, is a special case in which a state is skipped during the change.

Margaret Early, Bernard Mohan, and Hugh Hooper (1989) have been working for several years on a large-scale project with more than 150 teachers from K through 12 in the Vancouver School District. The objective of the project is to assist teachers in helping ESL students to improve both their academic achievement in content areas and their English proficiency. The use of graphic displays, which they call key visuals (Early, Thew, and Wakefield, 1986; Mohan, 1986), has been one of their major strategies. Key visuals are useful both (a) in teaching ideas and the relationships between ideas, and (b) in promoting academic language proficiency (Early, 1989).

Figure 11.1
Visual Representation of Changes of State of Matter

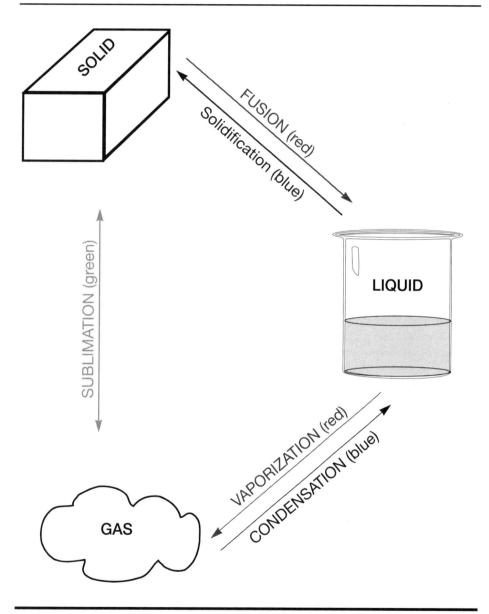

Source: Student assignment.

Ideas and Their Interrelationships

Mohan (1986) lists six major types of knowledge structures which he believes occur over and over again in different situations and in different content areas. The six types of knowledge structures are listed in Table 11.2. There are typical kinds of thinking that are associated with each knowledge structure. These also are shown in Table 11.2. Early, Thew, and Wakefield (1986) examined British Columbia Ministry of Education curricula and text books from kindergarten through grade 11 and found that these kinds of thinking skills recurred again and again across curriculum areas. Specific kinds of **key visuals** are suitable for representing the various kinds of knowledge structures. (See Table 11.2)

Visuals can be used in a variety of ways to help students master content. They may be used: to prepare students to read an academic text; to support a teacher's oral presentation; to revise material. Visuals can also be used to develop language skills.

Promoting Academic Language Proficiency through Visuals

For much of the history of foreign language teaching, instruction focused on pronunciation, vocabulary, and grammatical structures in isolation from meaningful tasks. Teaching language in conjunction with teaching content provides opportunities for involving students in particular types of real language use in contrast to exercises isolated from real communicative purposes. Visuals provide a valuable and natural opportunity for practising the use of grammatical structures.

Let us consider, as an example, the ESL teacher of the grade 4/5 class who generated with her students the classification tree for kinds of animals. (See Figure 8.1 on p. 181). With the classification tree in front of them, the teacher asked the class to give her sentences that would explain in words what was displayed in the tree (Early, 1990). Let us consider some of the sentences that might be generated:

- Animals can be divided into two groups (classes, kinds, categories), vertebrates and invertebrates.

- There are two kinds of animals, vertebrates and invertebrates.

- Vertebrates and invertebrates are two kinds of animals.

- The kinds of vertebrates are warm blooded and cold blooded.

- A mammal is a warm-blooded vertebrate.

- Fish and amphibians are cold-blooded animals.

Note that, in producing sentences such as these, students are engaging is language learning of the following kinds: practising vocabulary; practising sentence structures of varying kinds; practising a variety of alternate ways of

Table   **11.2**
Mohan's Knowledge Framework and Key Visuals

Types of Knowledge Structure	Types of Thinking Skills	Types of Key Visuals
Description	Observe, identify, label, locate, describe, compare, contrast	Picture/slide, map, diagram, table, plans/drawing
Sequence	Arrange events in order, note changes over time, follow directions, note cycles and processes	Timeline, action strip, flowchart cycle
Choice	Make decisions, select, propose alternative solutions, solve problems, form personal opinions	Decision tree, flow chart
Classification	Classify, define, understand, apply, develop concepts	Web, tree, table
Principles	Explain and predict; interpret data and draw conclusions; formulate, test and establish hypotheses; understand, apply causes, effects, means, ends, rules	Line graph, cycle, Venn diagram
Evaluation	Evaluate, rank, appreciate, judge, criticize	Grid, rating chart, table, mark book

Source: B. A. Mohan, (1986), *Language and Content* (Reading, MA: Addison-Wesley).

expressing the ideas and concepts displayed in the tree. The emphasis here is on forms of language, on particular sentence structures and particular vocabulary items. But the language forms are not practised in isolation; they are used in performing purposeful tasks.

Particular kinds of language forms are associated with each of the six knowledge structures shown in Table 11.2. Some of the kinds of language forms for each knowledge structure are shown in Table 11.3. If you were to look in an ESL text produced ten or fifteen years ago, you would note that chapters are devoted to many of the structures listed in Table 11.3; these structures would once have been taught and practised in isolation. By combining language instruction with content area instruction, you can make it possible for students to make progress in both areas simultaneously. Note, however, that specific attention needs to be paid to language development. It is not enough to teach content and assume that language learning will be enhanced.

If you are teaching grade 10 history or grade 11 business education or chemistry, you may feel that you have little time to engage in the kind of language teaching described above. The time you are able to spend can be supplemented if you enlist the assistance of the school's ESL specialist. Many ESL students who are integrated in regular classrooms will have one or two periods of specialized ESL instruction each week. If you suggest that students spend some of the time in their ESL class putting visuals into words, for example, you are likely to find the ESL teacher more than happy to cooperate. For example, it could be very useful for ESL chemistry students to describe in words the information presented in Figure 11.1 above: it would help them learn the important vocabulary items in the visual; it would give them practice in structuring both individual sentences and also a piece of extended discourse; and it would help them to learn the concepts that are illustrated in the diagram.

WRITING ASSIGNMENTS

The case for using writing as a means of learning has been made in Chapter 10. All the reasons for having students write are particularly relevant to ESL students. For example, a short free writing exercise allows students to gather their thoughts before contributing orally to a class or a group discussion. This kind of preparation is especially important for ESL students who find it even more difficult that other students to gather their thoughts and put them into words. All the kinds of writing assignments suggested in Chapter 10 are highly desirable for ESL students.

Writing exercises suggested in the preceding section, namely, translating visuals into prose, give important practice at all levels — word, sentence, and whole discourse. Figure 11.2 shows a piece of science writing by a sixth-grade

Table 11.3
Grammatical Structures Associated with
Mohan's Knowledge Structures

Types of Knowledge Structure	Grammatical Structures
Description	NP (noun phrase) + BE + NP/adjective; Prep. phrase; relative clauses; demonstratives; (*his, its*); articles (*a, the*); possessives (his, its); adverbs/adjectives of comparisons (*longer, shortest*, etc.)
Sequence	Prepositions and prepositional phrases of time, cause, and purpose; clauses of time, condition, reason; sentence time relaters (*first, earlier, later*); tenses— present tense, reported speech, imperatives
Choice	Modals (*can, will, must/ought, should, would, may*); *in my opinion …; I think that …; I choose …*
Classification	Verbs of class membership (*be*); verbs of possession (*have*); possessives (*his, its*); generic nouns (*animals, music*); species nouns (*kind, class, category*); nouns of measure (a *kilogram* of beans)
Principles	cause (*is due to, the result of*); condition and contrast (*if … then, unless*); generalization (in short, for example); scale of amount (*all, every, always, none*); prediction (*must, ought, should*); probability (*likely, may*)
Evaluation	describing emotions (*like/dislike, satisfactory/ unsatisfactory*); preference (*prefer, had rather*); standards (*good/bad, right/wrong, better/worse*); volition (*want, wish*)

Figure 11.2
A Report by a Sixth Grade ESL Student

Parts of a Spider

My Specimen, a spider, has two main body segments, and no exoskeleton. The two main body segments are the head and the abdomen.

The head of a spider is oval shaped and hairy. On the head there is eight smooth, dark, black eyes. Two of the eyes are at the top, two underneath, and four just beneath the others in a semicircle. It also has a mouth at the bottom, near the stomach. The mouth is kind of tube-shaped, and has a dull point. Although it has a mouth, spiders cannot chew on their food because they don't have a jaw! Instead they have two black, pointy fangs to suck the blood out from their prey. Spiders have eight legs, four on each side of the head. They are also hairy. These legs are excellent to walk forward fast. Attached to the head, is the abdomen. The abdomen contains all of the inside body parts, such as the heart and spinneret. The spinneret is also used in many ways. They are used for making the web and wrapping their prey before they eat it. The spiders also puts its victim into sleep by sending a sleeping liquid through their bodies. This is my description of spider's two main body segments, the head and the abdomen.

ESL student. The student has translated a visual into a piece of prose. The detail and organization make this an excellent piece of report writing for a sixth grader. It is easy to imagine how the visual supported the writing task.

It was customary in the past to postpone writing for second language learners until they had made considerable progress learning the language. Speaking and reading, it was believed, needed to come first. The same was true for first language learners. Ten or fifteen years ago, children in grade one and grade two were expected to compose little more than single sentences, and writing in kindergarten was virtually unheard of. Work in emergent literacy has transformed our understanding of the ways in which children acquire language processes. It is now common for children to begin writing in kindergarten (using invented spellings), and first graders commonly write stories that are pages long. We know now that oral language, reading, and writing are closely interrelated. Writing helps primary children learn to read, just as reading helps their writing. The same is true for second language learners. Hudelson (1984, p. 221), who reviewed research in second language reading and writing development, believes that second language learners' ability both to read and to write are frequently underestimated:

> … even children who speak virtually no English read English print in the
> environment; … ESL learners are able to read English with only limited control

over the oral system of the language; ... early in their development of English, (they) can write English and can do so for various purposes.

Writing has an important role to play in helping ESL students to develop their English proficiency, in general, and the language of academic discourse, in particular.

COOPERATIVE, COLLABORATIVE WORK IN SMALL GROUPS

Both first and additional languages develop in interactive, communicative situations (Snow, 1977; Wells, 1981). Children's language skills develop best when they participate in a rich language environment, and when they communicate with others for real purposes. They will not have sufficient opportunities to talk as much as they need to unless they spend substantial time working in pairs and small groups. Traditional classrooms, dominated as they are by teacher talk, give ESL students very little chance of practising and developing proficiency in academic discourse.

The importance of talk for learning in content areas was discussed in Chapter 6. Cooperative group work increases motivation, encourages active learning, increases academic performance, promotes literacy and language skills, and increases respect for diversity (Johnson and Johnson, 1987; Slavin, 1988). Student talk should occupy a central place in the classroom because of the importance of dialogue in promoting understanding and learning. Talking and working in cooperative groups is especially valuable in heterogenous and multicultural classrooms. For ESL speakers, talking is important not only to help them master content, but also to help them learn academic discourse. They will not practise academic discourse any place but in the classroom. Classrooms should be organized to facilitate interaction and collaboration in the interests of both content-area learning and language learning.

As discussed in Chapter 6, cooperative group work requires skills in both teachers and students. In addition to the general problems mentioned in Chapter 6, teachers in multicultural classrooms need to be sensitive to special problems that may arise. Students from a single language group, if allowed to work together in the same group, are likely to speak in their mother tongue rather than practising and developing proficiency in English. Certainly, the mother tongue should not be forbidden. Students recently arrived from another country may receive valuable and needed assistance from a buddy who speaks the same language. The language or languages that students bring to the class are important resources for learning. Students must be encouraged to value their mother tongue and the heritage of the culture to which they belong. However, in order to develop proficiency in English, ESL students need to be encouraged to work in English.

Students from some cultural groups may be reluctant to speak. They need to be encouraged to speak but not forced to do so. Unless fellow group members are trained in effective group interaction skills, reluctant participants who are culturally different may be ignored and isolated within the group.

Cazden (1988) points out that cultural differences may affect the kind of group structure that works best. If teenage girls are discouraged, in their culture, from speaking with boys, they will doubtless participate more comfortably if they work in groups of the same sex.

Working in cooperative groups offers benefits for all students. It is especially beneficial for ESL learners. In small groups they have many opportunities to speak and listen for a variety of purposes. They benefit from having English modelled by their peers. If they establish friendly relations with native-speaking students in their groups, they will be more comfortable asking for clarification than in the very public forum of the large group. Talk in small groups offers ESL students opportunities to learn and to practise academic discourse that they are unlikely to find through talking in any other place.

CONCLUSION

The large and continuing influx of immigrants and refugees into Canada has resulted in large numbers of classes with students from other lands and other cultures. Classrooms reflect the multicultural reality of the country. Within those classrooms are children with varying degrees of proficiency in English. Some have very limited proficiency. Some who appear to be fluent in English in social situations lack the kind of proficiency that would enable them to deal with academic language. This kind of proficiency comes only after several years.

Multicultural classrooms place extra demands on teachers. We need to be sensitive to cultural differences that may influence the behaviour of the students in our classes and the way they respond in classroom situations. We are all creatures of our own cultural background; we make assumptions and interpret the world and what happens on the basis of our cultural knowledge and values. The potential for misunderstanding, misinterpretation, and miscommunication is high between people of different cultures. As teachers, we need to be sensitive and alert to the possibility of misunderstanding both between us and our students and among students in our classes.

A second major demand placed upon teachers is to give assistance to students in developing their English proficiency as they study content area subjects. Since it takes many years for students to become proficient enough to deal with academic discourse, they cannot delay their study of math, science, history and literature until their English is up to the demands of these subjects. The kinds of strategies described throughout this book are ideally suited to producing the kinds of interactive classrooms and actively engaged students that give ESL students the best chance of learning in content areas. Specific strategies are described in this chapter that will help students to make good progress also in learning academic discourse. Content area teachers who are wise enough to collaborate with the ESL specialist available in many schools can multiply their own efforts to help students deal with the language of various content area disciplines. It is useful for teachers to have a special course in ESL methodology. However, most beginning teachers have to cope without specialized training. Much can be achieved, even without specialist training, by using the methods suggested in this chapter.

REFERENCES

Au, K. (1980). Participation structures in a reading lesson with Hawaiian children: An analysis of a culturally appropriate instructional event. *Anthropology and Education Quarterly. 11,* 91-115

Bevan, G.H. (1984). *Alberta Education Curriculum Review: Part I—Publication of the Curriculum Branch.* Edmonton: Alberta Education

Banks, J.A. (1988). *Multiethnic Education: Theory and Practice.* Boston: Allyn and Bacon.

Cazden, C.B. (1988). *Classroom Discourse.* Portsmouth, NH: Heinemann.

Cheng, L.R. (1987). *Assessing Asian Language Performance.* Rockville, Maryland: Aspen Publishers.

Collier, V.P. (1987). Age and rate of acquisition of second language for academic purposes. *TESOL Quarterly,* 21, 617-641.

Cummins, J. (1984). *Bilingualism and Special Education: Issues in Assessment and Pedagogy.* Clevedon, England: Multilingual Matters.

Damen, L. (1987). *Culture Learning: The Fifth Dimension in the Language Classroom.* Reading, MA: Addison Wesley.

Early, M. (1990). Enabling first and second language learners in the classroom. *Language Arts,* 67, 567-575.

Early, M. (1989). Using key visuals to aid ESL students' comprehension of content classroom texts. *Reading-Canada-Lecture,* 7, 202-212.

Early, M., B. Mohan and H. Hooper (1989). The Vancouver school board language and content project. In J. H. Esling (ed.), *Multicultural Education and Policy: ESL in the 1990's* (pp. 107-124). Toronto: O.I.S.E. Press

Early, M., C. Thew and P. Wakefield (1986). *Integrating Language and Content Instruction K-12: An ESL Resource Book*, Vol. 1. Victoria: Ministry of Education, Modern Language Services Branch.

Gibson, M.A. (1987). Punjabi immigrants in an American high school. In G. Spindler and L. Spindler (eds.), *Interpretive Ethnography of Education at Home and Abroad* (pp. 281-310). Hillsdale, NJ: Erlbaum.

Heath, S.B. (1983). *Ways with Words: Language, Life and Work in Communities and Classrooms.* Cambridge: Cambridge University Press.

Hudelson, S. (1984). Kan yuret an rayt en Ingles: Children become literate in English as a second language. *TESOL Quarterly, 18*, 221-238.

Hymes, D. (1981). Ethnographic monitoring. In H. T. Trueba, G.P. Guthrie, and K. Au (Eds.), *Culture and the Bilingual Classroom: Studies in Classroom Ethnography* (pp. 56-68). Rowley, MA: Newbury House.

John, V.P. (1972). Styles of learning — styles of teaching: Reflections on the education of Navajo children. In C.B.Cazden, V.P. John, and D. Hymes (eds.), *Functions of Language in the Classroom* (pp.331-343). New York: Teachers College, Columbia University.

Johnson, D.W. and R. Johnson (1987). *Learning Together and Alone: Cooperation, Competition, and Individualistic Learning.* Englewood Cliffs, NJ: Prentice-Hall.

Mohan, B.A. (1986). *Language and Content.* Reading, MA: Addison-Wesley.

Nova Scotia Human Rights Commission. (1981). General statement of major findings: Textbook analysis Nova Scotia. In P. Robinson (ed.), *Publishing for Canadian Classrooms* (pp. 191-198). Halifax: Canadian Learning Materials Centre.

Philips, S.U. (1972). Participant structures and communicative competence: Warm Springs children in community and classroom. In C.B.Cazden, V.P. John, and D. Hymes (eds.), *Functions of Language in the Classroom* (pp.370-394). New York: Teachers College, Columbia University.

Rowe, M.B. (1986). Wait time: Slowing down may be a way of speeding up! *Journal of Teacher Education, 37*, 43-50.

Scarcella, R. (1990). *Teaching Language Minority Students in the Multicultural Classroom.* Englewood Cliffs, NJ: Prentice Hall.

Slavin, R. (1988). Cooperative learning and student achievement. *Educational Leadership, 54*, 31-33.

Snow, C.E. (1977). Mothers' speech research: From input to interaction. In C.E. Snow, and C.A. Ferguson (eds.), *Talking to Children: Language Input and Acquisition* (pp. 31-49). Cambridge: Cambridge University Press.

Wells, C.G. (1981). *Learning through Interaction: The Study of Language Development.* Cambridge: Cambridge University Press.

Chapter 12
ASSESSMENT AND EVALUATION

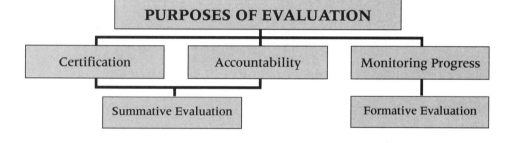

PURPOSES OF EVALUATION

- Certification
- Accountability
- Monitoring Progress
- Summative Evaluation
- Formative Evaluation

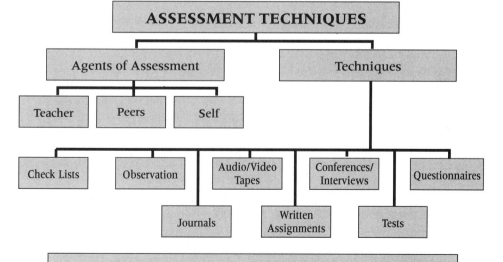

ASSESSMENT TECHNIQUES

- Agents of Assessment
  - Teacher
  - Peers
  - Self
- Techniques
  - Check Lists
  - Observation
  - Journals
  - Audio/Video Tapes
  - Written Assignments
  - Conferences/Interviews
  - Tests
  - Questionnaires

EVALUATING THE CULTURALLY DIFFERENT

If I had been asked to make a statement about evaluation when I began teaching, years ago, I would not have found it easy to come up with an answer. I knew about testing, of course. Testing was a prominent feature of classroom procedure. Graded assignments, weekly spelling tests, monthly tests, term examinations all had their place. The main purpose of testing and grading was to assign marks for reporting purposes.

My practice was congruent with traditional views of teaching and learning that continue to dominate much education. Learning, according to this view, is considered to be largely a matter of knowledge acquisition. The teacher's job is to transmit knowledge — to diagnose what students need to learn, to teach the missing information, and to test to determine whether students have learned. Evaluation, in the transmission-oriented tradition, concentrates on lower level cognitive skills like memorization, and on products rather than processes. By products, I mean correct answers to questions or problems, or well-written essays. It is, after all, easy to determine whether a math problem, for example, has the correct answer; it is more difficult to find answers to more important questions like: How did the student go about finding that correct answer? How much "correct" thinking went on even though the final answer is wrong?

Evaluation is a topic of critical importance because evaluation can easily dominate the educational scene. What is evaluated, measured, and tested comes quickly to be equated with the goals of education. Testing heavily influences and often dictates the curriculum. Rather than measuring what is valued, we often come to value what is measured.

Approaches to teaching and learning cannot change unless approaches to evaluation also change. But changes in evaluation attitudes and practices are not easily produced. Langer and Applebee (1987) describe how attempts to change teaching practice can be thwarted by teachers' inability to revise their ideas about evaluation. Langer and Applebee worked with seven experienced secondary teachers of science, English, social studies and home economics. The teachers were volunteers who were eager to learn ways of using writing to help their students to think and learn in content areas. The teachers received considerable help and support from personnel of the university-based project team who met frequently with the teachers for collaborative planning sessions, and for regular classroom observations, and who held numerous informal discussions with teachers in the staff room and by phone. Despite this most favourable situation — experienced teacher-volunteers who wanted to learn to use writing to promote learning, and who were supported by a highly-trained research team — only three of the seven changed their views of teaching and learning in substantial ways. Those who changed were able to do so only when they found new ways of handling the problem of evaluation. For the rest, their good intentions were undercut by their deeply rooted views of their roles as transmitter-of-knowledge and evaluator. Langer and Applebee comment (1987, p. 144) that the role of teacher-as-evaluator permeates almost all classroom exchanges, written and oral alike ... (The teachers') concerns with evaluation were deeply ingrained in the structure of their classrooms as well as in the schools and districts within which they taught.

The topic of assessment and evaluation is one that will have been dealt with in various subject-area methods courses that readers of this book have taken to prepare them to teach in a variety of content areas. The purpose here is not to repeat what has been well covered elsewhere or to attempt to provide a comprehensive scheme for evaluation in the various subject areas of the curriculum. The purpose, rather, is to consider assessment and evaluation in the light of the view of teaching and learning presented throughout the book, and in the specific context of language across the curriculum.

My argument throughout this book is that students learn when they are active makers of meaning, and that talking and writing about what they read and study, as well as representing material in graphic ways, are important ways of coming to know. In the elementary grades, talking, reading and writing will be a major focus of evaluation. Report cards, for example, usually require teachers to comment on students' achievements in these areas. If secondary teachers emphasize reading, writing and talking as important classroom activities, it is important that they also consider how they can assess how their students are doing in these activities, and what place, if any, talking, reading, and writing-to-learn ought to have in final grades in, say, mathematics, art, or history in the senior high school.

Purposes of evaluation

The evaluation carried out by the classroom teacher is of central importance in the educational enterprise because evaluation is inseparable from teaching. Yet evaluation is often poorly understood and poorly executed. Rexford Brown (1986, p. 114) an experienced, eminent evaluator in the field of English education claims that "most evaluations in education should never have been undertaken in the first place, are badly done when they are undertaken, and are misused or ignored when they are completed." One reason he gives for the unsatisfactory nature of much evaluation is that many evaluations are designed to "satisfy political rather than educational needs or are undertaken primarily in the interests of bureaucratic 'efficiency'." There are political ends that must be served by schools. The difficulty is that educational ends are sometimes lost sight of in the process.

The three main purposes of evaluation are: certification, accountability, and the monitoring of progress. Evaluation serves a certification purpose when it serves as the basis for a school or school division's affirmation that a student has satisfactorily completed the requirements for high school graduation, for example.

A second purpose of evaluation is to give to those who have a right to know an account of how the schools are doing. Parents and taxpayers have a right to hold the schools accountable. Administrators need access to the results of various kinds of evaluation in order to serve the politically necessary purpose of accountability.

The third purpose of evaluation is to monitor students' progress in order to promote further learning. Teachers assess and evaluate in order to diagnose students' strengths and weaknesses in order to plan further activities that will help students to learn. From an educational point of view, diagnostic evaluation is the purpose of central importance.

The different purposes of evaluation are sometimes referred to in the distinction that is made between **summative evaluation** and **formative evaluation**. Summative evaluation occurs at the end of a unit, a term, or a year. It is often expressed by means of a mark or a grade, especially in grades beyond the primary level. Summative evaluations are used for certification and accountability purposes. Formative evaluation occurs during the process of learning for the purposes of monitoring students' progress and planning further instructional activities.

Since student learning is the purpose for which schools exist, formative evaluation is at the heart of the educational enterprise. It is often the case, however, that major emphasis is placed on summative evaluation. Evaluation is thought of in terms of grades and reports. Certainly that was true for me when I was a young teacher. Evaluation is seen as something that happens after instruction has ended rather than as an integral part of teaching and learning.

The process of evaluation and its relationship to teaching and learning is illustrated in Figure 12.1. Both evaluation and instruction begin with and are dependent upon a clear definition of expectations as expressed through aims and objectives of the curriculum. Learning experiences are created to achieve the objectives of the program. The teacher assesses learning by observing ongoing activities in the classroom and by collecting products of various kinds. The results of observations and of examinations of students' work are documented and, subsequently, interpreted. After reflection and interpretation, the teacher revisits the program to determine ways in which it must be modified in order to achieve stated goals. Program modification may result in a sharpening and clarification of objectives. The process described thus far is continuous throughout the year. At the end of the year (or the end of the reporting period), however, the teacher's reflection and interpretation result in a report which may be oral, written, or both oral and written. In some cases, the whole enterprise has to be summed up in a single letter grade accompanied by a brief comment on a report form.

Figure 12.1
The Process of Evaluation

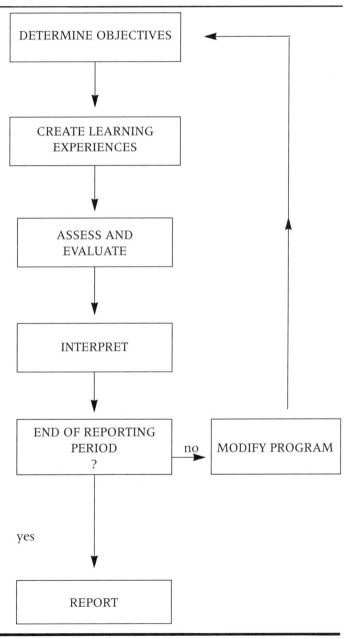

The main thing to note is that evaluation is an integral part of instruction. The goals of the program should be evident in every aspect of the instructional program: in instruction, in information-gathering procedures, in the way information is interpreted, in the judgements that are made, and in reporting procedures.

ASSESSMENT TECHNIQUES

Assessment should be continuous, manageable, fair, consistent with objectives and teaching strategies, and based upon a variety of measures and observations. In *The Curriculum from 5 to 16*, The Department of Education and Science in the United Kingdom (1989, pp. 52-53) puts it this way:

> Assessment involves a mixture of techniques, many of them subjective, which the teacher learns with experience to apply to day-to-day observation of how pupils perform across the range of tasks ... (T)hese forms of assessment have the virtue of being an integral part of classroom activity. A range of techniques should be used to suit the purpose and the activity. Much of the assessment ... has to go on in the busy environment of the classroom and must be largely impressionistic ... From time to time also, informal assessment needs to be supported by more objective forms of testing, such as class tests and examinations devised by the teacher ...

In carrying out the kind of assessment envisaged, there are assessment roles to be played by the teacher, by a student's peers, and by the student. Teacher assessment, peer assessment, and self assessment all have important contributions to make to the learning process.

TEACHER ASSESSMENT

The teacher's judgement is the primary means of assessing students' performance. It should be informed by a variety of measures and observations. If students are engaged in the kinds of active learning suggested throughout this book, the teacher is no longer on centre stage for the major portion of class time. With less emphasis on the teacher as lecturer, and director and controller of activities, and more emphasis on students engaging in learning activities individually, in pairs, and in small groups, the teacher has more time than in traditional classrooms to engage in a wide range of assessment techniques. The teacher's time is freed for observation, interviews, and conferences that can be very informative for diagnostic purposes, and that are difficult to find time for in the traditional class. Some of the assessment techniques available to the teacher are: check lists, observations, questionnaires, conferences and interviews, audio and video tapes, journals or learning logs, reading logs, written exercises, and tests of various kinds. The teacher's judgement, informed by a variety of information sources, is the main source of information about student performance.

Check Lists

Check lists are useful because they enable comment on a broad range of factors. Check lists do not give detailed comments about those activities. But judicious use of a check mark (✔) for "satisfactory," a check minus (✔–) for "some weaknesses," and a check plus (✔+) for "outstanding" can give an informative picture over many instances. Moreover, the record keeping is quickly and easily done.

Check lists allow teachers to select items that are interesting and informative. A great variety of items can be included. Figures 6.4 and 6.5 in Chapter 6 are examples of check lists that might be used to assess students' performance in small group discussions. These figures might be adapted to assess students' performance in other kinds of group tasks. Science teachers, for example, might want to keep observations about students' participation carrying out group experiments.

Figure 12.2 shows a check list that an English teacher might use to summarize information about a student's writing over time. A glance at the record sheet — which might be attached to the back of the student's writing folder — can give the teacher a great deal of information about the student's writing over a period of time. It will tell the teacher how many pieces have been completed, what kinds of writing have been attempted, how many pages have been written, and what some of the student's strengths and weaknesses are. The particular items on the form can vary according to the grade level, the student's needs, and the aspects of writing that the teacher may be concentrating on at a given time. The items in Figure 12.2 could easily be adapted for lab reports in science with check, check plus, or check minus given for the various parts of the report: objectives, procedure, materials, observations, and conclusions. Note how much more informative such a record is than a mere summative mark or grade. A row of Cs will tell you that there are improvements that a student needs to make but gives you no information about the areas in which you need to help her.

In many cases it is sufficient for a teacher to know whether or not a student has made a reasonable effort at completing a task — a writing-to-learn task; graphing a segment of text; a response to a poem in English, to a picture in art, or to a piece of music. Check lists (used either with or without the addition of plus and minus signs) are a useful way of recording this kind of information.

Check lists, then, have many purposes. They may be used to record observations while a class is in progress, to record impressions at the end of a class (for example, in regard to attendance, punctuality, courtesy, cooperativeness,

Figure 12.2

RECORD OF COMPLETED PIECES								
NAME DATE:								
Type of Writing								
Argument								
Story	✔							
Report								
Poem								
Business Letter		✔–						
etc.								
Length (in pages)	1.5	1						
Sentence Structure	✔–	✔–						
"Voice"	✔	✔–						
Word Choice	✔–	✔–						
Spelling								
Punctuation	✔	✔						
Structure	✔+	✔+						
Beginning	✔+	✔+						
Development	✔+	✔+						
Conclusion	✔	✔–						
Process								
Getting ideas	✔	✔						
Revising	✔–	✔–						
Proof reading	✔	✔–						
Attitude	✔	✔						

volunteering answers or comments, and so on), or to summarize information over several tasks of a similar kind. The benefits of check lists are: (1) their flexibility; teachers can select from among a large number of items those that seem important at a given time; (2) the ease of recording; and (3) the wide range of tasks or behaviours that may be assessed.

Observations

When students are working in groups, pairs or on individual work, the teacher has many opportunities to observe individuals and groups of students. Sometimes observations may be recorded on check lists as described above. A more informative record may be made about fewer students if the teacher makes anecdotal comments. Anecdotal comments may be made on 3 x 5 cards, with different cards for individual students. Alternatively, the teacher may keep a class notebook or journal with a page divided into two columns for each student. Notes about what students do, or say, or write may be made on the left leaving the right hand column for comments or interpretations. Notes might be made of good questions, comments, or contributions made by students, as well as misinterpretations or errors. Teacher journals of this kind should highlight what seemed most significant. If reviewed and summarized periodically, the journal can help a teacher to discover information about the progress of individual students, and also to identify useful information about the classroom interaction as a whole. Extensive documentation cannot be made about all students in the class. A detailed record might be kept, however, about a few students who are of particular concern. A detailed record on a few students can serve to sharpen the teacher's powers of observation of all students.

Audio and Video Tapes

Audio and video tapes are another means of observing and recording students' performance. Insights can be gained into students' thinking by taping groups solving a mathematical problem, discussing a science problem, or discussing a poem or a piece of art. Recording a whole-class session, as well as small groups, can also be an informative experience for teachers who are interested in assessing teaching and learning in the class. As students work to improve their group skills or to improve their performance on a piece of music in band, observing a videotape of a session can be very useful for promoting self and group assessment. Sometimes a video may be viewed and discussed by the class. Such observation and discussion can provide useful peer assessment and, at the same time, be a learning experience for those observing. Note, however, that you need to give clear instructions to guide students' observations. Have them look for instances of specific desired behaviours. While time limitations will affect the extent to which audio and video recording can realistically be used in assessment, judicious use is a useful technique.

Conferences and Interviews

The times when students are engaged working in small groups or pairs on tasks and problems of various kinds allows time for teachers to spend some class time on individual conferences with students. Conferences may serve many purposes: to give formative evaluation on a piece of writing or an assignment in progress; to listen to a student talk his way through a mathematical problem; to determine how the student is managing the reading of the course text. Listening to students is essential as a way of assessing progress, according to the DES (1979) booklet on mathematics. Kerslake (1982) points out that the written tests so much used by mathematics teachers can give only an approximate idea of students' understanding. Listening is the only way of finding out how and why students get the answers that they record on paper. The same is true for many subject areas.

Conferences are a regular part of the day in many elementary classrooms. Secondary teachers may also find conferences a useful assessment technique, especially for students with particular problems. You might, for example, confer with second language students about their progress in the course, or their degree of comfort with the course text. A student might prepare for a conference by completing a self assessment. For example, a student in a secondary science, social studies, or business education class might prepare for a reading conference by preparing answers to the following after he has read some assigned reading:

INSTRUCTIONS TO THE STUDENT

After you have read this chapter (or segment of a chapter), answer the following questions:

1. Did you finish the reading? If not, how much did you read?

2. How long did you spend reading?

3. Did you preview the chapter? How did you do that?

4. Which parts of the reading were hard to understand?

5. What made those parts hard to understand?

6. What did you do when you came to a part that was hard to understand?

7. Did you read any part twice? More than twice? Which parts?

Alternatively, while the class is engaged on some task related to a class reading, the teacher might use a conference with a student experiencing difficulty to show the student how to preview a reading selection by using procedures described in Chapter 8.

Questionnaires

Conferences allow a teacher to collect in-depth information from a single student on some aspect of her performance. Questionnaires allow teachers to collect information from all students. Many questions may be explored: attitudes towards the subject; what students like and dislike; what they find easy and difficult; what they find interesting; what their reading strategies are as they deal with the course text — to cite just a few examples.

Journals or Learning Logs

If students are asked to write entries in a course journal or learning log, teachers have many opportunities to assess their learning and thinking. Things to note are: what questions they ask; what comments they make that reveal thought, understanding, or misunderstanding; what attitudes towards the subject and the class their journals reveal. Sometimes the teacher will read and respond to a given entry for all students. But teachers need not necessarily read every journal entry by every student, especially in higher grades where a lot of writing may be done. Sometimes written responses may be shared with group members, and sometimes written responses may serve their purpose by having volunteers share their responses with the class as a basis for further discussion. The teacher may take journals in periodically and respond to a given number of entries selected by the student.

Written Assignments

Written assignments and exercises of many kinds will be given in most courses. Some of these may be formal assignments for which a mark or grade will be given in higher grades. But many should be assignments aimed at helping students to learn. Some, but not all, of these will be read by the teacher. If read, the purpose should be to determine the degree of understanding shown rather than to assign a grade or mark. Often a simple check mark indicating whether or not the assignment has been done is sufficient record to keep. If teachers believe that students will not complete assignments if no marks are given, the record of check marks can be translated into some part of the final mark or grade as described below under **Summative Evaluation**.

Tests and Examinations

Quizzes, tests and exams are an appropriate part of the assessment and evaluation procedure. Tests are extensively used to measure students' subject-area knowledge. Lytle and Botel (1990) suggest the following as ways in which tests and exams can link language and learning and thus be more congruent with the model of teaching and learning presented throughout this book:

1. Include questions that require students to develop ideas in writing.

2. Give take-home and open-book tests to encourage more thoughtful reflection. Take-home and open-book tests should be designed to call for reflection or application rather than for factual answers.

3. Allow students to work in teams to prepare tests and sometimes to do collaborative answers.

4. Allow a choice of questions to be answered.

5. Remove time limits to allow for review and revision.

PEER ASSESSMENT AND SELF ASSESSMENT

Students in the class are an invaluable resource in the process of teaching and learning, and in assessment and evaluation that are part of teaching and learning.

Self Assessment

To be involved in self assessment means that students are working at identifying their strengths and weaknesses. This gives them the kind of awareness necessary for improvement. When students are working on developing group skills, for example, the most valuable thing they can do is to examine their own participation in order to determine what they can do to improve the functioning of the group. Forms such as that illustrated in Figure 6.1 in Chapter 6 encourage self evaluation. Similar self evaluation forms might be used in other kinds of group performance like band, or team sports.

The approaches to writing suggested in Chapter 9 encourage students to identify problems with their writing and to seek help from a peer or the teacher with the problems that they themselves perceive. Students might similarly seek help with self-identified problems in art, or with design problems in home economics or industrial arts.

Students may play a role in their own evaluation by selecting one or two pieces of work from a portfolio of their work for the teacher to assign a grade to. In the writing class, for example, the teacher should not grade every piece of writing. When it comes to assigning a grade at the end of the reporting period, the teacher might grade two pieces of writing, one of which is selected by the student, or by the student in consultation with the teacher, and the second which is completed under test conditions, if the teacher wishes to ascertain what students can do independently. (Elementary teachers, and especially primary teachers, will likely be less concerned than secondary teachers about putting students under test conditions.) A similar procedure might be followed in other subject areas.

Some teachers have their students write regular self evaluations based on their portfolios of work in each subject area. (A portfolio consists of a collection of work of various kinds that is selected in order to display achievement and used by the teacher in summative evaluation. The following materials are examples of what might be included in a portfolio of work in social studies: writing of various kinds; graphic materials (charts, maps, drawings, etc.) based on individual research or on readings; constructed materials, for example, a model; tests.) For one evaluation, a seventh-grade teacher asked students to comment on the following:

1. What did you do well?

2. What disappointed you?

3. List three things that you want me to notice about your portfolio of work.

4. What are you proud of?

5. What do you need to focus on in the future?

Figure 12.3 shows the self evaluation written by one student for each of social studies and writing. Note that the student had been permitted to omit from her portfolio one test on which she had done less well than usual. Note also how useful it is for the teacher to have her attention focused on aspects of progress that the student has taken pride in. How disappointing to work hard overcoming a weakness or mastering a skill and receiving no acknowledgement of progress made because a busy teacher is swamped with the demands of evaluation and report writing.

There are many ways in which students can be involved in self assessment. The great value is that if students themselves identify areas that need improvement, they are more likely to work on those areas.

Peer Assessment

There are two major values of involving students in peer assessment. One is that students are well able to offer constructive comments on the performance of their peers in a wide variety of areas. The teacher's load is lifted considerably when she realizes that she does not need to read and respond to every piece of work each student does. Useful peer responses can be made by students even in the elementary years.

Figure 12.3
Grade 7 Student's Self Evaluation of Portfolios in
Social Studies and Writing

Social Studies

This term in social studies we have studied Early Man … I felt I took good notes and my work was always up to date. I did well on the test with the graph. It was hard it took a lot of thinking.

I was really disapointed in the other test (not enclosed in portfolio). I'm glad Mrs. Smith understands how noisy it was and impossible to take a test.

Three things I want you to notice are:

1. That my note book is neat and organized.

2. I know how to apply what I know to tests.

3. Im getting better at the big ideas not details.

One thing Im proud of is the mark I got on my stations. What a surprise.

One thing I need to focus on is being able to concentrate no matter how noisy it is.

Writing

I have written alot of stories and like the way my writing is changing. I prefere picking my subject. I dont mind being given subjects.
Three things I want you to notice are:

1. I still have run on sentences but not as much as before because I'm starting to understand sentences more.

2. I don't just write one type of writing. I know how to write poems and lots of other things thanks to Mrs. Smith.

3. I don't go on and on boring my reader to death anymore. I have learnt ways to make my storys more interesting.

Something I'm proud of is my early man story. Gisele said she wanted to make another copy and give it to her English teacher.

One thing I need to focus on is NO run on sentences.

The second value is that, when students examine the work of their peers for assessment purposes, their own learning is promoted. Janet West (1985), a teacher of senior high, college-bound English students, asked her students to write a biopoem (described in Chapter 10) about the author of a difficult piece of literature they were studying. She had them share their poems. She reports that "students spent almost half an hour criticizing, applauding, justifying, and challenging each other's adjectives in line two of the poem" (p. 176). When they saw what their peers had written, many gained new insights. Some of them decided to borrow a word a peer had chosen. Cheating? No; benefitting from the insights of their fellow students.

SUMMARY

A teacher, schooled in traditional attitudes towards assessment and evaluation, might read about the long list of assessment techniques described above, and ask sceptically, "When am I ever supposed to teach?" Such a question arises, however, only if assessment and evaluation are regarded as something separate from teaching, something that happens after teaching has taken place. Assessment is inseparable from teaching. Its major purpose is to improve students' performance. Assessment is essential in order to determine what else needs to be planned in order for further learning to take place. Assessment, in other words, is part of teaching. It is necessary, of course, that assessment and evaluation be manageable. Not all the techniques listed above will be used in all classes. Rather, the description is illustrative of the range of techniques that may be used. Beginning teachers, especially, should "hasten slowly" if they are working in a very traditional environment. You might consider trying different techniques, one by one, and adopting those that work well for you.

SUMMATIVE EVALUATION

In addition to the formative evaluation that is continuously undertaken in order to inform teaching decisions, it is part of the teacher's responsibility to make summative evaluations for reporting purposes. In many primary classes and some upper elementary classes, teachers write anecdotal reports in which considerable information can be given about students' strengths and weaknesses. In many upper elementary classes and most secondary classes, the teacher is required to sum up a student's multi-faceted performance throughout a term by a single letter grade.

Where a single letter grade is given, it is important that it, too, be based on a variety of tasks and observations. If talking, reading, writing, performing, solving problems, and doing experiments are important learning activities in the classroom, it is appropriate that some part of the final grade be assigned for work done in these areas. Note that, if you have been keeping records for purposes of formative evaluation as described above, you will have a rich set of data to use in preparing your summative report. Some ways of using this data are as follows:

1. One procedure is to assign some part of the term grade (perhaps 5 to 15 percent) to participation which might involve various factors depending on the content area, for example:

- attendance

- punctuality

- participation in group tasks and discussions

- satisfactory participation in clean-up activities in subjects like art, science, home economics, and industrial arts

- participation in whole-class discussions by offering comments, asking insightful questions, volunteering to read responses to free writing assignments, and so on.

If teachers observe frequently and use the check (✔), check plus (✔+), and check minus (✔–) system, they are likely to find, at the end of the reporting period, that the long string of checks against each student's name is not difficult to translate into an A, a B, or a C for participation. Teachers who give participation grades often consider participation as an aspect of the course work where students easily earn an A or a B if they make a real effort.

2. A similar procedure might be used to assign a percentage of the final grade for homework and/or writing-to-learn assignments. Teachers could use either the three levels of checks or, alternatively, might simply mark with a check if a satisfactory attempt has been made to do the work assigned. At the end of the reporting period, all those who have attempted all — or very nearly all — assigned work might receive an A for this portion of the grade.

3. You may wish to assign a specific portion of the summative grade for the course journal if you have used journal writing extensively. Approaches to giving marks or grades for journals vary, as discussed in Chapter 10. Some teachers opt for giving full marks provided students make a reasonable attempt to do assigned journal-writing tasks. Some teachers use what amounts to the check system described above. Students get a good mark if they keep their journals satisfactorily, but there is room for a bonus mark for those who do outstanding work, and a lower mark for those whose responses show little thought or effort. Butler (1982, p. 77) suggests that students should be involved in self-evaluation of their journals. On a day late in the course, he asks the students to bring their journals to class where they read through their journals, and then write an evaluation. He provided the following guide for his students who were pre-service education students:

Quantity How much did you write? How frequently? How regularly? Under what conditions? How long did you spend?

Variety What sort of topics did you choose? What forms of writing did you use? Did you shift topics? Or sustain topics?

Depth	What sorts of topics seem most intense? Which show most feelings? Which are most perfunctory? Which show most insight?
Interest	Which entries are most interesting to re-read? Which might interest another reader? Could you show any entries to a friend? a colleague? A relative? Your teacher?
Value	How valuable has the journal been to you? Was it just an assignment to get done? Or did you get involved in it? Will you continue your journal? Will you have your students write journals? Is your journal worth preserving?

If a grade is given for the journal, it might be based partially on the student's self-evaluation, and partially on the teacher's reading of the journal. Some teachers like to allow students to maintain the right of privacy over their writing by indicating pages that should not be read by others.

4. There will be, especially in higher grades, formal assignments, quizzes, and tests for which marks or grades are assigned.

It would be comfortable for both teachers and students if teachers could concentrate on organizing productive learning activities for their students without the necessity of categorizing students by means of grades. The political reality is, however, that schools and administrators are accountable to parents and taxpayers, and that marks and grades are required from most teachers as part of the accountability equation. Given the inescapable fact that teachers must assign grades, the task is to establish a grading system that is fair, that is based on a variety of tasks and observations, and that is congruent with the aims of the program and the instructional activities.

EVALUATION IN CULTURALLY DIVERSE CLASSROOMS

Special care is needed in evaluating those who belong to cultures other than mainstream, middle-class culture. People from different cultural groups sometimes have different ways of learning, as mentioned in Chapter 11, and they often differ in the ways they use language. This is true not only of those who are second language learners who have not yet developed full proficiency in English, but also of some whose mother tongue may be English but whose cultural, ethnic, or social background is different from the dominant middle-class mainstream.

Language normally plays a central role in evaluation — as it does in learning. Teachers depend heavily on students' writing and speaking when they are assessing learning. The danger is that knowledge and learning will be equated with the ability to *express* what has been learned. Content area teachers need to take care to try to separate content learning from the student's ability to express what has been learned in fluent, standard English.

If assessment is made continuously throughout the course by means of a variety of techniques and strategies, it is less likely that those who use nonstandard English or who are not proficient in English will be unfairly treated. It is especially important, when assessing those who are culturally different, to make sure to include procedures that do not require writing, like talking to students about their work and observing them as they participate in class and in small groups. Even tests may sometimes be administered orally with the assistance of a bilingual parent or aide to interpret, if necessary (Law and Eckes, 1990). Examining the work that students produce is another valuable source of information. A high school science department had the following as part of their departmental learning and assessment policy (Corson, 1990, p. 96):

> The output of students for assessment will not be confined to writing and talking. Students will experiment with different media including video, posters, charts, overhead transparencies, cartoons, models or demonstration experiments.

If written tests are given, care should be taken to use simple language with simple sentence structure.

If students do writing-to-learn exercises where the emphasis is on developing understanding rather than producing a polished piece of writing, they should not be penalized for limited language proficiency. Sometimes a formal written assignment is given and graded. If teachers feel that they must give some part of the grade for language, they should at least separate language and content, giving a proportion of the grade for each.

Teaching and assessing those whose language is different, for one reason or another, from the language of the middle-class mainstream, requires sensitivity and judgement. A balance must be found between valuing the language of students' home cultures, on the one hand, and, on the other hand, equipping students with the ability to use language in ways that will given them access to opportunities that will otherwise be denied to them. Striking the right balance requires careful thought.

CONCLUSION

Assessment and evaluation are an essential aspect of teaching. Teachers must assess and evaluate in order to report to those who have a right to know how students are doing. Such reporting is a political necessity. The most important reason for evaluating, however, is to inform teachers about progress and problems so that they can plan subsequent learning activities. Assessment is part of teaching. It should take place continuously by means of a variety of techniques, from informal observations and interviews to formal assignments and tests. Not only the teacher but learners themselves and their peers should be involved in the assessment process.

A variety of special concerns arise in the assessment of those whose language use is different from the language of the mainstream either because they are second language learners, or because, though native speakers of English, they speak a different dialect. Since assessment tends to depend heavily on language, students who are not proficient language users are likely to sustain double penalties — for failures in the content area, and for less than proficient skill in expressing themselves. Special judgement is called for in assessing such students.

EXERCISES

1. Meet with one or two of your peers who share a common interest in a particular content area and:

    a. Make a list of materials that might be included in a student's portfolio upon which you might base summative evaluation at the end of a reporting period.

    b. Use Figure 12.2 to create a check list that you think would be useful to you in the chosen content area.

    c. Make a list of uses for individual student conferences in the chosen content area.

2. Discuss the following in your group: Do you think students should be permitted to select work to be included in their portfolio for summative evaluation? Why or why not? What limits, if any, would you place upon their freedom to choose?

3. The two pieces of writing that follow were written by ESL students in an intermediate grade 5 science class.

STUDENT A

The bees are helpful because they make a honey for us and they make flower to beautiful our land. They hepl us to make food. Sometimes the bees sting people because the people hurt the bees.

STUDENT B

Bee are halpful beacuse the give honey to us to eat and halp the flowers to groe more and more it halps the trees to beacuse the can grow the worker bees halp the other bees too and I think there very halpful
        and now they are harmful they stinger pople
        they are halpful and harmful
I hope you injoy my bee story Thank you

a. How would you evaluate their content knowledge? their ability to express themselves in writing?

b. What diagnostic comments would you make about each student's work, that is to say, what kinds of help would you plan, if any?

c. What, if anything, do you find encouraging about each piece of writing?

REFERENCES

Brown, R. (1986). Evaluation and learning. In A.R. Petrosky, and D. Bartholomae (eds.), *The Teaching of Writing.* Eighty-fifth Yearbook of the National Society for the Study of Education (pp. 114-130). Chicago: University of Chicago Press.

Butler, S. (1982). Assessing the journal: An exercise in self-evaluation. *The English Quarterly,* 14 (4), 75-83.

Corson, D. (1990). *Language Policy Across the Curriculum.* Clevedon, Avon: Multilingual Matters.

DES. (1989). *The Curriculum from 5 to 16,* 2nd ed. London: Her Majesty's Stationery Office.

DES. (1979). *Mathematics 5-11: A Handbook of Suggestions.* London: HMSO.

Kerslake, D. (1982). Talking about mathematics. In R. Harvey, D. Kerslake, H. Shuard, and M. Torbe. *Mathematics* (pp. 41-83). London: Ward Lock Educational.

Langer, J.A., and A.N. Applebee (1987). *How Writing Shapes Thinking: A Study of Teaching and Learning.* Urbana, IL: National Council of Teachers of English.

Law, B., and M. Eckes (1990). *The More-than-Just-Surviving Handbook: ESL for Every Classroom Teacher.* Winnipeg: Peguis Publishers.

Lytle, S.L., and M. Botel (1990). *The Pennsylvania framework for reading, writing and talking across the curriculum.* Harrisburg, PA: Pennsylvania Department of Education.

West, J. (1985). Thirty aides in every classroom. In A. Gere (ed.), *Roots in the Sawdust* (pp. 175-186). Urbana: IL: National Council of Teachers of English.

INDEX